*Acquisitions Management
and Collection Development
in Libraries*

Second Edition

Acquisitions Management and Collection Development in Libraries

Second Edition

ROSE MARY MAGRILL
and
JOHN CORBIN

CHICAGO AND LONDON
American Library Association
1989

Designed by Frank Williams

Composed by Michael Brierton in Times Roman using Aldus
Pagemaker on a Macintosh IIcx and output on a Linotronic L-300

Printed on 50-pound Glatfelter B-16, a pH-neutral stock, and bound
in B-grade Holliston cloth by Braun-Brumfield, Inc.

The paper used in this publication meets the minimum requirements
of American National Standard for Information Sciences —
Permanence of Paper for Printed Library Materials,
ANSI Z39.48-1984

Library of Congress Cataloging-in-Publication Data

Magrill, Rose Mary.
    Acquisitions management and collection development in
libraries / by Rose Mary Magrill and John Corbin. — 2nd ed.
        p. cm.
        Bibliography: p.
        Includes index.
        ISBN: 0-8389-0513-7 (alk. paper)
        1. Acquisitions (Libraries)—Management. 2. Collection
development (Libraries) I. Corbin, John Boyd. II. Title.
Z689.M19 1989
025.2'1—dc20   89-6784

Printed in the United States of America.

93 92 91 90 89   5 4 3 2 1

Contents

Introduction

How does a library get the materials upon which its users depend? If the general library patron were asked this question, it is likely that the response would be: "Oh, I don't know. I suppose they buy some of them, or maybe they come as gifts. Actually, I don't really care as long as they have what I want when I need it."

This attitude has been characterized as the "black box" mentality: it does not matter to the library's clientele what goes on behind the scenes, so long as the needed material or information is available when required. To the librarian, however, the process of identifying what the library ought to acquire, determining how and from whom it can be obtained, and actually getting it is time-consuming and often quite complex. In many ways the work is hidden from the public; but without an effective acquisitions management and collection development program, the expectations of library patrons can never be met.

While, in earlier times, many libraries gained a book stock by purchasing a good private collection or obtaining a valuable donation, today's libraries utilize a variety of methods, computer assisted and manual, to develop an inventory of materials—books, periodicals, films, sound and video recordings, microforms, maps, music, etc.—that will meet the anticipated needs of their clientele. The collection that was once selected by the chief librarian and purchased by the librarian's secretary, who sent a letter to each publisher whose books were wanted, is now most likely being developed by a team of subject specialists who not only specify the new titles to be purchased but also draft policy statements and analyze the strengths and weaknesses of existing materials in various fields. The secretary's role has been transferred to a corps of professionals and assistants, technicians and clerks, who manage a multimillion-dollar budget, purchase and keep records on tens of thousands of separate items each year, negotiate individual and blanket orders and approval arrangements with dozens of vendors, and carry on correspondence with perhaps fifty or more nations, representing almost as many languages.

At the same time, however, there are library directors in small settings who do all the selection work and have their secretaries type the orders, while their counterparts in large research libraries are interacting with computer-based systems, soliciting gift collections worth thousands of dollars, and managing a staff of fifty to a hundred or more.

For the beginning student of library and information service, this range in the size and job responsibilities of acquisitions and collection development staff can obscure the fact that, no matter how old, how large, or how specialized a library may be, the same basic functions (identifying materials and their source of supply, acquiring them, paying for them or otherwise acknowledging their receipt, keeping records of their movement and their cost, and assessing their value in meeting patrons' needs) must be served. The variations occur mainly because some libraries have larger budgets, more staff, and a wider range of clientele to satisfy.

This book is intended primarily as an overview of the way in which library acquisitions programs are managed—what they try to accomplish and what methodologies are often used—and the processes through which the collection is designed, developed, and evaluated. The first three chapters, which outline the institutional, political, and economic factors that influence collection development policies and procedures, are followed by a general treatment (in the fourth chapter) of the relationship between collection development and the acquisitions function in a library. The largest part of the book (fifth through eleventh chapters) concentrates on the routines and problems associated with the acquisition of various types of materials. The final chapter focuses on ways in which to evaluate both the processes used to acquire materials and the final product, the collection, that results from those efforts.

Because of the variations between manual and computer-based systems, not every possible work procedure can be enumerated, nor can each nuance of collection development policy be illustrated. This book attempts to describe commonly used procedures in public, school, academic, and special libraries. The bibliographies, appended to each chapter, are designed to support and complement the text by pointing to more specific sources of technical details and system descriptions.

Collection development and acquisitions, while not ordinarily perceived by the public as particularly demanding or exciting, contain elements that bring great personal satisfaction to those whose careers are spent in the library. There is a distinct aesthetic joy in knowing that one has contributed to the building of a fine research collection or a well-selected municipal library that serves its citizens effectively. Little can excel the feeling that the librarian experiences when the material needed by a particular user can be placed immediately in his or her hand because that need was anticipated months earlier. Experienced staff in acquisitions units of large libraries often testify that they are called upon to use every bit of training and skill to interpret strange requests, correspond with remote dealers, and successfully handle complex and costly transactions to obtain materials from all parts of the world. If the following chapters reflect some of the challenges, as well as the difficulties, associated with acquisitions work and collection development, they will have succeeded in their purpose.

ONE

Overview of Collection Development

COLLECTION DEVELOPMENT has been described as one of the most discussed but least understood areas of librarianship. Libraries have always had collections that grew—and, in that sense, might be said to have developed. There is, however, more to the growth of a collection than simply acquiring materials; someone must decide which materials will be acquired and through which methods. This implies that selection decisions must be made, perhaps in accordance with an overall plan for the development of the collection. In recent years, the term "collection development" has come to encompass a broad range of activities related to the policies and procedures of selection, acquisition, and evaluation of library collections. As collection development began to be seen as a library function distinct from acquisition procedures, and broader than selection alone, the exact relations of the terms were not always clear.

In a paper presented at the 1977 Preconference on Collection Development, sponsored by the Resources and Technical Services Division of the American Library Association, Hendrik Edelman suggested that collection development, selection, and acquisitions are terms which represent a hierarchy. The highest level is collection development, which is the planning function. From the established collection development plans of the library flow the decisions about inclusion or exclusion of specific items in the collection—in other words, selection, the second level of the hierarchy.[1] Acquisitions, the next level, is the process that implements selection decisions and collection development plans.

"Collection development," as the term that includes all planning for the systematic and rational building of a collection, has come to be generally accepted. "Acquisition" refers to the process of verifying, ordering, and paying for the needed materials.

1

In one sense, collection development includes assessing user needs, evaluating the present collection, determining selection policy, coordinating selection of items, reevaluating and storing parts of the collection, and planning for resource sharing. However, in a broader sense, collection development is not only a single activity, or a group of activities; it is a planning and decision-making process. To speak of collection development "implies that collection response to changing conditions is to be part of a predetermined, definable system of relating the collection to the community managed by the librarian."[2] Of course, a library's collection development efforts cannot be effective unless its acquisition efforts are also businesslike and efficient.

COLLECTION DEVELOPMENT ENVIRONMENT

Since the mid-1970s, librarians have placed more emphasis on better management of library collections. They have been brought to the point of engaging in broad and rational planning for the growth and maintenance of their libraries' collections by a variety of factors. One of the major factors has been diminished financial resources, but measurement, analysis, and planning have also been encouraged by the prevailing public opinion favoring such activities. The changing structure of the knowledge distribution system, shifting government policies concerning the financing of education and research and the support or suppression of information, and variations in public attitudes toward schools and libraries also contribute to the pressure for planning and evaluation.

Government Policies

Government influences collection development in libraries through a variety of public policies that cover the financing of research and development and other kinds of data collection, the regulation of information technology, and the encouragement or restriction of the distribution of certain kinds of information. When the government provides funds for research and development in one area (e.g., defense) as opposed to another (e.g., agriculture), the demand for information in those fields shifts, as eventually does the amount of published information available. The federal government has in the past given direct grants to schools and libraries to make purchases in specified subject areas. The results of this policy decision can still be seen on the shelves of school libraries. Policies that regulate the granting of broadcast licenses, satellite transmission, etc., and all of the activities of the Federal Communications Commission have the potential of at least indirectly affecting collection development.

One example of how changing government policies toward research and development can have an impact on certain educational institutions and indirectly on their libraries is the way in which National Science Foundation (NSF) grants have been handled. In 1950, when NSF was created, it was directed to give roughly equal support to education and research. By 1959, when the United States was in a post-sputnik effort to strengthen science education, the National Science Foundation allocated 46 percent of its funds for education.[3] Even as late as the mid-1960s, a significant number of grants were awarded annually to elementary, high school, and college students and teachers. Twenty years later, educational projects were barely represented on NSF's list of programs. Most of the foundation's money was going for individual and institutional research grants.

Perhaps the area of government activity with the most direct effects on collection development is the one that involves policies concerning public access to information. The policies that determine which documents shall be classified as secret or which statistics and other data shall be collected by government agencies are of vital concern to libraries serving research specialists. A government's decisions about what shall be published with public funds, in which formats, and at what price can potentially affect even the smallest libraries. Every librarian engaged in collection development feels the effects of decisions about postal subsidies for the transportation of books, journals, and other library materials through the United States Postal Service. Anything that a government does to record or distribute information to the public opens up new possibilities for collection development. On the other hand, anything the government does to impede the public's access to information causes frustrations for librarians.

One of the areas in which government policy influences libraries indirectly by directly affecting nongovernmental publication is through laws governing copyright. The U.S. Constitution gives to Congress the power "to promote the Progress of Science and useful Arts, by securing for limited times to Authors and Inventors the exclusive Right to their respective Writings and Discoveries" (Article I, Section 8). Under that authorization, Congress has provided federal copyright protection since 1790. A number of revisions of the copyright laws have been made since that time, the most recent being Public Law 94-553, General Revision of the Copyright Law, signed on October 19, 1976, and effective on January 1, 1978.

The latest copyright law attempts—without total success—to provide copyright protection for all the new forms of information technology, such as cable systems and videotape. "Fair use" is recognized as a limitation on the exclusive rights of the copyright owner. Under the fair-use provisions, those scholars, critics, teachers, or researchers who need to make single copies of small amounts of material may do so. However, extensive, unlimited, or repetitive copying is not allowed. The copyright law has affected reserve collection policies in school, college, and university libraries and the interlibrary loan policies in all types of libraries. In many cases, collection development policies have been adjusted to provide for the necessary purchase of duplicate titles.

That the federal government's monetary policy can have direct effects on collection development was clearly shown in the early 1980s. The U.S. dollar has fluctuated widely in value since the early 1970s, when the U.S. government completed its abandonment of the Bretton Woods arrangements, which up to August 1971 had tied the dollar to a modified gold standard. After March 1973, the United States accepted a floating exchange rate based on market forces such as the international balance of trade. In general, the floating exchange rate is supposed to help ease imbalances in foreign trade. When the U.S. dollar goes down in value in relationship to the currency of another country, that country's products become more expensive for the U.S. consumer, who will then buy fewer of the foreign products and more domestically produced goods. Since library collection development programs that include many foreign publications are not in a position to switch from foreign to domestic purchases, librarians find their acquisitions expenses rising out of all proportion to the actual value of their purchases.[4]

Economic Conditions and Financial Support

The United States government began its direct financial involvement with library matters in 1956, the year of the Library Services Act. A ten-year review of acquisitions work, covering 1956 to 1966, emphasized the impact of this involvement: "In less than ten years the federal government has achieved an eminent role in promoting library development."[5] In 1969, however, federal appropriations started to decline, and they have been declining ever since. During the 1980s, the executive branch of the federal government did not support appropriations for libraries, but the Congress continued to provide some aid. An example of the lack of executive branch support was the proposal sent by the Department of Education in the spring of 1988 to Congress advocating that all federal programs for college and university libraries and the training of library personnel be abolished.[6] To compound the problem of declining federal support for some libraries, city and state funding of public libraries and education in general has been erratic in many parts of the country since 1971.

The economy of the United States during the late 1970s and early 1980s combined inflation with recession, producing higher prices and declining economic growth. This combination caused a severe problem for libraries, where expenses are mostly for staff and materials, both categories that rose in cost. Libraries were squeezed from two directions: their sources of revenue started drying up as their costs increased. Federal and (in most cases) state and local funding steadily decreased.

All libraries have been affected by the economy but not in exactly the same way. In the last half of the 1960s, large cities in the United States were faced with a variety of social and economic problems, one of which was that the costs of social services were rising at a faster rate than the tax base could support. With declining income and declining use, many public libraries in large cities had to adjust their services and collection development practices.

Academic libraries function within the environment of higher education and reflect the strength or weakness of their parent institutions. Higher education was affected by special economic factors in the early 1970s: student enrollments and tuition income decreased in some institutions; the value of institutional endowments declined; and public confidence in the value of higher education weakened. A 1988 report, "The Economics of Research Libraries," noted: "Over the last 20 years, total university budgets, in constant dollars per full time equivalent (FTE) student, have remained roughly constant. This same phenomenon has also held true for academic and research libraries as a group."[7] All of higher education has suffered from inflation; but, according to the *Higher Education Price Index*, the cost of books and periodicals showed a tendency to rise faster than the increase in prices paid by universities for other goods and services. In addition to inflated costs of library materials, research libraries have been forced to adjust to abnormal increases in the cost of serials. The concern of the mid-1980s for librarians trying to build collections for specialists who need materials produced in other countries was the decreasing value of the U.S. dollar and the phenomenal price increases of foreign publications, particularly serial publications.

Libraries which rely on corporate and private donations have found those sources increasingly less reliable. The major tax reform that went into effect in 1987 and the sharp decline of the stock market in the fall of 1987 appeared to have less effect on philanthropy than many had expected, but the 1987 news was not strongly encouraging.[8] Individual giving increased in absolute dollars, but the rate of giving decreased. The slowdown in growth of personal income was blamed for this decline. Foundation giving and bequests increased slightly in 1987, but corporate giving remained level with 1985 and 1986. One interesting feature of 1987 giving patterns was an increase in the percentage of donations by corporations to elementary and secondary education.

Academic Environment

School, college, and university libraries have also been affected by certain aspects, other than economic, of the academic environment. Changes in the size and composition of the student body and the faculty—in teaching methods, in areas of study, and in research methods and interests—have required more and different library materials, and more duplication of selected items. Cline and Sinnott identified several developments that affect particular academic library collections.[9] In addition to decreased buying power, declining budgets, and changes in the college or university, academic librarians have faced the increased visibility of their operations to college and university administrators and the expectations of those administrators that librarians will engage in businesslike planning and reporting.

Accreditation, the judgmental process whereby a group of educators or other specialists critically review a particular institution or program, is an important feature in the academic environment. Accreditation in the United States developed in the late nineteenth century as a voluntary method for colleges and secondary schools to provide self-regulation of educational quality. The general regional associations—such as the North Central Association, the Southern Association, the New England Association, etc.—date back to this movement. Early in the twentieth century, professional associations began assuming responsibility for monitoring quality of the education that prepared new entrants to their respective professions. A wide variety of general, specialized, and professional accrediting agencies is now recognized by the Council on Post-Secondary Accreditation. (There are also some groups claiming to provide accreditations that are not recognized by COPA.) In addition to national and regional accreditation associations, state agencies assume a somewhat similar role for educational institutions that operate within a particular state. All of these accreditation efforts are intended to benefit the consumers of education: the students who must make decisions about where to enroll and the general public who eventually will employ and be served by an institution's graduates.

Although accreditation is said to be voluntary, most governing boards and administrative officers of educational institutions feel little freedom of choice in the matter of general institutional or even graduate professional accreditation. Sometimes accreditation of undergraduate programs in such areas as music, business, and chemistry is a matter of choice.

(Where state recognition of a particular certification program, such as teacher education, is concerned, there is usually no question or hesitation about the need to apply for approval of that program.) The decisions that are made about which types of specialized or professional accreditation to pursue will be felt immediately in collection development, because such accreditation decisions represent major policy decisions about which schools or departments will be emphasized in the institution.

Standards are the starting point for the accreditation process, and all librarians need to be familiar with the ones written for their academic institutions. Although accreditation standards do vary in the amount of emphasis they give to the library, most have a section devoted to library resources and services. In the early years of accreditation, these standards were likely to be very quantitative, specifying the exact number of books, pieces of equipment, etc., that a library should have. Since the 1930s, standards have gradually been shifted from a quantitative to a qualitative approach, giving more emphasis to the suitability and use of a library's collection than to its total volume count. All of these changes potentially affect how a library collection will be built and how it will be evaluated.

Publishing

Problems with the economy have affected publishers, who were forced, in the 1970s, to adjust their strategies to preserve their cash flow. Shifts in ownership of publishing companies apparently resulted in pressure to emphasize bestsellers at the expense of works which might sell steadily but in small numbers. High manufacturing costs and rising interest rates, as well as a more restrictive Internal Revenue Service ruling on depreciation of inventory, have discouraged all types of publishers from heavy investment in backlists and contributed to rising book prices. It is difficult for either trade or scholarly publishers to cover future direct and indirect costs with future income expectations based on current costs. The changing relationship of mass-market and traditional hardcover-trade publishing, along with increased emphasis on trade, or quality, paperback publishing, has been an important trend over the last decade. Scholarly publishing has suffered as much as trade publishing from rising production costs and high interest rates. Recent predictions about the future directions of scholarly publishing emphasize the likelihood of shorter press runs and more reliance on electronic transmission of the text, at the same time that university presses increase the number of new titles they publish.

Statistics on books published in the United States indicate some of the problems of volume and cost that libraries must face. Over the decade of the 1970s, the total number of new book titles published in the United States ranged from 24,288 in 1970 to 36,112 in 1979.[10] Forty percent more new books were published in 1980 than 1970. The 1981 total of 37,259 new book titles was 9.5 percent higher than the 1980 total, but the final figures for 1982 production indicated a 3.8 percent decrease from 1981. However, the number of new book titles published annually had risen to 41,925 by 1986. In addition to new books, U.S. publishers also put out a substantial number of new editions each year. In 1986, 6,992 new editions were published.

Increases in new books and new editions were not even across all subject categories. A comparison of statistics for 1970 and 1980 indicates that the number of titles in some categories was lower in 1980, but the number in most was higher. In 1980, fiction, poetry, drama, literary criticism, and other subjects classified in the 800s of the Dewey Decimal Classification totaled only 5,700—approximately 75 percent of the 1970 total of 7,696. Books about education and music were also published in smaller number in 1980 than in 1970. Other categories showed increases, ranging from 8.3 percent more juvenile books in 1980 than in 1970 to an increase of 174 percent for home economics (a category including cookbooks and some craft books), 105 percent for technology, and 123 percent for medicine. Between 1980 and 1986, juvenile books (42 percent), books on religion (34 percent), and business books (33 percent) showed the largest increases in total number of new titles and new editions. Three categories—agriculture, language, and law—showed increases between 20 and 30 percent. Titles classified in the 800s had increased by 15 percent to a total of 6,550. Biography, history, home economics, philosophy, psychology, sociology, economics, and technology increased in the range of 10 to 20 percent. Overall, the total increase in number of books acquired between 1980 and 1986 was 15.4 percent.

The 1987 statistics, based on the *Weekly Record* database, reported $36.28 as the average price of a hardcover book, compared to a $19.22 average price per volume in 1977.[11] The most expensive subjects in 1987 were science ($62.16), technology ($60.24), and medicine ($57.68). The least expensive publications continued to be juvenile books ($11.48 in 1987, compared to $5.51 in 1970) and works of fiction ($18.19 in 1987; $5.51 in 1970).

A 1988 survey of prices of U.S. periodicals and serial services indicated the average subscription price of a periodical in that year was $77.93, a 9.1 percent increase from 1987.[12] During the 1970s, annual· average percentage increases in periodical subscription prices were never lower than 9.2 percent (in 1977). The highest annual increases were in

1970 (20.2 percent), 1972 (13.5 percent), 1973 (22.4 percent), and 1980 (13.7 percent). Between 1970 and 1988, increases ranged from lows of 8.6 percent in 1985 and 8.9 percent in 1986 to highs of 14.5 percent in 1982 and 13.3 percent in 1981. Libraries of all types are affected by subscription increases, but those that must buy most heavily in scientific, technical, and professional areas suffer the most. General interest periodicals had average annual percentage increases from 1979 to 1988 of only 5.1 percent. For the same period of time, each scientific and technical discipline included in the statistics had average annual percentage increases of more than 10 percent, as did a number of other areas: law and industrial relations (12.3 percent), sociology and anthropology (11.8 percent), psychology (11.4 percent), library and information sciences (10.8 percent), political science (10.2 percent), and business and economics (10.0 percent). Even children's periodicals increased at an annual average rate of 10.5 percent. Of course, the libraries with real problems are those that must buy many foreign periodicals, the price increases of which have far exceeded those of U.S. periodicals in recent years.

Although price indexes are not as readily available for material other than books and serials, the prices of nonprint media and newspapers have been increasing too. A price index based on *Previews* and published in 1981 showed average prices for nonprint media between 1972 and 1980.[13] During that period color films rose an average of 15.6 percent (to $279.09); filmstrips increased 67.8 percent (to $21.74); filmstrip sets (with cassette) rose 79.4 percent (to $67.39); multimedia kits went up by 80.6 percent (to $92.71); while sound recordings increased 27 percent for disks and 19.5 percent for cassettes. Newspapers also increased in the late 1970s: "the average subscription rate for a U.S. daily newspaper increased 52.8 percent between 1975 and 1978."[14] In 1987, *Library Issues* reported:

> Libraries fiscal experience with nonprint media was mixed in 1985. The average cost for 16mm film fell 2.6 percent to $16.50 per minute. The cost of a cassette sound recording also dropped 10 percent to $8.99 each. However, the cost of purchasing one minute of videocassette rose 21 percent to $10.24 and the cost of 35mm positive microfilm rose 10 percent to $.26 per foot. Finally, the average subscription cost to a U.S. daily newspaper rose 2.3 percent over 1984 to $111.31.[15]

All libraries, but especially the larger and more research-oriented ones, must cope with the increasing specialization of information needs. The information requirements of scientists, social scientists, and humanists are becoming more complex and require more costly library service. It is commonplace to talk about the exponential growth of knowledge, but the increase in the number of ways in which that information is packaged and distributed adds to the pressure on libraries. Since library materials budgets are not likely to increase significantly, librarians will be forced to make hard choices between print, nonprint, and electronic information sources.

The number of formats in which information is available has increased through the years, as technological advances have offered new forms of packaging without significantly reducing the need for information presented in traditional forms. In addition to the traditional print sources— monographs, serials, government documents, music scores, and pamphlets—libraries have for some time been increasing their holdings of microforms, audiovisuals, graphics, motion pictures, videorecordings, maps, machine-readable data files, manuscripts, and three-dimensional objects. Now, the various products of optical technology must be considered—CD-ROM, CD-I, compact audio disks, videodiscs, etc. Librarians are often advised that the format in which information is packaged should no longer be an issue for collection development, but format does continue to be an issue for unavoidable reasons: initial cost, equipment requirements, storage requirements, questions of preservation, and even questions of ownership (lease or subscription versus outright purchase).

Users' Habits

The attitudes of potential library users toward the various types of formats used to package and distribute information and those potential users' ingrained habits of seeking information must influence collection development planning. Since the 1950s, interest in understanding how scientists find the information they need has been growing. More recently, the habits of social scientists and of humanists have become targets for communication research. Several bibliographies have attempted to compile the references to these projects.[16]

While much still remains unknown or dimly understood about how people search for information, certain generalizations have been drawn from the many studies conducted. Librarians tend to accept these generalizations as operating assumptions. For example, scientists have been found to use journals far more than they use monographs; humanists tend to use monographs more than journals; and the habits of social scientists are somewhere in between these two patterns. The literature of science is cumulative, so that the latest research, which is based on earlier work, is the most important. The humanities are not cumulative, and older materials may often be more important to a researcher than current materials. Secondary sources, such as abstracting and indexing services, do not figure as prominently in the literature searching of the humanist as of the scientist. Whether that is because of the unavailability of truly useful indexes or because of an inherent lack of interest in secondary sources by humanists is not really known. Invisible colleges, important in science, are much less so in social science and hardly exist in the humanities. Humanists tend to work alone, to do their own literature searching, and to consider browsing to be important. The library is generally assumed to be more vital to a researcher in the humanities than in other broad disciplinary areas. In fact, the library is often referred to as the humanist's laboratory. Libraries provide the reports of research in all academic disciplines, but for the humanities scholar, the library provides the raw materials of research.

Although there is a tendency to speak of general patterns of literature use in the sciences, humanities, and social sciences, many differences have been observed within each of these broad disciplinary groupings. Marquis and Allen argued, as early as 1966, that the communication patterns of pure science and applied science or technology are quite different.[17] Literature generally occupies a much less important place in technology than it does in science. The creation of an engineer is likely to be a product or a piece of equipment, rather than a published paper describing a theory or research finding. Technological literature does not tend to build or cumulate and publication is seldom a part of the reward structure for engineers employed in industry or government. Fitzgibbons compared a number of citation studies done in various social science disciplines and found that, although social scientists as a group tended to use books and journals about equally, there were variations from this norm in certain disciplines. People in education cited books and journals about equally in their papers, but economists favored journals, sociologists cited books about 60 percent of the time, and political scientists cited books about two-thirds of the time.[18] Even the humanities, according to studies cited in Stone's work, cannot be regarded as homogeneous in research and information-seeking techniques.[19]

There is sometimes a tendency to think that scholars, as experts, will conduct a literature search in the best possible way and persevere until the best information is found. Research has shown that this is not true; scholars are human after all. Even scholars often choose the closest source or the one that is easiest to get rather than search for a better source. College students also display this information-seeking trait; they must be motivated to put forth effort in a search. Vigo-Cepeda conducted a questionnaire survey of 973 liberal arts undergraduates at the University of Michigan in 1976–77 and found support for the hypothesis that the greater a student's need for assigned class materials, the greater the student's efforts to search for and to use the materials.[20] The pressure of class assignments usually provides the motivation for students to use a library. For example, Knapp reported that 94 percent of the loans made from the Knox College library in the spring quarter of 1954 were course related.[21] During a three-week period in January 1966, Hostrop had circulation clerks question students about the books they borrowed from College of the Desert, a two-year institution. Nearly 90 percent of the items borrowed by full-time students were for courses.[22] In the 1981–82 academic year, Saunders interviewed a sample of 240 undergraduates who borrowed books at the Purdue University General Library. He found "86.6% of the titles were selected for subject matter relating to a specific course."[23] An additional trait of today's college students is a preference for certain formats—audio, video, computerized files—over the more traditional formats—books, journals, microforms.

Students in elementary and secondary schools resemble college undergraduates in their use of information sources. Class assignments provide the motivation to locate and use information. Teachers, through their recommendations and assignments, have the greatest influence on how students use the school library. In 1979, Mancall and Drott studied a sample of nearly 2,000 students from 15 high schools. They reported: "Student use of materials is controlled not only by what is available and suitable, but also by a more subtle factor—the students' perceptions of availability and suitability."[24] Unfortunately, teachers—even elementary school teachers—seldom provide the opportunities and activities in the classroom that lead to voluntary reading. In a critical appraisal of the way reading is often taught, Morrow argues for "the general recognition and acceptance of a systemmatic, programmatic development of voluntary reading as a primary objective within primary and elementary education."[25] He continues, "If our fundamental reason for teaching children to read is the belief that their own voluntary reading is necessary to their fullest participation in a civilized society, plus all the other lifetime benefits that ability to read brings with it, then we need to remedy our present approach to reading instruction in the elementary school."[26]

Research on how the adult who is not enrolled in formal education acquires general information and fulfills leisure reading, viewing, and listening interests again supports the proposition that people tend to put effort into their searches in proportion to the strength of their interests and motivations. Selections are often made on the basis of what is available. Back in the 1930s, Carnovsky found that adults in his study read books on topics of high interest when those titles were widely advertised, were readily accessible, were readable from the standpoint of style, and were written by reputable authors. However, he also found that books of relatively low interest were read when the above factors were present.[27] Public librarians can verify these generalizations about the importance of immediate access as a determining factor in actual use of materials. The finding that scholars take the closest source of information rather than search for a better one also applies to the general public. Even those from the educational and socioeconomic groups most likely to use libraries turn to their friends and the mass media to get the information they need for daily living.

Public Attitudes

The attitude of the public toward education generally and toward libraries specifically can create either opportunities or frustrations for those librarians engaged in collection development. When the public feels good about education and is willing to support it financially, library materials budgets usually benefit; when the public loses confidence in the quality of educational leadership, librarians may also find their collection decisions being questioned.

Every citizen, having had personal experience with the institution, has an opinion about elementary and secondary education. As a result, public education has always had a generous supply of critics. A Gallup Poll, conducted in the spring of 1988, found that "Americans rank the quality of public education neck and neck with the country's drug problem as the most important issues in this year's Presidential election."[28] The average person may always have an interest in educational issues, but the decade of the 1980s was a time when the educational establishment led the critics. In 1981, the Secretary of Education appointed a National Commission on Excellence in Education with the charge of examining the quality of education in the United States. His justification for creation of the Commission was "the widespread public perception that something is seriously remiss in our educational system."[29] Although the role of school libraries was not directly addressed in this report, ominously titled *A Nation at Risk*, many of the findings and recommendations dealing with strengthening instruction in English, science, social studies, foreign languages, etc., and providing challenges for gifted students do have implications for the school library's collection and services.

Post-secondary education also has its evaluators and critics. A panel appointed by the Council for Advancement and Support of Education warned college presidents in the summer of 1988 that higher education was in danger of losing public confidence unless it made substantive changes in methods of operation.[30] Administrators were advised to find better ways to assess the quality of education, to hold down tuition costs, to publicize special programs for minority and low-income students, and to emphasize the public service activities of colleges and universities. In 1987, the Carnegie Foundation for the Advancement of Teaching published a report on the educational experience of college undergraduates. The introduction of the Carnegie report points out that all educational levels are related and argues that there is "an urgent need to bring colleges and universities more directly into the national debate about the purposes and goals of American education."[31] Eight points of tension in higher education were identified: "the transition from school to college, the goals and curriculum of education, the priorities of the faculty, the condition of teaching and learning, the quality of campus life, the governing of the college, assessing the outcome, and the connection between the campus and the world."[32] Although identified as points of tension, these aspects of higher education were also noted as "points of unusual opportunity."

Collection development in tax-supported libraries (particularly school and public libraries) is affected very directly by the prevailing public view of why a library exists and what it should or should not make available to potential users. What society considers acceptable shifts from time to time and varies from place to place within the same period of time. Using data from the 1972–83 General Social Surveys of the National Opinion Research Center in Chicago, White documented this variation by analyzing the answers to questions about censorship of controversial authors and questions concerning the availability of sexual information and pornography.[33]

The American public library was begun in the nineteenth century as an agency to respond to certain basic needs of society. As society has changed, views toward the mission and structure of the public library have also been altered. However, the views of librarians about the library's mission and the views of the public do not always coincide. The Public Library Association expressed an official view of librarians in a 1982 document called "The Public Library: Democracy's Resource, A Statement of Principles":

> Without regard to race, citizenship, age, education level, economic status, or any other qualification or condition, public libraries freely offer access to their collections and services to all members of the community. The ideas and information available through public libraries range the entire spectrum of knowledge and opinions. The uses made of the ideas and information are as varied as the individuals who seek them. Only the public library offers that unique opportunity for each person by providing an open and nonjudgmental environment in which individuals and their interests are brought together with the universe of ideas and information. No other institution provides this service for the American people.

Free access to ideas and information, a prerequisite to the existence of a responsible citizenship, is as fundamental to America as are the principles of freedom, equality, and individual rights. This access is also fundamental to our social, political, and cultural systems.[34]

The latest set of school library standards, published in 1988, lists as one of the five major challenges facing school library media specialists "to ensure equity and freedom of access to information and ideas, unimpeded by social, cultural, economic, geographic, or technologic constraints."[35] That challenge is so important because, as the discussion in the standards notes: "Censorship efforts flourish in this time, as they always have. Some individuals and organized groups believe that schools should be purged of books, materials, and courses that contain ideas that conflict with their own convictions."[36]

Complaints about both school and public library collections come from parents who wish to protect the values of their own children, religious groups who are concerned about materials opposing their beliefs and views of society, political groups who fear materials advocating different political systems, ethnic groups who are offended by anything presenting their history or culture in a negative light, pressure groups who resent any type of stereotyping on the basis of race, age, sex, physical condition, etc., and individuals who may object to anything that opposes their own ideas or philosophies or aesthetic tastes.

School libraries have more often been the targets of attacks in the courts than have public libraries. A number of important school library censorship cases have been decided in the courts in recent years, and the school library media specialist needs to be aware of the implications of these decisions when planning collection development policy and procedure. As one authority on censorship in libraries observed: "Court decisions appear to be a part of a national balancing act that seeks to find a firm middle ground in the conflict among the traditional, statutory rights of school boards and the constitutional rights of teachers, parents, and students."[37]

Pressure groups opposed to some of the collection development actions of public and school libraries do not voice opposition to the basic principle of free and open access, but they do question the way librarians put this principle into practice. Such groups argue that librarians should be more aggressive in seeking out and making available books on *all* sides of controversial or sensitive issues. Some critics argue that their tax payments should not be spent for materials they consider offensive or that advocate positions with which they disagree. Others, realizing that if each person in the community were allowed to specify the kinds of materials his or her money could *not* buy, the library would probably have no collection, take a more realistic view by demanding more sensitivity to all points of view on the part of the librarian. This latter approach was illustrated by the General Legal Counsel of Moral Majority of Washington State, who spoke at the ALA Annual Conference in San Francisco in 1981 and made suggestions to librarians on how they could increase their sensitivity to certain groups within their communities. His three areas of primary concern were children's materials (particularly those treating sexuality or violence), adult materials (whatever is bought ought to have some "merit" and the collection as a whole should have balance), and mass-market materials dealing with sex, violence, etc. (libraries should have higher standards than television).[38]

More than three decades ago, Lester Asheim offered what became a much-cited explanation of the difference between censorship and selection. In 1983 he reaffirmed his view of the librarian's role in protecting the rights of those in a community whose reading, viewing, or listening tastes put them into the minority. "The librarian's responsibility is to identify interests and to make judgments with the entire collection and the entire community in mind, not just that part of it with the largest constituency or the loudest voices or the most intimidating threats."[39]

LOCAL FACTORS AFFECTING COLLECTION DEVELOPMENT

Our definition of collection development, which is not limited to one size or type of library, emphasizes that collection development, as a planning process, uses the methodology typically followed in planning: establishing mission and policy statements, describing the present state of affairs, reviewing relative strengths and weaknesses, considering environmental influences and other current trends, setting goals, and designing strategies to reach those goals. Collection development operates within the constraints of certain conditions that vary from one place to another and from one time to another.

The goal of those who are charged with collection development responsibilities is to build the best collection possible, given any combination of conditions. The local conditions that influence collection development may be grouped under five broad headings: the community or institution, the purpose(s) of the library, the clientele, the present collection, and the available resources. Each of these headings represents several variables—factors that vary from one library to another.

The Community or Institution

The first group of variables covers the community and/or institution in which a library is located. Library-oriented community analysis has been practiced in the United States at least since the 1930s, when faculty members at the Graduate Library School of the University of Chicago began encouraging community analysis, developing techniques and providing examples for others to follow. Knowing the community or the institution to be served is now a part of recommended (though not always practiced) procedure in all types of libraries. Many librarians give support to the idea of community analysis or institutional analysis, but relatively few have engaged in it in a systematic fashion or with any sophistication. Establishing goals and objectives for any library is difficult without thorough knowledge of the community. Meaningful policies cannot be formulated to guide the development of the collection, nor can a library "be a living, growing and changing force in any community—public, school, academic—unless it remains sensitive to the character and needs of the community it serves."[40]

Communities may be analyzed from several perspectives:

1. Individual citizens: their ages, educational levels, ethnic and religious background, general economic status, cultural and recreational interests, etc.
2. Organizations of the community: both formal and informal, including governmental, social, religious, educational, cultural, political, etc.
3. Business and economic life: types of business enterprises offering employment, occupational patterns, income levels, etc.
4. Educational, cultural, recreational lifestyle: public and private educational institutions, recreational facilities, museums, galleries, communication media, etc.

Libraries are particularly interested in the availability of other libraries and cultural and informational resources: bookstores, art galleries, information bureaus, etc.

Libraries within organizations are influenced in many ways by the communities in which they are located, but their primary concern is with the organization they are designed to serve. The role of the library collection in any academic institution is to further the purpose and mission of the institution as a whole. Special libraries, too, are designed to meet the needs of a specific agency or company. The standards for school library media centers specify the following as a guiding principle for their operation: "The school library media program that is fully integrated into the school's curriculum is central to the learning process."[41]

Two-year college learning resources programs operate in such a variety of settings that the compilers of the latest guidelines for those programs were moved to comment on the difficulty of establishing guidelines for institutions with such widely diversified purposes and size and with student bodies with such heterogeneous backgrounds.[42]   Institutional goals and objectives vary also among four-year colleges and universities. Some emphasize teaching, which is the primary purpose at most two-year institutions, while others aim for combinations of teaching, service, research, and (in larger and more complex academic institutions) interpretation and publication of research.

The present curriculum of an academic institution, as well as the path by which it developed and its anticipated future direction, is a vital part of the knowledge base for collection planning and development. How will collection development be affected, for example, if a liberal arts college phases out foreign language courses and builds up teacher education and business administration? If a community college shifts from a general academic emphasis to a vocational-technical emphasis? If a university suddenly receives authorization to develop several new doctoral programs?

The importance to collection development of institutional shifts in teaching and research was emphasized by Osburn in his study of the relationship between trends in research and the way in which academic research collections had been built.[43] His investigation led him to suggest that research libraries are unable to meet the needs of their users, not so much because of lack of money as lack of awareness of changes in the academic research environment.

Purpose of the Library

Closely related to the community or institution is the purpose (or purposes) for which the library was established, and sometimes community analysis leads to a new look at a library's purposes. A 1969 study of the Chicago Public Library reported that "the roles played in the past by the public library are increasingly provided outside the institution," and proposed that the library move toward "a series of specialized, discrete target programs for the remainder of the century."[44] Collections were to be built specifically in these areas:

1. Advanced resources for the many "specialists" not affiliated with universities or large special libraries

2. Cultural resources for the more intellectual and experimental segment of society
3. Basic, utilitarian, and self-development resources for the urban underprivileged
4. Information service, in a period dependent on facts and data
5. Subject and educational provision for students and adults
6. Provision of audiovisual resources (in which interest now runs high, but for which the distribution system is limited), other than the bland fare of television.

In a 1969 publication, emerging from the activities of the National Advisory Commission on Libraries, Lacy predicted that the library would move from being "an institution with rather general educational, cultural, and recreational aims" to one that would increasingly accept these responsibilities:

1. To support formal education, from prekindergarten through graduate and professional schools.
2. To sustain the increasingly complex operations of the government and the economy of the country.
3. To provide opportunities for continuing self-education and retraining.
4. To play a role in the reintegration into the society of groups now largely isolated and excluded by their lacks in education and training.
5. To provide resources for an informed public opinion and for personal cultural and intellectual growth and individuation.[45]

More recently, public librarians have shown a tendency to emphasize the provision of information as a fundamental purpose of the public library. Ballard noted, "this emphasis on information is a significant change in the service orientation of the public library" and pointed out a possible, significant implication for collection development—a shift away from the building of book collections toward other forms of service, such as electronic delivery of information.[46]

Unlike other types of libraries, public libraries do not have a set of standards specifying what the library should try to accomplish. According to the approach suggested in *A Planning Process for Public Libraries*, published in 1980, a public library administration is free—even required—to decide locally what its mission or purposes will be in terms of what the community needs and what resources are available to accomplish the chosen mission. At a conference on collection management in public libraries, Krueger gave these examples of choices that are available to those who lead public libraries:

> Will the public library try to be a center for research? Try to have in-depth collections for scholars and people needing original manuscripts?
>
> Will the public library provide primarily popular materials?
>
> Will it concentrate most of its energies on providing accurate, rapid access to information regardless of where that information is stored?
>
> Will it try to support the curriculum needs of elementary, secondary, and college students when those needs are also being met by other institutions?[47]

The standards statements for most other types of libraries have something to say about goals, objectives, or purposes. A school library media program is designed "to ensure that students and staff are effective users of ideas and information."[48] This broad mission is to be accomplished in the following ways:

> by providing intellectual and physical access to materials in all formats
>
> by providing instruction to foster competence and stimulate interest in reading, viewing, and using information and ideas
>
> by working with other educators to design learning strategies to meet the needs of individual students.[49]

Two-year college learning resources programs "exist to facilitate and improve learning, . . . are an integral part of instruction, [and] provide a variety of services as an integral part of the instructional process."[50]

The 1975 standards for college libraries acknowledged the library's responsibility to the curriculum, but also pointed out that a college library "now serves as a complementary academic capability which affords to students the opportunity to augment their classroom experience with an independent avenue for learning beyond the course offerings of the institution."[51] The 1986 standards noted that the role of the college library "has included collecting records of civilization and documentation of scientific pursuit," but also placed equal emphasis on the library's role in teaching users to retrieve and interpret these documents.[52] Standards for university libraries hint at a broader view of the library's purpose by assuming that the library exists "to support the instructional, research, and public service programs of the university."[53]

Clientele

A third group of variables that influences collection development is centered on the library's clientele: the real or potential users of its collection. According to accepted standards, a university library should give priority to the needs of students, faculty, and other academic staff of the university, who may be said to constitute the library's primary clientele. While it may also have obligations or commitments to other clienteles or constituencies, the library should recognize that these are secondary.[54]

School library media programs are expected "to provide learning experiences that encourage users to become discriminating consumers and skilled creators of information" and to "provide resources and activities that contribute to lifelong learning."[55]

The needs of users, demonstrated and perceived, are seen by many librarians as the primary basis upon which to develop, or discontinue, collections and services. Economists, looking at the problem of how libraries supply materials, have suggested that the public library may be viewed as a kind of cooperative that can reduce the cost of obtaining the material the members of the community wish to read. In this case, the library should supply those materials that people have indicated they want to borrow from the library. For example, Baltimore County Public Library has developed a reputation for building collections geared to high circulation rates; yet in 1981 its head of materials selection reminded possible critics that catering to the user's interest is not a revolutionary approach to collection development: "All libraries consider their audience when choosing books."[56] From an academic librarian's point of view, McGrath argues that analysis of past use of a collection enables the librarian to predict future use—a prediction which ought to be a determining factor in the formulation of collection development policy.[57] Public libraries have the most diverse clientele to consider, but even school and academic libraries have variety. From a numerical point of view, students make up the major part of an academic library's clientele, and members of the student body vary widely. Moreover, the student body of an institution may change from year to year; and students at one institution tend, as a group, to differ from those at other institutions in interest, abilities, motivation, and appreciation for the various forms of media.

Another important group of users of the school or academic library is the faculty, who also differ in interests, abilities, and motivation. Subtle shifts in the composition of the faculty may be important signals to those who work in collection development. A variation in the proportion of the faculty with various disciplinary interests, for example, is a clue that the faculty is changing in ways that may be significant for collection planning. Adjustments in the criteria by which faculty members are evaluated—a shift, for example, in emphasis among teaching, research, and service activities as accepted indicators of faculty productivity in a college—give other clues to the experienced librarian that part of the clientele may be changing its habits.

Alteration of teaching methods has obvious effects on collection use—perhaps the most immediately obvious of any variable in this group. A simple example is the change in demands on the library that occurs with a move from heavy reliance on the lecture method to more self-instruction, independent study, and problem-oriented methods of instruction. An individual faculty member may seldom make drastic changes in his or her teaching methods, but the faculty as a whole changes with the movement of faculty from one institution to another. Librarians in smaller institutions can often detect the effects on library use of one faculty departure or arrival.

Special libraries in academic institutions face all of these situations in regard to changing faculty and students, and have the same need to follow trends closely. In nonacademic settings, special libraries may find demands on their collections changing because of new services, new product development, new marketing approaches, etc., undertaken by their agencies or corporations.

Present Collection

In addition to the library's purposes and users, the collection which has been built and preserved through the years is itself a variable in the collection development process. This is not to suggest that the library collection should live a life of its own or that what it has been in the past must be the primary determinant of what it ought to be in the future. How much the present collection will influence future development depends on variables discussed earlier: the purposes of the library and the ways it is used, as well as the additional variables of size and age. The larger and older the present collection and the more research oriented the library, the more influence the present collection may have on future collection development plans, because of the tendency in such libraries to build on strengths that already exist in the collection. But in any collection, large or small, the weaknesses must be determined, rated as to their importance for users, and accepted or alleviated.

Hazen goes further than this in his effort to develop a model of collection development behavior by proposing that an outstanding collection in a particular subject will reinforce user demand and interests, as well as possibly affect publishing and reprinting in that discipline. "The historical commitment reflected in such a strong collection will, in turn, contribute to its continued support and strength."[58]

Available Resources

The fourth group of variables comes with the label "available resources." Resources, as the term is used here, include human resources;
financial resources; all the informational, inspirational, recreational, and
other kinds of resources that might be available for a library to purchase;
and the bibliographical and evaluative resources that help identify that
supply.

Human resources for collection development vary from one library to
another, in the sense that the number of qualified participants in selection,
evaluation, or collection management varies. A library director with a
large staff and other interested parties—faculty, students, researchers,
board members, etc.—who have diverse subject backgrounds, wide
knowledge of print and nonprint resources, an understanding of the
library's purposes, and are also eager to assist in building the collection,
can approach development from a different perspective than the director
who feels that he or she must do the job alone. The emphasis placed on
collection development skills in job announcements may give a hint
about a particular library's approach to this important function. Also,
libraries with good collection development programs are likely to be the
ones where staff members are provided continuing professional development in areas related to that effort.

Variation in the materials budget is so obvious a factor in collection
development that little comment on its significance is required. One of the
likely indicators of the quality of a library's collection is the amount of the
materials budget over a long period of time. It may not be possible to
control, or even influence, the level of the budget, but it is at least possible
to monitor it carefully. Fully documented budget requests and carefully
developed allocation procedures are useful techniques for dealing with
this variable.

The available supply of materials which might appropriately be acquired for a library's collection varies in total volume, in volume of
publications in various subjects, in mix of formats which publishers and
distributors use, and in terms of what librarians know about the supply.
Again, librar-ians may not be able to control the available supply, but they
can increase their knowledge of it. There are two levels of awareness: one
may know about the bibliographic tools which lead to the supply, or about
the available supply itself.

How much a selector needs to know about the available supply depends
on the size and purpose of the library, the subject under consideration, and

the pattern of publishing and use of materials on that subject. Sometimes, when a block of materials (such as all published histories of the community) has been identified as appropriate for a given library, it is sufficient to determine that an item (or group of items) exists. At other times, evaluative information is needed for item-by-item selection. Although improving one's knowledge of the available supply of materials is important for those who are involved in building library collections, this topic will not be emphasized here; and techniques of block buying, in one form or another, will be covered in a later chapter. For sources of evaluative information and considerations in item-by-item selection, the reader should consult the titles cited under General Works on Collection Development in the bibliography at the end of this chapter.

Resources also include materials that may be made available to users of a library even when they are not owned by that library. Standards for each type of library recognize this interdependence of library collections. The latest standards for school libraries put great emphasis on participation in resource sharing. "Promoting effective physical access to information resources and intellectual access to the content is the central unifying concept of these guidelines."[59] One of the sections in the chapter on resources and equipment is headed "Information Access beyond the School" and includes the specific guideline that "the library media center provides access to information outside the center through union catalogs, network arrangements, and resource-sharing options."[60] The latest college library standards also recognize this by recommending: "While it is important that a library have in its collection the quantity of materials called for in Formula A, its resources ought to be augmented whenever appropriate with external collections and services."[61] The university standards note: "University libraries should recognize that, to one degree or another, they share a responsibility with all research libraries to support higher education in general and each other in particular through cooperative efforts."[62] Even stronger is the statement in the guidelines for two-year college learning resources programs: "Every two-year college, whether privately or publicly supported, has a responsibility to help meet the resource material needs of the larger community in which it resides."[63]

A factor that has encouraged, or at least allowed, resource sharing to develop is the changing view of how to evaluate a library's service. There is less emphasis now on how many items a library can count in its collection and more on how well the library serves its clientele. Providing prompt access to an appropriate volume and range of materials (through resource-sharing agreements, if necessary) is beginning to be considered as acceptable as owning and storing those materials. From the user's point of view, prompt access is the key criterion of good service, not who owns and stores the item.

BIBLIOGRAPHY

Bibliographies

Bullard, Scott R., and Mollie K. Arthur. "The Literature of Library Acquisitions: A Selective Bibliography." *Library Acquisitions: Practice & Theory*, 1(1977):33-79.

Godden, Irene P., Aren W. Fachan, and Patricia A. Smith. *Collection Development and Acquisitions, 1970–80: An Annotated, Critical Bibliography*. Metuchen, N.J.: Scarecrow, 1982. 138p.

Kohl, David F. *Acquisitions, Collection Development, and Collection Use*. Santa Barbara, Calif.: ABC-Clio, 1985. 409p.

Magrill, Rose Mary, and Constance Rinehart. *Library Technical Services: A Selected, Annotated Bibliography*. Westport, Conn.: Greenwood, 1977. 238p.

Schmidt, Karen A. " 'Buying Good Pennyworths?' A Review of Literature of Acquisitions in the Eighties." *Library Resources & Technical Services*, 30(October/December 1986):333-340.

Thompson, James. "Current Awareness for Better Library Acquisitions." *Library Acquisitions: Practice & Theory*, 1(1977):23-32.

Wynar, Bodhan S. *Library Acquisitions: A Classified Bibliographic Guide to the Literature and Reference Tools*. 2d ed. Littleton, Colo.: Libraries Unlimited, 1971. 239p.

Review Articles

Hudson, Judith, and Geraldene Walker. "The Year's Work in Technical Services Research, 1986." *Library Resources & Technical Services*, 31(October/December 1987):275-286.

Pankake, Marcia. "Technical Services in 1984 and 1985: Resources." *Library Resources & Technical Services*, 30(July/September 1986):218-237.

Welsch, Erwin K. "Resources: The Year's Work in 1982." *Library Resources & Technical Services*, 27(July/September 1983):315-329.

Wortman, William A. "Collection Management, 1986." *Library Resources & Technical Services*, 31(October/December 1987):287-305.

General Works on Collection Development

Broadus, Robert N. *Selecting Materials for Libraries*. 2d ed. New York: Wilson, 1981. 469 p.

Collection Development in Libraries. Edited by Robert D. Stueart and George B. Miller. Greenwich, Conn.: JAI Press, 1980. 2v.

Collection Management in Public Libraries: Proceedings of a Preconference to the 1984 ALA Annual Conference, June 21–22, 1984, Dallas, Texas. Edited by Judith Serebnick. Chicago: American Library Assn., 1986. 148p.

Curley, Arthur, and Dorothy Broderick. *Building Library Collections.* 6th ed. Metuchen, N.J.: Scarecrow, 1985. 339p.

English and American Literature: Sources and Strategies for Collection Development. Edited by William McPheron. Chicago: American Library Assn., 1987. 272p.

Evans, G. Edward. *Developing Library and Information Center Collections.* 2d ed. Littleton, Colo.: Libraries Unlimited, 1987. 443p.

Gardner, Richard K. *Library Collections: Their Origin, Selection, and Development.* New York: McGraw-Hill, 1981. 354p.

Katz, William A. *Collection Development: The Selection of Materials for Libraries.* New York: Holt, 1980. 352p.

Pankake, Marcia. "From Book Selection to Collection Management: Continuity and Advance in an Unending Work." In *Advances in Librarianship*, vol. 13, pp. 185-210. Edited by Wesley Simonton. New York: Academic Press, 1984.

Selection of Library Materials in Applied and Interdisciplinary Fields. Edited by Beth Shapiro. Chicago: American Library Assn., 1987. 287p.

Selection of Library Materials in the Humanities, Social Sciences, and Sciences. Edited by Patricia McClung and John Whaley. Chicago: American Library Assn., 1985. 405p.

Van Orden, Phyllis J. *The Collection Program in Schools: Concepts, Practices, and Information Sources.* Englewood, Colo.: Libraries Unlimited, 1988. 347p.

Collection Development Environment

Book Reading and Library Usage: A Study of Habits and Perceptions. Princeton, N.J.: Gallup Organization, 1978. Various paging.

Boyer, Ernest L. *College: The Undergraduate Experience in America.* New York: Harper & Row, 1987. 328p.

Brittain, John M. *Information and Its Users: A Review with Special Reference to the Social Sciences.* New York: Wiley, 1971.

Chronicle of Higher Education. 1966- . (weekly)

Cummings, Martin M. *The Economics of Research Libraries.* Washington, D.C.: Council on Library Resources, 1986. 216p.

Hamaker, Charles. "The Least Reading for the Smallest Number at the Highest Price." *American Libraries*, 19(October 1988):764-768.

Intellectual Freedom Manual. 2d ed. Chicago: American Library Assn., 1983. 210p.

Jones, Frances M. *Defusing Censorship: The Librarian's Guide to Handling Censorship Conflicts.* Phoenix, Ariz.: Oryx Press, 1983.

Librarian's Guide to the New Copyright Law. Chicago: American Library Assn., 1978.

Library Issues: Briefings for Faculty and Administrators. 1981- . (bimonthly)

Lytle, Susan S., and Hal W. Hall. "Software, Libraries, and the Copyright Law." *Library Journal*, 110(July 1985):33-39.

Mancall, Jacqueline C., and M. Carl Drott. *Measuring Student Information Use: A Guide for School Library Media Specialists.* Littleton, Colo.: Libraries Unlimited, 1983. 145p.

Newsletter on Intellectual Freedom. 1951- . (monthly)

Publishers Weekly: The International News Magazine of Book Publishing. 1872- . (weekly)

Reading in America 1978: Selected Findings of the Book Industry Study Group's 1978 Study of American Book Reading and Book-Buying Habits. . . . Washington, D.C.: Library of Congress, 1979.

Tough, Allen M. *The Adult's Learning Projects.* 2d ed. Toronto: Ontario Institute for Studies in Education, 1979.

United States. Commission on Excellence in Education. *A Nation at Risk: The Imperative for Educational Reform: A Report to the Nation and the Secretary of Education, United States Department of Education by the National Commission on Excellence in Education.* Washington, D.C.: The Commission, 1983. 64p.

United States. Copyright Office. *General Guide to the Copyright Act of 1976.* Washington, D.C.: Library of Congress, 1977.

Zweizig, Douglas, and Brenda Dervin. "Public Library Use, Users, Uses: Advances in Knowledge of the Characteristics and Needs of the Adult Clientele of American Public Libraries." In *Advances in Librarianship*, vol. 7, pp. 231-255. New York: Academic Press, 1977.

Local Factors Affecting Collection Development

Atkinson, Ross. "The Citation as Intertext: Toward a Theory of the Selection Process." *Library Resources & Technical Services*, 28 (April/June 1984):109-119.

"Community Analysis and Libraries." Issue editor, Larry Earl Bone. *Library Trends*, 24(January 1976):429-642.

Hartje, George N. "The Parameters of Developing and Managing a Library Collection." Collection Management, 3(Summer/Fall 1979):247-257.

Hazen, Dan C. "Modeling Collection Development Behavior: A Preliminary Statement." *Collection Management*, 4(Spring/Summer 1982):1-13.

Kennedy, Gail. "The Relationship Between Acquisitions and Collection Development." *Library Acquisitions: Practice and Theory*, 7(1983): 225-232.

Martin, Murray S. "A Future for Collection Management." *Collection Management*, 6(Fall/Winter 1984):1-9.

Miller, Marilyn L. "Collection Development in School Library Media Centers: National Recommendation and Reality." *Collection Building*, 1(1978): 25-48.

Osburn, Charles B. *Academic Research and Library Resources: Changing Patterns in America.* Westport, Conn.: Greenwood, 1979. 187p.

Perdue, Albert. "Conflicts in Collection Development." *Library Acquisitions: Practice and Theory*, 2(1978):123-126.

Weintraub, Karl J. "The Humanistic Scholar and the Library." *Library Quarterly*, 50(January 1980):22-39.
Williams, Gordon R. "The Function and Methods of Libraries in the Diffusion of Knowledge." *Library Quarterly*, 50(January 1980):58-75.
Wilson, Patrick. "Limits to the Growth of Knowledge: The Case of the Social and Behavioral Sciences." *Library Quarterly*, 50(January 1980):4-21.

Standards, Guidelines, and Related Documents

American Association of School Librarians and Association for Educational Communications and Technology. *Information Power: Guidelines for School Library Media Programs*. Chicago: American Library Assn., 1988. 171p.
Association of College and Research Libraries. "An Evaluative Checklist for Reviewing a College Library Program." *College & Research Libraries News*, 40(November 1979):305-316.
_____. "Guidelines for Branch Libraries in Colleges and Universities." *College & Research Libraries News*, 36(October 1975):281-283.
_____. "Guidelines for Library Service to Extension/Noncampus Students: Draft of Proposed Revisions." *College & Research Libraries News*, 41(October 1980):265-272.
_____. "Guidelines for Two-Year College Learning Resources Programs (Revised)." *College & Research Libraries News*, 43(January 1982):5-10; 43(February 1982):45-49.
_____. "Standards for College Libraries, 1986." *College & Research Libraries News*, 47(March, 1986): 189-200.
"Guidelines for Branch Libraries in Colleges and Universities." *College & Research Libraries News*, 36(October 1975): 281-283.
Joint Committee of the Association of Research Libraries and the Association of College and Research Libraries. "Standards for University Libraries." *College & Research Libraries News*, 40(April 1970): 101-110.
McClure, Charles et al. *Planning and Role Setting for Public Libraries: A Manual of Options and Procedures*. Chicago: American Library Assn., 1987. 168p.
"The Mission of an Undergraduate Library (Model Statement)." *College & Research Libraries News*, 40(November 1979):317-319.
Van House, Nancy, et al. *Output Measures for Public Libraries: A Manual of Standardized Procedures*. 2d ed. Chicago: American Library Assn., 1987. 99p.
Palmour, Vernon E., Marcia C. Bellassi, and Nancy V. DeWath. *A Planning Process for Public Libraries*. Chicago: American Library Assn., 1980. 304p.
Public Library Association. Goals, Guidelines, and Standards Committee. *Public Library Mission Statement and Its Imperatives for Service*. Chicago: American Library Assn., 1979. 24p.

TWO

Collection Development Policies

A WRITTEN COLLECTION DEVELOPMENT POLICY is an important tool for guiding all activities related to planning, budgeting, selecting, and acquiring library materials. It is one of the first pieces of evidence in deciding whether a library is engaged in true collection development. The ideal collection development policy clearly indicates the general intent of the library administration with regard to the collection and is both generally applicable and adequately flexible. Policies are sometimes confused with procedures, which are entirely different. A procedure statement documents the best way to carry out a specific activity, giving detailed, step-by-step instructions. While procedures leave little room for individual judgment, policies spell out limits of acceptable action and grant freedom to exercise professional judgment when operating within those limits.

Standards for various types of libraries make firm statements about the need for collection development policies. As early as 1966, the public library standards contained this statement:

All materials should be selected and retained or discarded in keeping with stated objectives of each system. . . . Every system and every library within the system should have a written statement of policy, covering the selection and maintenance of its collection.[1]

The standards for school library media centers published in 1975 made this recommendation:

Selection of collections is guided by a selection policy formulated by media staff, administrators, consultants, teachers, students, and representative citizens, and adopted by the board of education.[2]

The 1988 standards for school library media programs were even more specific about the importance of a selection policy, as shown by these two recommendations:

> The school district has a selection policy that has been approved by the school board and includes criteria and procedures for the selection and reconsideration of resources.

> Each school building has its own collection development plan that supplements a district policy and provides specific guidelines for developing the school's collection.[3]

The 1975 standards for college libraries did not specifically mention a collection development policy, but the 1986 standards did:

> Although the scope and content of the collection is ultimately the responsibility of the library staff, this responsibility can be best fulfilled by developing clear selection policies in cooperation with the teaching faculty.[4]

The standards for university libraries read:

> A university library's collections shall be developed systematically and consistently within the terms of explicit and detailed policies.[5]

The guidelines for two-year college learning resources programs further this theme:

> A written statement regarding acquisition and production of learning materials has such an important and pervasive effect on the instructional program and the services of the Learning Resources Program that all segments of the academic community should be involved in its development. The statement should be readily available in an official publication.[6]

Public libraries have a longer tradition of articulating the principles behind their collection efforts than do other types of libraries. Not only did the public library standards offer specific recommendations on policies at an earlier date, but many public libraries have also published their policies, thus providing models for other institutions. School librarians have received great encouragement to write policies and have been provided with models from the American Association of School Librarians, as well as from various state agencies.

University librarians were slower to accept written collection development policies as an appropriate tool for planning, but they have made great progress over the past decade in producing such documents. Before the 1970s, a few university librarians emphasized the value of collection and acquisition policies and discussed how to construct them, but by the early

1970s, more evidence of interest in policy statements began to appear. The publication and wide distribution of policy statements by Stanford University in 1970 and Northwestern University in 1972 prompted increased activity in many libraries. A collection development survey, conducted in 1974 by the Association of Research Libraries, found that 65 percent of the large university libraries responding had a formal, written collection development policy.[7]

RATIONALE FOR A WRITTEN POLICY

A written statement of policy is needed not only because it publicly expresses the relationship of collection development to the objectives of the institution, but also because of the need for practical guidance in everyday selection problems and for support and assistance in justifying the selections made for the library. Decisions about the way in which the collection will be developed, expressed through such policy statements, are basic to planning for a broad range of library operations. The written policy can function as a training tool for those who participate in collection decisions, especially those who are new to the library or to the process.

For some librarians, the main pressure leading to a written collection development policy is the need to provide a more rational guide for budget allocation. Policies should be clearly written using standard terminology and then disseminated widely in order to facilitate interlibrary loan and cooperative acquisitions projects. In general, a collection development policy can help the library make the best use of its limited resources by indicating who will be served, for what purposes, and with what types of materials.

Almost every library has some vestige of a collection development policy, whether or not it is written (library materials are generally not added to the collection at random). Those who participate in selection use some principles, stated or unstated, good or bad. Development of the collection will be better if it is backed by a policy statement and guidelines that are based on library objectives and the needs of users. These can be discovered and stated for every library, although the complexity of the exercise will vary greatly—in, say, a public library that serves a homogeneous community, as opposed to a special library that serves a utilitarian information function, or a major research library with diverse clienteles and goals.

The process followed in formulating and recording a collection development policy has value in itself, particularly in a large, complex library. Those who participate gain knowledge of the existing collection and become better able to make appropriate reference referrals. The coordinator of the University of California at Berkeley's collection development policy statement commented that as selectors met to discuss various subject policy statements, "fruitful exchanges of information took place, a sense of an organically whole library was being built up informationally bit by bit in the minds of the participants, and some ingrained attitudes began to change."[8]

In spite of the wide acceptance of the value of collection development policies within the profession, there are those who believe that these policies are unnecessary. One set of objections is based on the difficulties that surround planning in any rapidly changing situation. Public libraries in areas of rapid growth may require so many reviews and revisions of policy that collection development librarians may not have the time to develop written plans. Academic librarians have always complained of the difficulty of adjusting collections and services to an institution where new courses of study rise up unannounced and budgets are unpredictable. The high cost in staff time required to develop a policy that is widely understood and accepted may be an unaffordable expense. In certain types of libraries (for example, special libraries), where the main focus of collection development is to respond to immediate, expressed needs of a well-defined clientele, any written policy beyond the most general statement of objectives may be of little practical use.

PREPARING THE WRITTEN POLICY

As a library staff begins a written collection development policy, it must analyze its present situation to determine what the users of its library need and what it is doing to meet those needs. This means gathering documents and interviewing staff and other interested parties to establish what kinds of opportunities and constraints exist in the institution or community being served; the policies and procedures which, though unwritten, may already be in effect; the cooperative agreements and other obligations binding the library; the limitations imposed by the physical facilities and anticipated materials budgets; and the strengths and weaknesses of the present collection. This is the stage where community or institutional analysis and collection evaluation or assessment play a part.

Guidelines must also be established for the project. Those who have reason to participate—who may be able to contribute something to the drafting of the policy—need to be identified. Plans should be made for involving as many knowledgeable persons as possible in the process, although all need not be involved in the same way. Some may provide input for assessing the present situation; a few may cooperate on the actual writing; and others may read and react to successive versions of the document. Establishing a timetable, providing for several rounds of drafting and review, is also important.

ELEMENTS OF THE POLICY

Decisions about the format of the document—which elements will be included and how they will be arranged—must be made early in the planning process. Elements to be included in a policy statement, as recommended by the Collection Management and Development Committee of the ALA's Resources and Technical Services Division in its *Guide for Written Collection Policy Statements*, published in 1989, can be grouped under three headings: introduction to the policy, general collection management and development policies, and detailed analysis of subject collections.[9]

According to the *Guide for Written Collection Policy Statements*, the first section of the policy—the introduction to the policy—"describes the context of a library's collection management and development programs, lists the mission and goals of the program, and summarizes basic principles common to all aspects of the program."[10] This section of the statement is designed to introduce the philosophy behind the library's collection development efforts and to define and explain the scope of the operations to be covered by the policy. This is also the section in which legal and delegated responsibility for collection development may be indicated, the organization of the process described, and, if desired, the participants identified. The specific topics to be covered in this first section include the purpose of the policy and its intended audience, a description of the institution and its clientele, and an overview of how the collection has developed. Official statements on the library's approach to intellectual freedom issues and cooperative collection agreements should also be included. This introduction to the policy is the logical place to discuss preservation, storage, replacement, and weeding in relationship to the total effort to develop and manage the collection.

The second main section of the policy specifies the way in which materials of certain types or on certain subjects will be added to the collection. In the past, some libraries have chosen to divide this section by method of acquisition, listing separately what will be acquired through approval plans, standing orders, gifts and exchange, etc. Public libraries often divide their policies by client groups, discussing materials for adult, for children, for young adults, for home bound, etc. According to the *Guide for Written Collection Policy Statements*, the section of a policy dealing with "general collection management and development policies" is the place for "general policies that transcend subject boundaries and govern the collection of material by format, language, or use."[11] Specifically, there may be statements on formats (newspapers, microforms, maps, etc.); special collections (rare books, archives, etc.); languages; multiple copies; reserve materials; reference works; or government documents.

The third broad section suggested for a collection development policy is the detailed analysis of the collection by subjects. The *Guide for Written Collection Policy Statements* recommends that the "breadth and depth of subject collections" be described "in a standard, uniform, and detailed manner."[12] Public librarians have sometimes chosen to divide the main section of the policy further, into fiction, nonfiction, reference, or to comment separately on materials dealing with medicine, law, religion, genealogy, sex, drugs, pseudoscientific topics, or those written in foreign languages. Certain academic librarians have made their divisions on the basis of academic department, physical location, or administrative unit (such as a departmental library).

In the early stages of formulating collection development policies, there appeared to be more variety among libraries in the way that subjects were outlined in a policy. The recommendation of the 1979 ALA guidelines on collection development policies—that the subject analysis be organized by a standard library classification scheme—did not have an immediate effect on library practices, but the collection assessment movement that began with the RLG Conspectus appears to have done a great deal to achieve that desired uniformity in collection development policies.

The RLG Conspectus was a product of the Research Libraries Group, Inc., working through its Collection Management and Development Committee, which undertook a study beginning about 1980. The Conspectus grew out of a desire to analyze collection development strengths and weaknesses at each member institution in order to allocate "primary collecting responsibilities" for subjects, geographical areas, forms of material, etc. Representing a joint or cooperative collection development policy, the Conspectus is a summary of existing collection strengths and future collecting intensities of RLG members. It is arranged by a version of the Library of Congress Classification System and uses codes similar to those recommended in the ALA guidelines of 1979.

Although only a few dozen of the country's largest research libraries were involved in the original development of the RLG Conspectus, its influence has spread to smaller and other types of libraries. The Association of Research Libraries (ARL), with a membership similar to, but less exclusive than, RLG, also recognized the need to identify collection strengths nationally and, in 1981, tested the methodology of the Conspectus in five non-RLG libraries. Eventually, the Conspectus approach was adopted by ARL for its North American Collection Inventory Project. Among the advantages expected by the ARL were "development of the capacity to relate local collection development policies to collection levels at other institutions and to serve as the basis for cooperative collection development, both nationally and regionally" and "development of the capacity to relate collection development strengths to cataloging and preservation needs."[13]

Regional groupings of libraries, such as the Association for Higher Education of North Texas, which includes several university libraries of more than 1,000,000 volumes and several college libraries of less than 500,000 volumes, tried out the Conspectus approach for cooperative planning. Statewide and multistate projects incorporating public, academic, and special libraries of widely varying size also developed modifications of this collection assessment tool. In the latter types of projects, where many participating libraries had collections classified by the Dewey Decimal Classification, conversion tables were developed and classification schemes were outlined at more than one level of detail. The net effect of all this activity was to make it more likely that collection development policies for libraries of all sizes and types could be found using a standard library classification scheme.

Guide for Written Collection Policy Statements specifically recommends that the Conspectus approach to collection evaluation and description be used, regardless of the size of the library. Two sets of subject listings are suggested: RLG's version of the Library of Congress Classification subject fields or the subject fields and worksheets developed for the Pacific Northwest Conspectus database, a project of LIRN (Library and Information Resources for the Northwest).[14] The latter set of subject fields and worksheets offers two levels of specificity, which makes it more suitable for smaller collections.

CODES FOR LEVELS OF COLLECTING

Once the outline for subject analysis has been chosen, the next step is to describe each subject. For each subject, the *Guide for Written Collection Policy Statements* suggests noting existing collection strengths, current collecting intensity, desired collecting intensity, languages collected, chronological and geographical emphases, and any special features of the collection.[15]

Coding of collection strengths and intensity has evolved from schemes using three or four broad groupings to the latest recommendations in the 1989 *Guide to Written Collection Policy Statements*, which uses five broad groups (three of these have subdivisions) and a set of language codes.[16] The codes range from 0 (out of scope) through 4 (research level) and 5 (comprehensive level). Codes 1 (minimal level), 2 (basic information level), and 3 (study or instructional support level) are the ones with subdivisions. Language codes provide a way to indicate foreign-language materials. The other important aspects of a particular subject collection may be described in narrative scope notes.

Many public librarians found the levels of collecting recommended in the 1979 ALA guidelines unsuitable for describing their collections. Adaptations of collection-level codes have been developed for use by smaller, less exhaustive collections. A collection-coordinating committee of the Library Council of Metropolitan Milwaukee developed a six-level set of descriptors to rate the strength of subject collections in a mixed group of libraries that included university, large public, small college, special subject, etc.[17] The Subject Strength Scale, used by the Northwest Missouri Library Network for a cooperative collection development project, had five points:

1. Some basic reference tools.
2. Highly selective reference and circulating collection. . .
3. General coverage of the subject, including current and limited retrospective coverage. . .
4. Most aspects of the subject covered, including both current and retrospective materials but with varying depth. . .
5. All aspects of the subject covered, including strong retrospective coverage. . . .[18]

The same project allowed collections to be described according to the User Orientation Scale, which provided for six categories: recreational, independent, study, professional, student (primary and secondary level), academic (college study up to the master's degree level), and research.

OTHER FEATURES OF POLICIES

In any library in which the written policy is viewed as protection from unwarranted interference in collection development, a large part of the policy may be devoted to procedures for reconsideration of materials. The model policy developed by the American Association of School Librarians includes statements about responsibility for selection and criteria for selection, but its most detailed section is a step-by-step procedure for handling complaints. Sample forms are provided for recording information about the materials being challenged. Public library policies often contain similar sections. The *Intellectual Freedom Manual*, compiled by the Office for Intellectual Freedom of the American Library Association, is a useful source for those who wish to use a collection development policy to promote unrestricted access to materials and to defend against censorship.

A policy document which covers all aspects of collection development will also include statements on discarding, replacement, duplication, and possibly preservation. Collection evaluation is an integral part of collection development and is occasionally included. Provision for periodic review and possible revision is essential if the policy is to offer real guidance in collection development.

An issue that causes librarians to hesitate about becoming involved in writing a collection policy is the frame of reference to be used: whether the policy should be limited to what the library is *currently* doing or focus on what the library *ought* to be doing to develop its collections. If the process of developing the policy uncovers user needs not presently being met, what the library ought to be doing may be more important than what it is doing. The 1979 ALA guidelines, as well as the 1989 publication, *Guide for Written Collection Policy Statements*, suggest that both present practice and future intentions may be included in the written policy. Osburn's comment on this point is worth considering: "The common and most evident feature of the policy should be its tendency toward the ideal, tempered by a sense of the real on all occasions. Ultimately, the application of sound professional judgment will be fundamental to the quality of the policy."[19]

The collection development policy establishes ground rules for planning, budgeting, selecting, and acquiring library materials and usually identifies where final responsibility for these activities will reside. It does not ordinarily specify the way in which the staff will be organized or the exact procedures to be followed in carrying out these activities. The next chapter will outline factors affecting the organization of the collection development function and will describe typical procedures used in various kinds of libraries.

BIBLIOGRAPHY

Adams, Helen R. *School Media Policy Development.* Littleton, Colo.: Libraries Unlimited, 1986. 174p.

American Association of School Librarians. "Policies and Procedures for Selection of Instructional Materials." *School Media Quarterly,* 5(Winter 1977):109-116.

Association of Research Libraries. Office of University Library Management Studies. Systems and Procedures Exchange Center. *Acquisition Policies in ARL Libraries.* Washington, D.C., 1974. 132p. (SPEC Kit No. 12)

_____. *Collection Development in ARL Libraries.* Washington, D.C., 1974. 132p. (SPEC Kit No. 11)

_____. *Collection Development Policies.* Washington, D.C., 1977. 109p. (SPEC Kit No. 38)

Atkinson, Ross. "The Language of the Levels: Reflections on the Communication of Collection Development Policy." *College Research Libraries,* 47(March 1986):140-149.

Boyer, Calvin J., and Nancy L. Eaton. *Book Selection Policies in American Libraries: An Anthology of Policies from College, Public, and School Libraries.* Austin, Tex.: Armadillo Pr., 1971. 222p.

Collection Development Policies. Chicago: Assn. of College and Research Libraries, American Library Assn., 1981. 131 p. (CLIP Notes #2-81).

Conway, Suzy, Kathy Gallagher, and Barbara Halbrook. "Selection and Acquisitions Manual Development." *Bulletin of the Medical Library Association,* 67(January 1979):54-58.

Dowd, Sheila T. "The Formulation of a Collection Development Policy Statement." In *Collection Development in Libraries.* Edited by Robert D. Stueart and George B. Miller. Greenwich, Conn.: JAI Pr., 1980, pp. 67-87.

Evans, Robert W. "Collection Development Policy Statements: The Documentation Process." *Collection Management,* 7(Spring 1985):63-73.

Farrell, David. "The NCIP Option for Coordinated Collection Management." *Library Resources & Technical Services,* 30(January/March 1986):47-56.

Feng, Y. T. "The Necessity for a Collection Development Policy Statement." *Library Resources & Technical Services,* 23(Winter 1979) :39-44.

Ferguson, Anthony W., Joan Grant, and Joel S. Rutstein. "The RLG Conspectus: Its Uses and Benefits." *College & Research Libraries,* 49(May 1988):197-206.

Forcier, Peggy. "Building Collections Together: The Pacific Northwest Conspectus." *Library Journal,* 113(April 15, 1988):43-45.

Foster, Eloise C., and C. Poole. *Collection Development Policy of the Library of the American Hospital Association.* Chicago: American Hospital Assn., 1983. 127p.

Futas, Elizabeth, ed. *Library Acquisitions Policies and Procedures.* Phoenix, Ariz.: Oryx Pr., 1977. 406p.

_____, ed. *Library Acquisitions Policies and Procedures.* 2d ed. Phoenix, Ariz.: Oryx Pr., 1984.

Gardner, Charles A. "Book Selection Policies in the College Library: A Reappraisal." *College & Research Libraries*, 46(March 1985):140-146.

Guidelines for Collection Development. Edited by David L. Perkins. Chicago: American Library Assn., 1979. 78p.

Haley, Anne, and Douglas K. Ferguson. "The Pacific Northwest Collection Assessment Project." *Resource Sharing and Information Networks*, 2(Spring/Summer 1985):185-197.

Intellectual Freedom Manual. 2d ed. Chicago: American Library Assn., 1983. 210p.

Koenig, Dorothy. "Rushmore at Berkeley: The Dynamics of Developing a Written Collection Development Policy Statement." *Journal of Academic Librarianship*, 7(January 1982):344-350.

Kreuger, Karen. *Coordinated Cooperative Collection Development for Illinois Libraries.* Springfield, Ill.: Illinois State Library, 1983. 3v.

Lein, Edward. "Suggestions for Formulating Collection Development Policy Statements for Music Score Collections in Academic Libraries." *Collection Management*, 9(Winter 1987):69-101.

Merritt, LeRoy Charles. *Book Selection and Intellectual Freedom.* New York: Wilson, 1970. 100p.

Nisonger, Thomas E. "Editing the RLG Conspectus to Analyze the OCLC Archival Tapes of Seventeen Texas Libraries." *Library Resources & Technical Services*, 29(October/December 1985):309-327.

Oberg, Larry R. "Evaluating the Conspectus Approach for Smaller Library Collections." *College & Research Libraries*, 49(May 1988):187-196.

Osburn, Charles B. "Planning for a University Library Policy on Collection Development." *International Library Review*, 9(1977):209-224.

_____. "Some Practical Observations on the Writing, Implementation, and Revision of Collection Development Policy." *Library Resources & Technical Services*, 23(Winter 1979):7-15.

Overmier, Judith, and Mary H. Mueller. "Collection Development Policies and Practices in Medical School Rare Book Libraries." *Bulletin of the Medical Library Association*, 72(April 1984):150-154.

Pacific Northwest Collection Assessment Manual. Portland, Ore.: Fred Meyer Charitable Trust, Library and Information Resources for the Northwest, 1986. 90p.

Parr, Virginia H. "Case Study: A Collection Development Policy for an Academic Library Endowed Enrichment Area and Collection." *Collection Management*, 6(Fall/Winter 1984):83-92.

School Library and Media Center Acquisition Policies and Procedures. Edited by Mary M. Taylor. Phoenix, Ariz.: Oryx Pr., 1981. 272p.

School Library and Media Center Acquisition Policies and Procedures. 2d ed. Edited by Betty Kemp. Phoenix, Ariz.: Oryx Pr., 1987. 280p.

Stam, David H. "Collaborative Collection Development: Progress, Problems, and Potential." *Collection Building*, 3(1985-86):3-9.

Stanford University Libraries. *Book Selection Policies of the Libraries of Stanford University.* Compiled by Peter A. Johnson; edited by E. M. Grieder. Stanford, Calif., 1970. Unpaged.

_____. *Collection Development Policy Statement 1980.* Stanford, Calif., 1981. Various pagings.

University of California, Berkeley. General Library. *Collection Development Policy Statement.* Prelim. ed. Berkeley, 1980. Unpaged.

University of Texas at Austin. General Libraries. *Collection Development Policy.* 2d ed. Austin, 1981. Unpaged. (Contributions to Librarianship, No. 2)

Ward, K. Linda. "Collection Policy in College and University Libraries." *Music Library Association Notes*, 29(March 1973):432-440.

THREE

Organization of Collection Development

THE ORGANIZATION OF collection development activities in libraries varies with the size of the library, the purposes for which it was established, and the composition and location of the clientele it was designed to serve. In small libraries, all activities—from developing policy, allocating funds, selecting individual items, verifying bibliographic information, ordering and receiving, to fund accounting— may be done by one person, or at least in one department. Observation of the evolution of library organizational structures indicates that responsibility for collection development may be retained by the library director longer than responsibility for cataloging or circulation or reference. When separation of collection development tasks becomes necessary, the director may delegate order preparation, bookkeeping, certain selection decisions, and liaison with users before finally relinquishing direct control of the budget. In large, complex libraries, the activities connected with planning, allocating, and selecting may be either highly centralized or widely dispersed, and may be separated both administratively and physically from the business activities of purchasing materials.

The administrative location of the collection development function also varies from one library to another. Collection development may operate as a department within either technical or public services, may actually be directed from the acquisitions department, or may be organized as a separate unit, parallel to public and technical services and reporting to the director. In large libraries, collection development often has closer ties to public service departments, particularly to the general reference department and departments that serve specific disciplines, than to the acquisitions department.

In a 1987 review of the status of collection development organization, Bryant offered the following list of seven configurations, while pointing

41

out, at the same time, that "creative thinking can add to this list of possibilities."

1. collection development that is performed by a single librarian;
2. separate subject-oriented segments of the library, each of which has its own collection developer(s) who may or may not report to a collection development officer (other than the director);
3. collection development that is the function of a committee that reviews suggestions from patrons and staff, making final purchase decisions;
4. a group of librarians who come together to perform collection development activities and then disperse to their primary assignments throughout the library;
5. a unit of full- or part-time collection developers that is subsumed by a larger division of the library;
6. a unit of collection developers that is separate from other divisions of the library; or
7. the collection development unit that subsumes one or more other library functions, such as acquisitions, special collections, or interlibrary loan.[1]

One of the most significant factors affecting the organization of the collection development function in a library is the perspective—present or future—from which the collection is viewed. Is the collection seen as a current resource, designed to meet the immediate needs of users and to be changed as often as those needs change? Or, is it seen as a permanent resource, a collection that will meet the as-yet-unknown needs of scholars far into the indefinite future? Although not all public library collections are built from the perspective of current needs, that is a common approach. As one public librarian expressed it: "In public libraries, every title that is purchased is expected to be used today."[2] The emphasis in these libraries is on identifying popular materials as soon as they are announced for distribution, predicting the volume of local demand, and then buying quickly and in appropriate quantities. When public interest in certain authors, subjects, or formats wanes, the unwanted materials are removed from the collection to make room for those of rising popularity.

Educational libraries, particularly those serving students below the level of graduate or upper division undergraduate courses, may also be built from the perspective of current needs. In such cases, the demands of the curriculum play the role that popular demands and interests do in public libraries. Materials will be regularly selected and discarded from the collection in order to provide direct instructional support. Collections are most likely to be viewed as permanent resources when they are intended to support graduate instruction and scholarly research programs.

Research collections are seldom reviewed for the purpose of discarding materials and generally do not include multiple copies of the same item. Funds are spent in a way that will secure the greatest depth and breadth of coverage in the chosen subjects. As the collection development perspective varies from current demand to future needs, organization and participation in collection development may also vary.

Another factor affecting the organization of the collection development function in a library is the degree to which the library staff—as opposed to library users or those completely outside the library's community, such as book dealers—influences the development of the collection. Bryant has suggested that a library may represent one of three different postures in the organization of collection development: "an *acquisitions* posture which acknowledges minimal staff investment; a *selection* posture which proclaims the library's intent to bear responsibility for new additions to its collections and for consultation with the library's patron community regarding purchases; or a *collection management and development* posture which perceives the library's collections as comparable in importance to its more visible services."[3]

Since the basic characteristic of an acquisitions posture is identified as being a reliance on external selection, many school, academic, and special libraries would fall into this category. Library collections in educational settings—from elementary schools to universities with graduate programs—are influenced (to varying degrees) by the faculty and students who use them. In some college and university libraries, the faculty maintains tight control over departmental allocations and the selection of titles; in other libraries, the faculty is willing to leave these matters to the library staff. Special libraries try to respond so promptly to the demands of their users that librarians may find the range of their decision-making responsibility quite limited. Also falling into this category might be libraries where responsibility for initial selection decisions is turned over to publishers and book dealers, through standing orders, blanket orders, and approval-plan arrangements.

The rise of blanket order and approval plans has usually been credited to the sudden expansion of materials budgets between the late 1950s and the mid-1960s. Some librarians, particularly in developing universities, saw their materials budgets suddenly double or triple, forcing them to drop traditional methods of selection and acquisition and try new approaches. In general, a blanket order plan is one in which a publisher agrees to supply everything published (within specified limits of the plan), generally without return privileges for the buyer; and an approval plan is one in which a dealer assumes the responsibility for selecting and supplying (subject to return privileges) all materials that fit with the library's profile and needs, specified in terms of subjects, levels, formats, prices, etc.

Large public libraries often use an arrangement called the Greenaway Plan (named for Emerson Greenaway, former director of the Free Library of Philadelphia, who worked out the original arrangement with the J. B. Lippincott Company in the spring of 1958). Greenaway Plan terms vary from one publisher to another, but generally the library receives, for a nominal price, one copy of each trade title in advance of publication. This enables the library staff to review each title early and make recommendations for purchases, so that books can be ordered in advance of publication. No return privileges are allowed, since the price is set so low that returns would not justify the paperwork involved. Books that are not of interest to the library can be discarded, which is cheaper than trying to arrange for their return. This type of plan does not really involve selection decisions on the part of the publishers, since most plans are designed to send one copy of everything published. For this reason, a library using it may fit into the second category in Bryant's typography—the selection posture.

A library with a selection posture toward collection development provides for some type of liaison with users, but decision making is assigned to librarians, who have the responsibility for building the collection. In public libraries, for example, the library staff ordinarily has complete responsibility for the collection. Users may be asked for suggestions, or they may volunteer them, but librarians make the key decisions. Academic libraries sometimes have formal arrangements for consultation with academic departments, while still retaining final collection development responsibility for the library staff.

The third of Bryant's categories—the collection management and development posture—requires a strong commitment of staff. Librarians are assigned specific subject areas in which to monitor publication, select new materials, evaluate the present collection, and remove unneeded materials. Attention may also be given to policy development, budget allocation, resource-sharing commitments, preservation, and interpretation of the collection. The design and monitoring of approval and blanket plans may be among the duties of such specialists. In this type of situation, some proponents of blanket plans argue that a dealer's staff is an extension of the library's staff. If a detailed profile or plan for the library's collection has been provided to the dealer, then, theoretically, the dealer's staff should be able to match new publications with the library's needs in the same way the library staff does. When materials are needed in a language that few, if any, library staff members can handle easily, dealers can be instructed to select and ship. If, as supporters claim, blanket orders and approval plans mean that the library staff spends less time on current acquisitions work, then they ought to be able to spend more time evaluating the collection, identifying weak areas, and doing retrospective buying.

PUBLIC LIBRARIES

For most of this century, public librarians have been engaged in serious debate concerning the basis on which materials should be added to a public library collection. The arguments have usually focused on how much emphasis should be given to user demands as opposed to evaluating the quality of materials available to be purchased (or otherwise acquired). Although following demands of the public does not necessarily mean acquiring materials of dubious quality, putting first priority on those materials in greatest demand will probably produce a different collection from the one built by a librarian who looks first at the quality of what is available. In some ways, how a library's mission statement places its collection development efforts on the user-oriented to supply-oriented continuum is related to the current versus future perspective. The organization of the staff for collection development is also likely to vary among libraries with varying approaches to the quality versus demand issue.

Size of staff and materials budget does not necessarily indicate whether a public library will stress meeting current demands or building a collection for the future. However, long-established public library systems in large cities are likely to have at least one unit that is viewed as a research collection. For that reason, large public libraries may be characterized by subject departmentalization, specialized professional staff in the central library, and large branch systems with generalists in charge of the branches. Possible differences between collection policies and procedures of the main library and the branch libraries are important, as the two types of collections may respond to different purposes and priorities within the system. The main or central library in a system may be viewed as a composite of many special-subject collections, rather than as a large general library which duplicates the current popular titles in branch libraries. The branch libraries are the demand-oriented part of the library system.

Large public libraries usually have a department to coordinate collection development activities, with responsibility for checking and circulating reviews to staff members, acquiring approval and review copies of books and other materials, and compiling lists of materials approved for purchase. These libraries often have standing orders for some categories of materials, and also maintain approval and Greenaway Plan arrangements. Not every public library has a written collection development policy, but most now follow recommended practice and state their policies publicly. In general, the larger the system, the more likely a written policy.

Department or division heads in the central library are usually specialists in their fields and ordinarily have responsibility for checking selection aids related to their subjects. These specialists have the advantage of knowing their collections well and concentrating upon a relatively narrow area of subject material. Branch collections and the collection for popular reading in the central library will probably be handled in a different way. Typically, a rotating committee, drawing membership from both the central library and the branches, has the responsibility of considering titles on the lists compiled by the collection development department, as well as those recommended by subject specialists. In addition, members of this committee may examine approval copies (particularly for marginal or controversial materials) and write reviews for circulation to other staff members. Meeting regularly, such a selection committee will reach agreement on a list of materials approved for purchase by any library in the system.

Selecting and discarding children's (and often young adults') materials are usually handled separately from the routines established for adult materials. When a system is large enough to justify the hiring of coordinators, the children's, young adults, and adult coordinators are responsible for organizing the selection of their respective materials.

Large public library systems that are more demand oriented in their collecting efforts may place more responsibility on a central selection department and make less use of committees involving branch librarians. In some of these systems, there is no central library or other collection that might have a specific research mission. Thus, there will be few subject specialists with narrow collection development assignments and little time spent on writing reviews for circulation to other staff members. This approach to collection development emphasizes quick decisions on new purchases, heavy duplication of popular items, and speedy processing of materials received. While branch librarians may be asked for advice and, in some library systems, may be organized into committees to do this, the head of selection and the staff assigned to that department make most of the decisions.

In many medium-sized and small public libraries, all librarians are likely to participate in selection of materials. Much of the routine selection is based on standard reviewing sources, preference being given to those that provide the quickest coverage. The reviewing sources are read and checked by staff members, according to their subject specialties. (These specialties may reflect the formal educational background of the librarians or they may be based on hobbies or personal reading interests.) Selections are typically coordinated by the head librarian, who reviews recommended materials in the light of the overall collection and the budget. Children's materials may be chosen through separate, but roughly similar, procedures.

Collection development in the smallest public libraries may be carried out by one person, as there may be only one librarian on the staff. The librarian reads reviewing sources to identify appropriate new titles, selects titles for purchase, and orders them. In such a library, members of the library board and patrons with special backgrounds and interests can help. Small libraries usually have small budgets, and small budgets mean restricted selection in more than one way. The librarian in this setting typically relies on selection aids and other bibliographical tools to suggest materials appropriate for the collection. Because the library cannot afford a wide variety of selection aids, the librarian makes choices based on a narrow view of what is available. The expressed interests of library users are likely to carry more weight in small public libraries than in some of the larger systems.

LIBRARIES IN EDUCATIONAL SETTINGS

School Library Media Centers

Collections built to support the instructional programs of K–12 institutions are usually expected to meet current needs with high-quality materials. Materials are to be selected carefully, according to a collection development plan that adheres to district-wide policy but also addresses the needs of the individual school. To emphasize the level of quality expected in the collection, the national guidelines include selection criteria:

1. intellectual content of the material: scope, arrangement and organization, relevance and recency of information, special features, and overall value to the collection
2. philosophy and goals of the school district: resources support and are consistent with the educational goals of the district and with goals and objectives of individual schools and specific courses
3. characteristics of the user: resources are appropriate for the age, emotional development, ability levels, learning styles, and social development of the students for whom the resources are selected.[4]

In multicampus school districts, collection development activities are usually distributed between individual schools and the district office, possibly with a district coordinator who supervises the whole operation. In smaller districts, without coordinators, individual librarians may be responsible for all selection and acquisition. The activities that must be performed at the building level include those related to gaining knowledge of the curriculum and of the teachers' and students' needs, securing and routing selection aids to those who participate in selection, and previewing certain types of materials requested by teachers. Verification of requests, writing orders, checking invoices, and processing new materials may be handled efficiently at the district level. If there is no centralized ordering at the district level, the building-level librarian must also verify order information, place the order, and maintain all records related to acquisitions.

Wide participation in selection is emphasized in this type of library. The latest national guidelines for school library media programs call for cooperation among librarians, teachers, administrators, and even students in selecting and producing "materials to meet the overall goals of the school and the learning objectives designed by teachers for specific curricula."[5]

Some library media centers operate the selection process through selection committees, sometimes organized separately for faculty, students, curriculum areas, and/or grade levels. In other schools, the librarian sets a procedure for routing reviewing journals, other selection aids, and preview copies of books, magazines, films, etc., to those who want to participate in selection, collecting recommendations from them directly. When there is more than one librarian to a campus, each may work directly with certain curricular areas or individual teachers.

Large school districts often maintain evaluation and selection sections which assist individual librarians. The purpose of such district-level units is generally to improve the quality of the media collection in the district, but some systems attempt to do this through maintaining centralized control of most selection and acquisition, while others concentrate on assisting the efforts of individual school librarians. Such units may coordinate policies—for example, by taking the lead in developing written policies—or they may establish and supervise procedures. Typical activities include organizing district-wide selection committees, developing approved buying lists, maintaining examination centers (where librarians may preview materials before purchase), building professional collections on library science and educational technology, or conducting workshops to improve evaluation skills of librarians.

College Libraries

College libraries have sometimes been treated as miniature research libraries—similar to university libraries in most ways except total size. This is no longer the prevailing view. The standards for college libraries state, "there is no substitute for a strong, immediately accessible collection," but they also note that providing access to materials is the top priority.[6] Resource sharing arrangements are encouraged where appropriate. Quantity of effort in collection development is important, but quality of selections is even more important, given typically inadequate materials budgets. "The best way to preserve or improve quality is to adhere to rigorous standards of discrimination in the selection of materials to be added, whether as purchases or gifts."[7]

Maintaining rigorous standards of selection in the college library is difficult, because participation in the various collection development activities is likely to be widely dispersed among faculty, librarians, and sometimes even students. Perhaps because of this dispersion, college libraries have been slow to show formal evidence of collection development, in terms of systematic and rational planning. According to a 1979 study of ten prominent liberal arts colleges, the typical library had only a minimal organization for collection development, with no one assigned to coordinate the development, and no written policy statement.[8] In a few libraries that were studied, not all selections were subject to review by a librarian, and in most libraries the materials budgets were allocated to departments on the basis of historical precedents. Findings such as these have caused some to conclude that, in many college libraries, the library staff serves as purchasing and processing agent for the faculty, who do most of the selection. The latest standards for college libraries make it clear that librarians are (or should be) ultimately responsible for the collection, while acknowledging a role for the teaching faculty in making collection development policy.

Because the college library collection is usually centered on the curriculum, it is particularly important that librarians and faculty work together. A typical arrangement is a sizable portion of the materials budget be allocated to academic departments. Faculty members then participate in selection by making recommendations to their department head or to the departmental library committee, who approves or disapproves such expenditures from the departmental allocation. Some libraries have a formal faculty liaison structure to ensure that librarians communicate with faculty about collection development matters and provide for the regular routing of review journals, *Choice* cards, publishers' announcements, and other sources of bibliographical information. If there is a library committee for the college as a whole, it may also become involved in the process. Establishment of review committees of librarians, faculty, and students—sometimes for a single problem area, such as serials—is one way in which collection development has become more formalized in recent years, even in college libraries.

A survey of medium-sized academic libraries was conducted by Cubberly to determine their organizational structure for collection development. "Medium-sized" was defined as those libraries listing a professional staff of between 18 and 30 librarians in the 1986 edition of the *American Library Directory* (actual staff sizes of participating libraries ranged from 14 to 29 librarians). Only five of the 43 libraries studied reported having a separate collection development unit. Sixteen libraries had the type of structure in which acquisition, allocation of funds, and selection were dispersed among several library units. The remainder of the participating libraries drew staff from various functional departments of the library to carry out collection development activities on a part-time basis. Most of the librarians with collection development responsibilities were from public service departments. Overall, Cubberly concluded that "when librarians are appointed to do collection development in a library that has identified it as a separate activity worthy of its own department, more time is devoted to it, and more activities associated with collection development are accomplished."[9]

University Libraries

Although most university libraries are viewed as research collections, they still vary widely in size of collections, size of staff, and patterns of organization for collection development. At one, there may be no department or librarian with designated responsibility for collection development, but departmental and reference librarians may be heavily involved in selection and evaluation of parts of the collection. At another, a corps of subject and area bibliographers may carry the major responsibility for developing the library's collection. Still another may have an assistant or associate director for collection development, who operates primarily at the level of planning and policy formulation, chairing policy review committees, allocating the budget, and coordinating cooperative agreements and evaluation projects. In such a library, selection might be done by bibliographers, reference librarians, departmental librarians, faculty, or various combinations of these groups.

One of the reactions of university libraries to the economic problems that arose in the 1970s was to begin formulation of collection development policies, creating formulas for budget allocation, initiating explicit long-range planning, and increasing coordination of collection development within the institution. During the 1960s, many large university libraries added subject specialists with various kinds of collection development responsibilities to their staffs, but in the 1970s, the trend was to add upper-level staff to coordinate the activities of all librarians involved in selection and to lead in the formulation of policies and procedures. The establishment of collection development committees appears to be a response to requests for increased staff involvement in library decisions, as well as to a need for more formalized collection development procedures.

The organization of collection development among members of the Association of Research Libraries was studied in the mid-1980s by Sohn, who observed that "the image of collection development as the stepchild within the organization is disappearing among ARL libraries."[10] She found that only two libraries in her sample did not have a collection development unit. Administratively, collection development was a separate unit in 57.1 percent of the libraries, within technical services in 17.1 percent, and a part of public services in 14.3 percent. In the remainder of the libraries, it was attached to a planning, administrative, or other unit. Sixty percent of the 73 libraries represented among the respondents had a collection development officer, usually at the rank of assistant or associate director, who was administratively in charge of all the collection development activities in the library. Among the 40 percent of collection development officers without total administrative control, the most typical exclusions were special collections or certain branch libraries.

In large academic libraries, a staff of full-time bibliographers is often primarily responsible for acquiring material for the system's central library. Since the turn of the century, German universities have employed subject bibliographers or specialists whose primary responsibility has been selection. This German system of concentrating selection for the university library in a few highly qualified members of the staff has been described by Danton. He contrasted the German pattern with the American tendency to rely heavily on faculty participation in selection, and he emphasized the strengths of the German system. In his 1963 study, he predicted that if a library with enough staff members (qualified through subject and bibliographical knowledge) gave these individuals the responsibility and sufficient time for book selection, the results would be "a more *objectively, consistently, thoroughly* built-up book collection than can otherwise be the case."[11]

Many university libraries adopted blanket order and approval plans in the 1960s. Some libraries had as many as 30 or 40 separate plans, operating at once and covering both foreign and domestic publications. In some cases, large percentages of the book funds were spent through this method, although other libraries were very selective in their choice of plans. Librarians were encouraged to consider blanket plans when their selection procedures reached the point where decisions on titles had become perfunctory, when they were already acquiring almost all new publications in specified subject areas, or when the regularly appropriated budget seemed to be covering the purchase of all current imprints in a specified subject area. Such conditions are most likely in large university libraries during times of economic prosperity, and least likely when budgets are tight and priorities must be reviewed.

Approval plans are still a major acquisitions channel in many libraries. As budgets became tighter, some libraries pulled back from approval plans and other vendor-designed systems for identifying the collection's needs and turned to more careful local selection. Declining staff due to decreasing budgets; concern about changing inventory policies of publishers, which may lead to shorter in-print times for new books; and general inefficiency of some acquisition systems, leading to slow arrival of needed materials, have led some librarians to reconsider their approval plans. A 1977 survey of 482 libraries of various types found that 178 (37 percent) used approval plans, 95 (20 percent) used blanket orders, and 380 (79 percent) used standing orders of one type or another.[12] A 1980 national survey of 95 randomly selected academic libraries found that nearly three-quarters of those responding were using an approval plan, and librarians in these institutions averaged four (of a possible five) points when they rated their satisfaction with their plans.[13]

In academic libraries, blanket order and approval plans have usually offered more systematic coverage of current publishing in fields of interest than the traditional method of relying on faculty selection. Faculty members need not be excluded from the selection process as a result of an approval plan; but since they do not have to initiate orders, any negligence on a faculty member's part will not be reflected in an unbalanced collection. According to supporters, approval plans simply mean that faculty members or librarians who want to select books can do it with the book in hand. Opponents of approval plans point out that reviews are not available at the time of selection, and emphasize the tendency of those in charge to take the path of least resistance by accepting a marginal book that has already arrived, rather than taking the trouble to reject it and return it.

Faculty Participation in Collection Development

One of the key questions for any school, college, or university library is who will be involved in the collection development process, and to what degree. If the faculty assumes responsibility for all important decisions relating to collection development, then the library is concerned only with processing requests—in other words, the order function. In general, there are three categories of faculty participation: (1) the faculty can have total responsibility for spending the materials budget, with aid and advice from librarians; (2) the faculty and librarians can share the responsibility; or (3) the librarians can have total responsibility, with aid and advice from faculty.

Even among librarians in liberal arts colleges—where faculty influence is traditionally strong—opinions vary widely about faculty participation. One director of a liberal arts college library suggests that selection for academic libraries be left to the faculty and that arguments for selection by librarians are "less than persuasive if not simply wrongheaded."[14] Another college librarian takes a different point of view:

> A great mistake made by many college libraries is to leave all or most selection of current books to the faculty. This is a mistake because of the delay in selection, the danger of too many areas not being covered, and the real possibility of selection not taking place. The bulk of the selection should be done by library staff. The faculty do not have the time to do this. . . . What the faculty should do is to participate in the establishment of collection development policies.[15]

Often the big question is whether faculty would actually participate, given the opportunity. A study of faculty at one midwestern institution found that older, more experienced faculty members, who were active in publishing and professional affairs, were more likely to be active participants in selection.[16] One generalization from Cline and Sinnott's study of seven academic libraries is that as faculty begin to feel less identification with a library collection (such as a large central library), its level of involvement declines.[17] Each condition appears to feed on the other: lower involvement may result in even less identification with the collection. Where faculty feel closer involvement with the library (such as a departmental library or a small college library), they are more likely to participate.

In university libraries, faculty participation in collection development is likely to be less than in college libraries. Cubberly also observed a trend away from faculty selection in medium-sized academic libraries. The librarians in nearly half of the libraries in her survey reported having full responsibility for selection.[18] In recent years, the faculty has appeared more and more willing to leave major collection development decisions, and even item-by-item selection, to librarians. This trend has probably been influenced by many factors, and one of them may be the addition of subject or area bibliographers to university library staffs. The first specialist bibliographers to be hired were usually familiar with the languages and publishing patterns of the area of the world in which a university was beginning (or expanding) area or interdisciplinary studies. The success of bibliographers in those areas led to appointment of specialists for other, more traditional areas of collecting, or to assignment of librarians (already on the staff) to spend part of their time evaluating and developing the collection in a particular subject area. Most of those who assume that librarians will have the major responsibility for selection also assume that the library staff will contain subject specialists and that the faculty will be asked for advice when it is needed. A university professor puts the case, as viewed by many faculty members: "For college and university libraries that are currently developing into significant research centers, the presence of specialist bibliographers is essential, and a closely organized interrelationship between them and departmental chairpersons is an invaluable means of ensuring the faculty influence."[19]

In general, the reasons why library staff should have major responsibility for collection development may be summarized this way: Faculty members, in any type of educational setting, do not have the time to concentrate on the library collection, nor do they have access to all the necessary bibliographic information. Since they are not ordinarily evaluated for promotion and tenure on their contributions to the library's collection, but on teaching, research, or public service, they have little incentive to become actively involved in collection development. Faculty selection tends to lead to unbalanced collections, because most faculty members think primarily of their own courses or research interests when they make selections. Even if the library has a collection development policy, faculty may not follow it closely—sometimes because they do not know about or understand it. Some may argue about who best knows the library needs of students, but the observation of many librarians is that what students *actually* use may be far different from what faculty *think* they use. On the other hand, faculty can be very helpful in determining policy, in building retrospective collections, and in sharing information about the typical publication and use patterns in its disciplines.

The proportion of the materials budget spent by faculty members, by library staff, and through standing orders or approval plans varies widely from one educational setting to another. Observing these proportions and how they have (or have not) changed tells something about the relative weights of these groups in the collection development process. Cline and Sinnott, in their survey of seven academic libraries of varying sizes, found that the amount spent on blanket orders and other contracts with vendors ranged from 0 to 15 percent of the total budget in 1977–78.[20] Funds assigned to faculty ranged from 0 to 73 percent, and funds assigned directly to librarians ranged from 10 to 78 percent.

SPECIAL LIBRARIES

Special libraries range from a few hundred volumes to hundreds of thousands of items, but many of them are one-librarian operations. Among the variety of duties forced upon a librarian who has total responsibility for operation of the library, collection development can easily be overlooked. In fact, "collection development" may be tantamount to preparing purchase orders for items that are specifically requested by users.

Those in charge of collection development in special libraries have one advantage over their counterparts in other types of libraries, in that they have a rather precise idea of the purposes of their collections. Special libraries have the most restricted purposes and homogeneous clienteles of all types of libraries. They are often created to support the research or business activities of one organization and to serve a small group.

The range of subjects collected in a special library may be very restricted, but the variety of forms and types of materials can be great. Written collection development policies are not common in special libraries because many special librarians prefer to rely on specific purchase requests. Large, academically related libraries (for example, law or medical) are more likely to have policies, specifying depth and extent of subject coverage, types of materials collected, exchange agreements, and other special considerations. The use of published reviews and the inspection of approval copies are rare in the special library that supports current research (the material it needs is probably not reviewed or available for inspection). Instead, the special librarian turns to lists of recently published research reports, government documents, etc., or to other lists that fit the subject needs of the collection. Some special librarians keep in close touch with their counterparts in similar libraries, in order to exchange bibliographic information on elusive items.

BUDGETING FOR COLLECTION DEVELOPMENT

Budgeting is an important facet of collection development work; the materials budget makes the collection development policy a reality. Funding requests illustrate the relationship between collection goals and financial expenditures. "The budget process involves identifying specific program goals and objectives through the planning process, specifying the physical and human resources required to accomplish these, and communicating the financial requirements for supplying these resources."[21]

Allocation of the materials budget involves assigning the available collection development funds to two or more accounts, which presumably reflect important divisions of the collection. Most libraries have some allocation or subdivision of the funds budgeted for materials. Proponents of allocation see it as an important means of monitoring and controlling collection devlopment—a way of demonstrating that funds are being spent systematically and rationally in support of collection needs and priorities.

Opponents argue that allocations take too much time to calculate and to monitor, tend to remain fixed over long periods of time, and may waste money, because some accounts receive larger allocations than can be used profitably. The disadvantage of inflexibility is countered with arguments that library directors can have great flexibility in the way budgets are allocated and the amount of control that may be exercised over the use of the accounts.

When a library uses budget allocation procedures, certain key aspects of that process affect the results. The first important decision that must be made is to decide which units or categories will receive allocations. A library may limit its allocations to relatively few categories. The collection development coordinator must be able to estimate amounts needed to build an adequate materials budget base and project the costs of maintaining that base in future fiscal years. Budget planners are forced to give initial consideration to continuing obligations, such as serial subscriptions, standing orders, memberships, approval plans, etc. Then discretionary purchases (anything purchased on a title-by-title basis, new serial subscriptions, sets, major retrospective purchases, etc.) can be considered. Money may be set aside to renew subscriptions, to continue payment for standing orders, to sustain programs of cooperation with other libraries, and to replace worn-out or missing volumes and pay for binding and rebinding—with the balance in a general fund from which all other purchases are made. In research libraries, the amount required for obligations already incurred, such as standing orders and subscriptions to periodicals, may constitute over 50 percent of the budget for materials; and in some special libraries it will be even higher, because of heavy dependence upon serials.

Different types of libraries tend to favor different allocation units. Public libraries may divide funds by departments (for example, reference, children's, branches), or by subjects, or by a combination of form and subject. Separate allotments usually are made for adult, young adult, and juvenile books. School libraries typically allocate by format (books, periodicals, audiovisual materials), but larger budgets may be further subdivided by subject. In academic libraries, allocations may be made on the basis of administrative unit (for example, departmental library, undergraduate library, or special collection), form of material (for example, monographs, serials, microforms, audiovisuals, or CD-ROM products), broad subject, specific subject, academic unit, individual or group responsible for selection (for example, individual librarian, departmental faculty), or language or country of publication. In some academic libraries, online database services are funded from the materials budget and, therefore, become an allocation unit. Other budget categories arise from gifts and endowments and from grants from government or other agencies. Separate accounts usually will have to be maintained for these funds, sometimes to the specifications of the grant, as is the case with federal funds, and selection of materials may be governed by the terms of the gift or grant.

A second major aspect of a budget allocation system is the set of criteria which are used to decide how much money will be assigned to each allocation unit. Allocation may be carried out by using a highly structured formula, or it may be done somewhat more informally and subjectively. Libraries that do not use allocation formulas prepare their draft budgets by considering historical and current patterns of spending (paying particular attention to over- and underspending), expected expenses for new programs, changes in faculty research, price indexes, the total amount available for materials, etc. Allocation formulas use factors that can be assigned numerical values: rating of strength of existing collections, number and cost of books currently published, number of faculty members, number (and level) of courses, circulation counts, interlibrary loans, inflation rates, ratings of the importance of a discipline, and the like. In a given formula, any combination of factors may be chosen, and any factor in the formula may be assigned a weight to represent its importance in the allocation decision. For example, each graduate student may be assigned higher weight than an undergraduate student, because the graduate student typically demands more from the library in terms of range of resources.

Many opinions have been offered about how budget allocation systems should be structured. Shirk argues that allocation formulas ought to be theoretically and empirically sound, while criticizing most existing formulas for being "merely notationally simplified expressions of arbitrary procedures."[22] In fact, budget allocation procedures do often represent political, rather than theoretical, decisions. Schad proposes that "the appearance of fairness in the allocation process can be as important as actual fairness."[23] He suggests that six procedural rules can give the appearance of fairness: allocations should be consistent over time; bias should be suppressed by separating adversarial and judicial roles in the process; allocations should be based on accurate information; appeal procedures should be provided; allocations "must reflect the basic concerns, values, and outlooks of all departments;" and "allocation procedures must be fundamentally moral and ethical."[24]

Actual budget allocation formulas demonstrate some of the ways that collection goals and political pressures are balanced. At one medium-sized academic library the materials budget allocation formula provides for one-third of the budget to be divided equally among all academic departments. To allocate the remaining two-thirds of the budget, equal weight is given to three factors assumed to influence potential need for library materials: (1) total number of students enrolled in the department; (2) total number of semester hours generated by the department; and (3) level of courses taught in the department. New departments are given an extra weight in order to increase slightly their allocations. To facilitate computation the formula has been converted to a computer program.

A new allocation plan for one university library proposes that 25 percent of the materials budget be set aside for general reference materials, special collections, and other purchases that cannot be directly related to specific academic programs. An additional 25 percent would be allocated directly to individual academic departments for purchase of materials that would likely be needed only for instruction and research in a single department. The remaining 50 percent of the budget would be allocated to eight disciplinary clusters, made up of academic units sharing research interests and likely to have similar needs for library materials. The amount of the allocation given to each disciplinary cluster and to each individual department would be based on factors commonly used in budget allocation formulas: (1) number of student credit hours generated; (2) number of student credit hours by academic level; (3) number of full-time faculty by department; (4) average cost per book by department; and (5) average cost per periodical by department.

Budget allocation formulas can be set up to try to achieve specific objectives, such as increasing the involvement of faculty in collection development. At one liberal arts college, revision of the budget allocation procedures became an opportunity to involve faculty members in various aspects of collection development and bibliographic instruction. As part of the revision process, faculty were asked to rate each course in the curriculum on amount of use required. This rating was incorporated into a formula that also included number of faculty in the department, number of majors being graduated (five-year average), number of courses, semester credit-hour enrollment, and average cost of a volume in that discipline.[25]

Hodowanec has proposed a budget allocation formula for academic libraries based on APWs (acquisition priority weights) assigned to each division of the library's subject classification.[26] The APW is calculated after extensive analysis of a library's annual circulation statistics. For each division of the subject classification, values are obtained for the year after acquisition in which the books in a subject area reach their highest circulation, the number of books in a subject area circulated per one hundred acquired, the subject's rank among all subjects in circulation, and the subject's rank in terms of how many academic departments use books on that subject. The APW for each subject is finally represented as a percentage of the budget to be assigned to the subject. The total of all APWs equals 100 percent.

Another proposed approach to materials budget allocation has been offered by McGrath.[27] Subject categories to which budget allocations are to be made are identified and described in terms of the appropriate classification numbers. Annual circulation figures, also analyzed by classification numbers, are matched with each subject category. In addition, average costs for books in each subject category are obtained. Three cost-use figures are calculated for use in the budget allocation formula: cost-use for each subject category (average cost of a book multiplied by the amount of circulation); total cost-use (sum of cost-use for all subject categories); and percent cost-use (each subject category's cost-use divided by the total cost-use). Allocations are then determined by multiplying the percent cost-use of each subject category by the total materials budget. This formula could presumably be used in any type of library in which circulation rates and average cost of materials are the major factors in determining budget allocations.

Some libraries, or the agencies of which they are a part, control expenditures through the periodic release of funds. Most commonly, this is done quarterly, so that, for example, an allocation for children's books of $10,000 for a fiscal year will allow the encumbrance of $2,500 at the beginning of each quarterly period in the year. Usually this device ensures that there will be sufficient funds to provide for purchases throughout the year, or to protect against overly zealous selectors. It also helps distribute the processing of orders throughout the year. If a library encumbers all of its funds within a few months of the beginning of a fiscal year, it is an indication of extreme undersupport or poor management—or, most probably, both.

An interesting variation in allocations is practiced in *some* public libraries and has potential for *all* libraries. This is the allocation of units instead of dollars. A unit may be the average cost per volume, or other predetermined translation of dollars into rough equivalents. For instance, each $5 (or a part thereof) may be one unit, based upon a determination of average volume costs. The advantage is in record keeping. Each department can maintain a simple record of the number of units it has used, and know how many more it can use during a budget period. No elaborate system of accounting is necessary, and frequent statements of balances from the library's order or finance department are not necessary. Usually, under the unit system, the agency responsible for accounting makes a financial reckoning each quarter for each allocation and adjusts the available units accordingly.

A third aspect of importance in budget allocation is where the decision-

making power resides—who decides what the allocation units and allocation criteria will be and who applies the criteria. Determining who plays
the principal role in budget allocation is one way of determining where the
real responsibility for collection development lies. In most libraries,
particularly in public libraries, the head librarian has the responsibility
(although it may be delegated to the librarian in charge of coordinating
collection development). In a school library, the principal or district staff
may specify how the budget is to be allocated; and in some academic
libraries, the faculty library committee has more control over budget
allocations than does the head librarian. In academic libraries, control of
the budget can be expected to follow one of three patterns. Grieder
summarizes the situation this way: (1) some academic libraries have
somehow managed to lose all budget control—and, subsequently, most
powers of collection development and guidance—to the faculty, producing the consequence of very spotty collections created almost entirely by
the particular and often obscure specialties of particular scholars; (2) other
academic libraries maintain partial control of funds, reserving some
monies for the purchase of reference and special collections materials and
some for general collection development, with the faculty controlling the
remainder of the budget; and (3) still other libraries retain control over all
of their budgets, in which event rational policies of selection development
are greatly facilitated.[28]

Even when faculty members have a great deal of control over the
budget, one or more librarians may play important advisory roles. The
librarian in charge of acquisitions is the person best able to provide and
interpret records of expenditures for previous years, and should be most
familiar with changes in the book market. Librarians who are closely
involved with the broad range of collection development activities are
most likely to be aware of needs for new materials and capable of weighing
the demands for changes in selection policies and procedures. In the
structure of fund distribution it is important to provide resources to allow
the librarian in charge of collection development to meet unexpected
demands. These might include the unexpected offer of a scarce but much
needed set, or prepublication offers that could not be anticipated but
provide substantial savings for order or payment before publication.

Estimating Costs of Materials

No matter what kind of budget allocation procedure is used, a library's
collection development program cannot be successful unless the materials
budget is large enough to meet collection goals. The collection development coordinator must be able to estimate amounts needed to build an
adequate materials budget base and project the costs of maintaining that

base in future fiscal years. This process of budget preparation and justification requires close cooperation with the acquisitions staff, since that department has the records on amounts spent in various categories during previous fiscal years. Local information on costs of materials in various categories is important, even though national price indexes are available, because local buying patterns may not exactly match any of the assumptions that underlie national indexes. Statistical evidence of price changes not only justifies increases in total allocations but can determine the distribution of funds within a library's budget for materials.

Some formulas have been developed primarily to justify budget requests. One that could be used in a library with a collection development policy specifying levels of collecting intensity by subject area has been published by Welsch, who suggests that relying on inflation rates and increases in book and serial prices derived from commonly available sources is inadequate. He proposes "a new measure of collection development needs that factors the change in percent of coverage and in size of the literature into funding cost."[29] In other words, if a library's collection goal is to acquire 50 percent of the new publications in a discipline, its budget must take this percentage into account, as well as the number of new titles and their average cost. The amount needed for each subject area in the collection may be calculated by multiplying the total number of volumes published by the percentage level of coverage to be achieved; then multiplying that result by the average price of a publication. The total materials budget request would represent the sum of each individual projection. Variations in the value of the dollar against foreign currencies and variations in foreign purchases by subject area can also be added into these calculations.

The latest national guidelines for school library media programs propose a formula for calculating budget requests to maintain a school's current materials allocation. Factors in the formula are variation in student population (increase or decrease from the previous year); attrition by weeding (percent of the collection that was weeded in the past year); attrition by date (sample estimate of the percent of the collection that is 15 years old or older); attrition by loss (percent of collection that was lost in the previous year); and inflation rate (based on the Consumer Price Index or on a library materials price index).[30] The number produced from all this calculation is multiplied by the amount spent for library materials in the current year. As the guidelines point out, this is a maintenance formula—not an enhancement formula that takes into account curriculum changes, etc.

Since most procedures for estimating collection development budgets include a price factor, price indexes are valuable tools for those who must make such estimates. A price index is obtained by dividing the average cost of a group of materials published or released in a year by the average cost of the same group of materials in a base period. The resultant index figure is the percentage increase over the base period. Base periods tend to vary according to the agency that prepares the index, and this can cause confusion; but the essential exercise, projection of costs for budgeting, can be done satisfactorily, irrespective of the base period. It is more important that a library apply an index consistently. A subcommittee of the American National Standards Institute Z39 Committee developed the standard, Criteria for Price Indexes for Library Materials (ANSI Z39.20—1974), which provides definitions and criteria for the measurement of price changes for books, paperback books, periodicals, serial services, and library-produced microfilm.

Choosing the best available price index requires careful consideration. The group of materials included in the price index should be as close as possible to the type of materials the library in question will be collecting. When studying a price index, one must note carefully the time period of the data covered, the country (or countries) of publication, and exactly what has been included or excluded. The subject classification used by the price index must be compatible with the library's planning categories. Finding a price index that meets all of the above requirements is hard enough that some collection development staffs have chosen to compile their own, based on local experiences and buying patterns.

The index of prices of hardcover trade books published in the United States (subdivided by subject) is prepared by the R. R. Bowker Company and includes all hardcover books listed in *Weekly Record*. This index, along with one for paperback prices, appears in *Publishers Weekly*— usually in preliminary form, soon after the end of the calendar year, and in final form a few months later. The calculations in *Publishers Weekly* involved the same three-year base as that for serials (described below) until 1970, when a change to a one-year base was made. *Choice*, which publishes reviews of books appropriate for liberal arts college libraries, is used as the source for an annual college book price index (usually published in the March issue of *Choice*). Vendors who supply approval and blanket plan books to American academic libraries have also made data available for an academic book price index.

The price indexes for U.S. periodicals and for serial services are prepared by the Library Materials Price Index Committee of the Resources Section of the American Library Association's Resources and Technical Services Division and have been published annually in an issue of *Library Journal*. It originally used the three-year period, 1947–49, as a base; then 1957–59. In 1971 it used 1967–69, and in 1981 it also provided information based on 1977–79. Beginning in 1982, a 1977 base was used to maintain comparability with the Bureau of Labor Statistics and its Consumer Price Index. *Law Library Journal* has produced a price index for legal publications using 1973 and 1974 as base years. The formats indexed include monographs, legal periodicals, looseleaf services, commercially published court reporters, and legal continuations. *Bowker Annual* has published price indexes for U.S. nonprint media, U.S. library microfilm, and U.S. newspapers, as well as reprinting other types of price indexes. The Music Library Association *Notes* has published price indexes for standard editions of musical scores, using 1977 as the base year.

The Library Materials Price Index Committee of ALA continues to work on price indexes that would better reflect the costs of the kinds of materials purchased by college and university libraries. The available price indexes are primarily for American and British materials, but a large proportion of the books and periodicals purchased by a university or research library may be in languages other than English and published outside the United States and the United Kingdom. Lynden gathered information about which sources of foreign price data are most reliable for academic librarians and reached these conclusions:

1. Academic libraries should use academic price indexes because they differ from the general price indexes.
2. Vendor data can be a reliable source of information because they are up-to-date and are frequently supplied from computerized records.
3. When there is no depository system, vendor selections of current titles for academic libraries can be an excellent source of information.
4. Vendors classify the books that they supply by subject in order to tailor their selections to libraries' interests.[31]

Indexes for materials from other countries are sometimes published in the *Bowker Annual*, but it may be necessary for librarians to establish their own cost figures, based upon local experience and, possibly, upon the experiences of other libraries that purchase similar materials. In fact, Lynden's study of fourteen of the largest private university libraries found that almost none relied on national price indexes.[32] They preferred to analyze their own cost data, because these data reflect the buying patterns of the individual institution—its emphasis on research reports and other scholarly materials, rather than on ordinary trade books—and show the cost of materials after discount, rather than list price. The Association of Research Libraries has published a SPEC kit to provide examples of the ways in which large university libraries have handled the problem of estimating costs of library materials.[33]

Other published statistics are relevant in planning for collection development. The number of book titles published in the United States each year is recorded in the issue of *Publishers Weekly* that contains the price indexes. This figure can be important to a library in budgeting, especially when exceptional changes in the number of books published in certain subject areas might change the amount of money required to keep pace with current publication.

TRAINING COLLECTION DEVELOPMENT STAFF

As the number (and percentage) of librarians involved in collection development activities has increased, more attention has been given to the problems of training and evaluating collection development staff. Identifying collection activities has sometimes been a first step for those who wanted to plan orientation programs. Identification has often been followed by attempts to determine the knowledge base required to carry out those activities. Ways of assigning fair work loads and judging the level of performance of collection development activities continue to be major concerns for collection development coordinators.

One of the difficulties encountered by administrators of collection development is that the activities identified with the collection development function range from policy making to purely clerical. Many activities involve intellectual activity that is invisible to the observer. Cubberly, in her survey of medium-sized academic libraries asked library directors and collection development librarians to check the same list of sixteen activities, indicating which should be carried out by a collection development librarian.[34] Both groups gave the five highest ratings to selecting current materials, maintaining liaison with academic departments, weeding the collection, evaluating the collection, and doing retrospective selection. There was less agreement about the remaining eleven activities. The collection development librarians' next five ratings were given to monitoring fund balances, writing collection policies, doing circulation studies, searching titles, and handling gift and exchange programs. Directors rated writing policies, maintaining approval plan profiles, monitoring fund balances, and building desiderata files in the sixth through ninth positions. Four activities tied in ratings for tenth position among the directors: liaison with other libraries, gift and exchange operations, budget justification, and circulation studies. Other collection development activities listed in that study and elsewhere include conducting user surveys, preparing order forms, designing and monitoring routines, and transferring materials from one collection to another. Because of the many patterns used to incorporate the collection development function into a library's organizational structure, there is no standard job description for a collection development librarian. The variety of activities and the differing perceptions about their relative importance present the collection development coordinator with interesting challenges.

The first challenge is to determine the skills and knowledge required to carry out the above activities. Collection development librarians need to have knowledge of the purposes, policies, and procedures of their particular libraries, as well as thorough knowledge of that library's present collection. The library's setting is important. Effective collection development requires knowledge of the special characteristics of the community or institution, of the present users and potential users, and of resources available in the area or through cooperative agreements with other libraries. Collection development librarians are expected to be particularly knowledgeable about patterns of research and publication, including the structure of the publishing industry; the structure and research methods of disciplines assigned for collection development or, where appropriate, the methods used in hobbies and practical fields; and bibliographic tools, sources of evaluation, etc. Bookkeeping skills and facility with statistical techniques are also needed by today's collection development librarian. Some individual libraries have identified other areas of knowledge required by their special local needs.

Because collection development units are relatively recent arrivals in library organization charts and because so much of collection development is cerebral, collection development coordinators have found it difficult to establish (and defend) fair distributions of work load among the staff. Expectations of directors and other staff members are still unclear, making this area of administration an extra challenge for the collection development coordinator. In a 1986 paper, Bryant attempted to break down collection development activities into measurable units for the purpose of establishing work load, identifying some as citation-centered decisions and others as people-oriented activities. She suggests counting "the number of citations (whether a bibliographic reference found in a selection tool, a patron request, or a book in hand) that are given either a positive *or* a negative resolution during the course of a given time period."[35] Such decisions might also be subdivided and weighted on the basis of whether they can be made immediately or whether they require research. Another type of citation-centered decision is related to collection maintenance and includes monitoring standing orders, periodical subscriptions, etc. These activities would vary in effort required, depending on the budget and on the number of titles already owned by the library. The people-oriented activities of the collection development librarian would include both planned and casual communication with users and other librarians about collection development matters. In presenting her quantitative model, Bryant acknowledges that the experience and expertise of the collection development librarian will greatly affect the amount of time required for any of the above activities. Therefore, evaluating librarians on how many tasks they accomplish within a specified period of time will probably not be acceptable. Some have suggested that the only way to handle evaluation of collection development librarians is to evaluate the collection that has resulted from their efforts.

Although there is no agreement on exactly what a collection development librarian should do or how that position should be evaluated, most people now agree that special training for collection development is necessary. New participants in a library's collection development efforts need specific information about the library's organization, procedures, and collections; they need to be instructed in techniques for gathering needed information and evaluating collections; and they must have opportunities to practice, under supervision, what they have learned. Formal, structured programs usually begin with an effort to indoctrinate the new collection development librarian with the local philosophy concerning collection development, as well as to provide an introduction to local policies and procedures. Since communication among all those involved in collection development is important, newcomers need an opportunity to exchange ideas and discuss their understandings with experienced librarians. This needed communication can be accomplished when a group works together on developing a policy or preparing a collection conspectus. If those activities have already been finished in a particular library, orientation may begin by having a new librarian study the documents that resulted—the collection development policy or worksheets from the conspectus project.

Some collection development coordinators prepare checklists for new selectors and meet with them regularly to review decisions that have been made. Manuals for collection development librarians are also an accepted way of providing direction. The Collection Management and Development Committee of the American Library Association's Resources and Technical Services Division published in 1987 *Guide for Writing a Bibliographer's Manual*. These manuals often include organization charts, position descriptions, outlines of responsibilities, statements of priorities, notices of deadlines that must be met, and copies of any documents or report forms that will be particularly useful for the collection development librarian. In addition to providing manuals and local training sessions, some coordinators bring in consultants to conduct short workshops on such topics as writing policies, conducting circulation or user studies, or collection evaluation techniques.

Although collection development work can be very satisfying, collection development librarians have problems and pressures not experienced in other units of the library. As noted previously, there is a wide variety of activities that may legitimately be included in a collection development librarian's work load. These activities require a person who has a depth of knowledge and great interest in one or more subject fields, who can attend to details carefully, and who can work easily with all of the people who want to make demands on the collection. Some collection development activities are invisible and therefore not valued by other library staff members. Other activities are clerical, but essential. Even these clerical tasks must often be performed by the collection development librarian, because the typical collection development unit does not have enough clerical workers. Collection development librarians often complain about lack of time to carry out all the duties that should be performed in effective collection development. Time appears to be a problem of particular concern in collection development, because so many collection development staff have only part-time appointments in that area. Of course, expectations of collection development staff vary from one library to another. In some situations where collection development has a low priority, the library director may develop the habit of raiding the collection development unit in order to focus personnel resources on other areas that appear to need emergency help.

BIBLIOGRAPHY

Bryant, Bonita. "The Organizational Structure of Collection Development." *Library Resources & Technical Services*, 31(April/June 1987):111-122.

Kennedy, Gail A. "The Relationship Between Acquisitions and Collection Development." *Library Acquisitions: Practice and Theory*, 7(1983):225-232.

Osburn, Charles. "Toward a Reconceptualization of Collection Development." In *Advances in Library Administration and Organization*, vol. 2. pp. 175-198. Greenwich, Conn.: JAI Press, 1983.

Public Libraries

Bone, Larry Earl, and Thomas A. Raines. "The Nature of the Urban Main Library: Its Relation to Selection and Collection Building." *Library Trends*, 20(April 1972):625-639.

68   ORGANIZATION OF COLLECTION DEVELOPMENT

Collection Management in Public Libraries: Proceedings of a Preconference to the 1984 ALA Conference, June 21–22, 1984, Dallas, Texas. Edited by Judith Serebnick. Chicago: American Library Assn., 1986. 148p.

Moore, Carolyn. "Core Collection Development in a Medium-Sized Public Library." *Library Resources & Technical Services,* 26 (January/ March 1982):37-46.

Norman, Ronald V. "A Method of Book Selection for a Small Public Library." *RQ,* 17(Winter 1977):143-145.

Polacheck, Dem. "A Method of Adult Book Selection for a Public Library System." *RQ,* 16(Spring 1977):231-233.

Turow, Joseph. "The Impact of Differing Orientations of Librarians on the Process of Children's Book Selection: A Case Study of Library Tensions." *Library Quarterly,* 48(July 1978):276-292.

School Library Media Centers

American Association of School Librarians and Association for Educational Communications and Technology. *Information Power: Guidelines for School Library Media Programs.* Chicago: American Library Assn., 1988. 171p.

"Collection Management for School Library Media Centers." Edited by Brenda H. White. *Collection Management,* 7(Fall/Winter 1985-86):1-383.

Ho, May Lein, and David V. Loertscher. "Collection Mapping: The Research." *Drexel Library Quarterly,* 21(Spring 1985):22-39.

Loertscher, David V. "Collection Mapping: An Evaluation Strategy for Collection Development." *Drexel Library Quarterly,* 21(Spring 1985):9-21.

_____, and May Lein Ho. *Computerized Collection Development for School Library Media Centers.* Fayetteville, Ark.: Hi Willow Research and Publishing, 1986.

Miller, Marilyn L., and Barbara Moran. "Expenditures for Resources in School Library Media Centers FY '85-'86." *School Library Journal,* 33(June/July 1987):37–45.

Nickel, Mildred L. *Steps to Service: A Handbook of Procedures for the School Library Media Center.* Rev. ed. Chicago: American Library Assn., 1984.

Van Orden, Phyllis J. *The Collection Program in Schools: Concepts, Practices, and Information Sources.* Englewood, Colo.: Libraries Unlimited, 1988. 347p.

Academic Libraries

Association of Research Libraries. Office of Management Systems. Systems and Procedures Exchange Center. *Collection Development Organization and Staffing in ARL Libraries.* Washington, D.C.: Assn. of Research Libs., 1987. 121p. (SPEC Kit no. 131)

Baatz, Wilmer H. "Collection Development in 19 Libraries of the Association of Research Libraries." *Library Acquisitions: Practice and Theory*, 2(1978):85-121.

Cline, Hugh F., and Loraine T. Sinnott. *Building Library Collec- tions: Policies and Practices in Academic Libraries*. Lexington, Mass.: Lexington Books, 1981. 170p.

Cogswell, James A. "The Organization of Collection Management Functions in Academic Research Libraries." *Journal of Academic Librarianship*, 13(November 1987):268-276.

Cubberly, Carol W. "Organization for Collection Development in Medium-Sized Academic Libraries." *Library Acquisitions: Practice and Theory*, 11(1987):297-323.

Danton, J. Periam. *Book Selection and Collections: A Comparison of German and American University Libraries*. New York: Columbia Univ. Pr., 1973. 188p.

Hannaford, William E. *Collection Development in Ten Small Academic Libraries: A Report to the Council on Library Resources.* Middlebury, Vt.: Middlebury College Library, 1979. 37p. (ED 190 074)

Library Resources for College Scholars: Transactions of a Conference Held at Ashington and Lee University, Lexington, Virginia, February 14–15, 1980. Edited by Robert E. Danford. Lexington: n.p., 1980? 55p. (University Library Publication No. 8)

Magrill, Rose Mary, and Mona East. "Collection Development in Large University Libraries." In *Advances in Librarianship*, vol. 8, pp. 1-54. Edited by Michael H. Harris. New York: Academic Pr., 1978.

Miller, William, and D. Stephen Rockwood. "Collection Development from a College Perspective." *College & Research Libraries*, 40(July 1979):318-324.

Sohn, Jeanne. "Collection Development Organizational Patterns in ARL Libraries." *Library Resources & Technical Services*, 31(April/June 1987):123-134.

Worley, Joan H. "Collection Development in a Small College Library: Can Less Be More?" *Choice*, 25(June 1988):1512-1517.

Special Libraries

Cohen, Jackson B. "Science Acquisitions and Book Output Statistics." *Library Resources & Technical Services*, 19(Fall 1975):370-379.

Gensel, Susan, and Audrey Powers. "Collection Development and the Special Library." *Bookmark*, 41(Fall 1982):11-15.

Grattan, Mary C. "Collection Development in Texas State Agency Libraries: A Survey with Recommendations." *Special Libraries*, 68(February 1977):69-75.

Levy, Charlotte L., and Gregory E. Koster. "Starting a Law School Library." *Law Library Journal*, 70(August 1977):290-308.

Miranda, Michael. "Developing College Business and Economics Collections." *Collection Management*, 10(1988):53-62.

Peterson, Stephen L. "Collection Development in Theological Libraries: A New Model—A New Hope." In *Essays on Theological Librarianship: Presented to Calvin Henry Schmitt.* pp. 143-162. Edited by Peter DeKlerk and Earle Hilgert. Philadelphia: American Theological Library Assn., 1980.

Root, Nina J. "Decision Making for Collection Management." *Collection Management*, 7(Spring 1985):93-101.

Sloan, Elaine. *Collection Development and Selection Decision-Making at the Smithsonian Institution Libraries: A Survey of the Curators of the National Museum of Natural History and the National Museum of History and Technology, Sept. 1970–June 1971.* Washington, D.C.: Smithsonian, 1971. 56p.

Truelson, Stanley D. "Selecting for Health Sciences Library Collections When Budgets Falter." *Medical Library Association Bulletin*, 64(April 1987):187-195.

Participation in Collection Development

Bell, Jo Ann, Paul J. Bredderman, Margaret K. Stangohr, and Kevin F. O'Brien. "Faculty Input in Book Selection: A Comparison of Alternative Methods." *Bulletin of the Medical Library Association*, 75(July 1987): 228-233.

Buckeye, Nancy. "A Plan for Undergraduate Participation in Book Selection." *Library Resources & Technical Services*, 19(Spring 1975):121-125.

Byrd, Cecil K. "Subject Specialists in a University Library." *College & Research Libraries*, 27(May 1966):191-193.

Dickinson, Dennis W. "A Rationalist's Critique of Book Selection for Academic Libraries," *Journal of Academic Librarianship*, 7(July 1981):138-143.

Dickinson, Dennis W. "Subject Specialists in Academic Libraries: The Once and Future Dinosaurs." In Association of College and Research Libraries. *New Horizons for Academic Libraries.* pp. 438-444. Edited by Robert D. Stueart and Richard D. Johnson. New York: K. G. Saur, 1979.

Evans, G. Edward. "Book Selection and Book Collection Usage in Academic Libraries." *Library Quarterly*, 40(July 1970):297-308.

Hardesty, Larry. "Book Selection for Undergraduate Libraries: A Study of Faculty Attitudes." *Journal of Academic Librarianship*, 12(March 1986):19-25.

Kim, Ung Chon. "Participation of Teaching Faculty in Library Book Selection." *Collection Management*, 3(Winter 1979):333-352.

Messick, Frederic M. "Subject Specialists in Small Academic Libraries." *Library Resources & Technical Services*, 21(Fall 1977):368-374.

Ryland, John. "Collection Development and Selection: Who Should Do It?" *Library Acquisitions: Practice and Theory*, 6(1982):13-17.

Sandler, Mark. "Organizing Effective Faculty Participation in Collection Development." *Collection Management*, 6(Fall/Winter 1984):63-73.

Sellen, Mary. "Book Selection in the College Library: The Faculty Perspective." *Collection Building*, 7(Spring 1985):4-10.

"Six Responses to 'A Rationalist's Critique . . .'." *Journal of Academic Librarianship*, 7(July 1981):144-151.

Thomas, Lawrence. "Tradition and Expertise in Academic Library Collection Development." *College & Research Libraries*, 48(November 1987):487-493.

Vidor, David L., and Elizabeth Futas. "Effective Collection Developers: Librarians or Faculty?" *Library Resources & Technical Services*, 32(April 1988):127-136.

Budgeting for Collection Development

Association of Research Libraries. Office of Management Studies. *The Allocation of Materials Funds*. Washington, D.C., 1977. Unpaged. (SPEC Kit No. 36)

Bach, Harry. "Why Allocate?" *Library Resources & Technical Services*, 8(Spring 1964):161-165.

Bender, Ann. "Allocation of Funds in Support of Collection Development in Public Libraries." *Library Resources & Technical Services*, 23(Winter 1979):45-51.

Benedict, Mike. "Long Range Budget Planning in Large Public Libraries." *Collection Management*, 3(Winter 1979):313-317.

Bentley, Stella, and David Farrell. "Beyond Retrenchment: The Reallocation of a Library Materials Budget." *Journal of Academic Librarianship*, 10(January 1985):321-325.

Bonk, Sharon C. "Rethinking the Acquisitions Budget: Anticipating and Managing Change." *Library Acquisitions: Practice and Theory*, 10(1986):97-106.

Evans, Glyn T., Mary H. Beilby, and Roger Gifford. *Development of a Responsive Library Acquisitions Formula*. Albany: SUNY Central Administration, Office of Library Services, 1978. 95p.

Genaway, David C. "PBA: Percentage Based Allocation for Acquisitions: A Simplified Method for the Allocation of the Library Materials Budget." *Library Acquisitions: Practice and Theory*, 10(1986):287-292.

_____. "The Q Formula: The Flexible Formula for Library Acquisitions in Relation to the FTE Driven Formula." *Library Acquisitions: Practice and Theory*, 10(1986):293-306.

Goehner, Donna M. "Allocating by Formula: The Rationale from an Institutional Perspective." *Collection Management*, 5(Fall/Winter 1983):161-173.

Gold, Steven D. "Allocating the Book Budget: An Economic Model." *College & Research Libraries*, 36(September 1975):397-402.

Goyal, S. K. "Allocation of Library Funds to Different Departments of a University—An Operational Research Approach." *College & Research Libraries*, 34(May 1973):219-222.

"Guidelines for the Allocation of Library Materials Budgets." In *Guidelines for Collection Development*. pp. 31-41. Chicago: American Library Assn., 1979.

Hanes, Fred W. "Another View on Allocation." *Library Resources & Technical Services*, 8(Fall 1964):408-410.

Hitchcock-Mort, Karen. "Collection Management in the Eighties—Where Are We Now?" *Library Acquisitions: Practice and Theory*, 9(1985):3-12.

Johnson, K. Suzanne, and Joel S. Rutstein. "The Politics of Book Fund Allocations: A Case Study." In Association of College and Research Libraries. *New Horizons for Academic Libraries*, pp. 330-340. Edited by Robert D. Stueart and Richard D. Johnson. New York: K. G. Saur, 1979.

Kohut, Joseph J. "Allocating the Book Budget: A Model." *College & Research Libraries*, 35(May 1974):192-199.

————, and John F. Walker. "Allocating the Book Budget: Equity and Economic Efficiency." *College & Research Libraries*, 36(September 1975):403-410.

Lynden, Frederick C. "Financial Planning for Collection Management." *Journal of Library Administration*, 3(Fall/Winter 1982):109-120.

Lynden, Frederick C. "Library Materials Budgeting in the Private University Library: Austerity and Action." In *Advances in Librarianship*, vol. 10, pp. 89-154. Edited by Michael H. Harris. New York: Academic, 1980.

McGrath, William E. "Determining and Allocating Book Funds for Current Domestic Buying." *College & Research Libraries*, 28(July 1972):269-272.

McGrath, William E. "A Pragmatic Book Allocation Formula for Academic and Public Libraries with a Test for Its Effectiveness." *Library Resources & Technical Services*, 19(Fall 1975): 356-369.

————, Ralph C. Huntsinger, and Gary R. Barber. "An Allocation Formula Derived from a Factor Analysis of Academic Departments." *College & Research Libraries*, 30(January 1969):51-62.

McPheron, William. "Quantifying the Allocation of Monograph Funds: An Instance in Practice." *College & Research Libraries*, 44(March 1983):116-127.

Martin, Murray S. "The Allocation of Money within the Book Budget." In *Collection Development in Libraries*, pp. 35-66. Edited by Robert D. Stueart and George B. Miller. Greenwich, Conn.: JAI Pr., 1980.

Martin, Murray S. *Budgeting Control in Academic Libraries*. Greenwich, Conn.: JAI Pr., 1978. 219p.

Mulliner, Kent. "The Acquisitions Allocation Formula at Ohio University." *Library Acquisitions: Practice and Theory*, 10(1986): 315-327.

Pierce, Thomas J. "An Empirical Approach to the Allocation of the University Library Book Budget." *Collection Management*, 2(Spring 1978):39-58.

Poole, Jay Martin, and Glorianna St. Clair. "Funding Online Services from the Materials Budget." *College & Research Libraries*, 47(May 1986):225-229.

Reed-Scott, Jutta. "Management of Resources." *Collection Management*, 7(Spring 1985):85-92.

Sampson, Gary S. "Allocating the Book Budget: Measuring for Inflation." *College & Research Libraries*, 39(September 1978):381-383.

Sanders, Nancy P. "A Review of Selected Sources in Budgeting for Collection Managers." *Collection Management*, 5(Fall/Winter 1983):151-159.

Schad, Jasper G. "Allocating Materials Budgets in Institutions of Higher Education." *Journal of Academic Librarianship*, 3(January 1978):328-332.

_____. "Fairness in Book Fund Allocation." *College & Research Libraries*, 48(November 1987):479-486.

Scudder, Mary C. "Using Choice in an Allocation Formula in a Small Academic Library." *Choice*, 24(June 1987):1506-1511.

Sellen, Mary. "Book Budget Formula Allocations: A Review Essay." *Collection Management*, 9(Winter 1987):13-24.

Senghas, Dorothy C., and Edward A. Warro. "Book Allocations: The Key to a Plan for Collection Development." *Library Acquisitions: Practice and Theory*, 6(1982):47-53.

Shirk, Gary M. "Allocation Formulas for Budgeting Library Materials: Science or Procedure?" *Collection Management*, 6(Fall/Winter 1984):37-47.

Sweetman, Peter, and Paul Wiedemann. "Developing a Library Book-Fund Allocation Formula." *Journal of Academic Librarianship*, 6(November 1980):268-276.

Vasi, John. *Budget Allocation Systems for Research Libraries*. Washington, D.C.: Office of Management Studies, Association for Research Libraries, 1983. 39p. (Occasional Paper Number 7)

Welwood, R. J. "Book Budget Allocations: An Objective Formula for the Small Academic Library." *Canadian Library Journal*, 34(June 1977):213-219.

Werking, Richard Hume, and Charles M. Getchell, Jr. "Using *Choice* as a Mechanism for Allocating Book Funds in an Academic Library." *College & Research Libraries*, 42(March 1981):134-138.

Willmert, John Allen. "College Librarians and Professors: Partners in Collection Building and Fund Allocation." In *Academic Libraries: Myths and Realities*. pp. 293-297. Edited by Suzanne C. Dodson and Gary L. Menges. Chicago: Assn. of College and Research Libraries, 1984.

Yunker, James A., and Carol G. Covey. "An Interdepartmental Allocation Formula for the Maximization of Use of Library Materials." *Collection Management*, 3(Winter 1979):363-369.

_____, and Carol G. Covey. "An Optimizing Approach to the Problem of Interdepartmental Allocation of the Library Materials Budget." *Library Acquisitions: Practice and Theory*, 4(1980):199-223.

Estimating Costs of Materials

Association of Research Libraries. Office of Management Studies. Systems and Procedures Exchange Center. *Indirect Cost Rates in Research Libraries*. Washington, D.C., 1980. 87p. (SPEC Kit No. 64)

————. *Library Materials Cost Studies*. Washington, D.C., 1980. 108p. (SPEC Kit No. 60)

Axford, H. William. "The Validity of Book Price Indexes for Budgetary Projections." *Library Resources & Technical Services*, 19(Winter 1975):5-18.

Clack, Mary E., and Sally F. Williams. "Using Locally and Nationally Produced Periodical Price Indexes in Budget Preparation." *Library Resources & Technical Services*, 27(October/December 1983):345-356.

Emery, Charles D. "Forecasting Models and the Prediction of Periodical Subscriptions Costs." *Library Journal*, 106(April 1, 1981):714-717.

Lynden, Frederick C. "Library Materials Cost Studies." *Library Resources & Technical Services*, 27(April/June 1983):156-162.

————. "Prices of Foreign Library Materials: A Report." *College & Research Libraries*, 49(May 1988):217-231.

Sauer, Tim. "Predicting Book Fund Expenditures: A Statistical Model." *College & Research Libraries*, 39(November 1978): 474-478.

Smith, Dennis. "Forecasting Price Increase Needs for Library Materials: The University of California Experience." *Library Resources & Technical Services*, 28(April/June 1984):136-148.

Welsch, Erwin K. "Price Versus Coverage: Calculating the Impact on Collection Development." *Library Resources & Technical Services*, 32(April 1988):159-163.

Williams, Sally F. "Budget Justification: Closing the Gap between Request and Result." *Library Resources & Technical Services*, 28(April/June 1984):129-135.

Training for Collection Development

Bryant, Bonita. "Allocation of Human Resources for Collection Development." *Library Resources & Technical Services*, 30(April/June 1986):149-162.

Gamble, Lynne. "Assessing Collection Development Organization in a Small Academic Library." In Association of College and Research Libraries. *Energies for Transition*. pp. 82-85. Edited by Danuta A. Nitecki.

Gleason, Maureen L. "Training Collection Development Librarians." *Collection Management*, 4(1982):1-8.

Guide for Writing a Bibliographer's Manual. Chicago: American Library Assn., 1987. 24p.

Parker, Diane C., and Eric J. Carpenter. "A Zero-Based Budget Approach to Staff Justification for a Combined Reference and Collection Development Department." In Association of College and Research Libraries. *New Horizons for Academic Libraries.* pp. 472-482. Edited by Robert D. Stueart and Richard D. Johnson. New York: K. G. Saur, 1979.

Pasterczk, Catherine E. "Checklist for the New Selector." *College & Research Libraries News*, 49(July/August 1988):434-435.

Perkins, David L. "Writing the Collection Development Manual." *Collection Management*, 4(Fall 1982):37-47.

_____, and Carol Bedoian. *Manual for Collection Developers.* Northridge, Calif.: California State University Libraries, 1975. 113p.

University of Texas at Austin. General Libraries. *Bibliographer's Manual: A Guide to the General Libraries Collection Development Program.* Austin, 1982. 42p. (Contributions to Librarianship No. 7)

FOUR

Organization of Acquisitions Work

THE IMPORTANCE OF ACQUISITIONS work in the modern library is so obvious that it is sometimes taken for granted. In earlier times, when libraries depended largely upon donations of books to stock their shelves, there was little need for a formal ordering procedure. Since the end of World War II, however, only small, independent community libraries have had collections based primarily upon donations. Many libraries have increased their purchases to such an extent that acquisitions work has become a dominant aspect of their daily activities, while some technical expertise in placing and handling orders is expected in even the smallest of school library media centers.

The process of obtaining library materials and assuring that they are properly recorded is the major focus of acquisitions work. This activity is usually completed by the cataloging and processing staff who, with the acquisitions staff, comprise what is often called the technical services or technical processes unit of the library. In small settings, one or two persons may constitute the entire unit, while in the large research library, more than a hundred staff members may be apportioned among the acquisitions, cataloging, and processing departments.

Contemporary emphasis upon economy in technical services has fostered two trends in acquisitions work: automation, to improve and enhance operations, and increased reliance upon cooperative and centralized organizational structures, to minimize duplication of effort in library systems. No matter how much the work is automated or what portion of it is placed in the hands of an outside agency, acquisitions staffs are still needed to make certain that the library secures the materials needed by its clientele, that these materials are appropriately entered into the library's files, and that they are purchased within the constraints of the library's budget.

MEANS OF ACQUIRING MATERIALS

Traditionally, there have been four basic means of acquiring materials for a library's collection: purchases, gifts, exchanges, and deposits. These methods often are used as a basis for organizing acquisitions work, particularly in large libraries. For example, one unit may be organized to handle materials that are purchased, and another unit to handle gifts, exchanges, and deposits.

Purchases

Materials can be acquired by purchasing them from jobbers, dealers, or their publishers. Items can be purchased through orders placed with a vendor for a specified time and price (firm orders and subscriptions); arrangements with vendors to supply all volumes or parts of specific titles as they appear (standing orders); plans under which vendors agree to supply one copy of all publications as outlined in an agreement (blanket purchases); or plans whereby vendors agree to supply selected materials as outlined in a profile (approval plans).

Gifts

Materials can be acquired as gifts from individuals, groups, other libraries and organizations, and sometimes from publishers. Gifts may be received as individual items or as part of a collection of materials.

Exchanges

A library can exchange materials it publishes, those published by its parent institution, or those published by others and given to the library, for materials published by other libraries or institutions, usually on a one-for-one basis. Most often, the material used as the basis for an exchange is a serial.

Deposits

Materials can be placed on deposit in the library by a group, organization, or publisher as a means of making items more readily available to readers. The library usually retains the material permanently in its collection.

FUNCTIONS OF AN ACQUISITIONS UNIT

The variations in acquisitions work from library to library make it difficult to generalize; nonetheless, almost every acquisitions unit, however it may be subdivided or combined with other units, performs certain fundamental tasks. The basic responsibilities of a typical acquisitions unit include those described below, although some may be assigned in a particular library to other units or to outside agencies.

Obtaining Information about Materials

One basic responsibility of an acquisitions unit is obtaining information about the materials the library wishes to acquire.

This involves: (1) securing from selectors a record of the basic bibliographic information such as title, author, publishing information, series relationship, etc., for materials to be acquired, often obtained through the use of an order request form; (2) completing and verifying the bibliographic information provided by comparing the request with the listings of materials in national, international, and other bibliographies, both those printed and those in online databases; (3) determining that the library does not already own and has not previously ordered the requested item so that unwanted duplication is prevented; and (4) identifying the expected price and possible sources of supply for each item.

Initiating the Purchasing Process

A second responsibility of an acquisitions unit is initiating the purchasing process, which involves: (1) selecting an appropriate vendor such as a jobber, a dealer, or the publisher with whom to place the order; (2) encumbering or placing a "hold" on the funds needed to pay for the item when it is supplied; (3) preparing the order; and (4) dispatching the order.

Maintaining Records for Materials Ordered

A third responsibility of an acquisitions unit is maintaining records for materials ordered.

This involves: (1) maintaining files, either manually or by computer, which show the status of each firm order, usually accessible by the title of the item and possibly by its author, series relationship, or standard number such as its International Standard Number; and (2) maintaining long-term records on continuations, which are items issued in parts over a definite period of time, and other serials whose parts are expected to be received indefinitely.

Receiving and Checking Materials

A fourth responsibility of an acquisitions unit is receiving and checking materials, which involves: (1) opening packages of materials shipped to the library, making sure that the items are undamaged, and preserving any enclosed records such as invoices, packing slips, etc.; (2) verifying that the items are the ones ordered by comparing their bibliographic information with that listed in the order record; (3) checking the items against any enclosed or separately shipped invoices to assure that the materials received match the list supplied by the vendor; and (4) determining that each item appears to be physically complete and in acceptable condition.

Authorizing Payment for Materials

Another responsibility of an acquisitions unit is authorizing payment for materials, which involves: (1) recording the actual price of each item on its order record; (2) releasing the encumbrance and entering the actual cost of an item in the financial records; and (3) preparing payment or creating the authorization required to release payment for the materials.

Clearing Order Records

An acquisitions unit is responsible for clearing order records after materials have been received.

This involves: (1) recording the fact that an item has been received, usually by entering the receipt date in its order record; (2) preparing an appropriate transmittal record to accompany the material to the next stage of preparation, which usually is the cataloging unit; and (3) either at this point or at the end of the cataloging and processing stages, changing the status of the order record from "current" or "on order" to "completed."

Claiming and Canceling Orders

Another important responsibility of an acquisitions unit is claiming and canceling orders as necessary.

This involves: (1) monitoring the files to detect if an order has been outstanding for so long a time that it should be claimed, that is, a query sent to the vendor to determine the status of the order; (2) informing the vendor that an order for an item is to be canceled; and (3) updating the order record to reflect these claims and cancellations.

Handling Materials That Need Special Treatment

An acquisitions unit is responsible for handling materials that need special treatment.

This involves a wide variety of activities such as developing a program for soliciting, maintaining records for, and acknowledging gift materials, depository collections, and items received through exchange programs, as well as developing the routines needed to handle materials supplied through standing orders, blanket orders, and approval plans.

Dealing with Special Situations

An often overlooked responsibility of an acquisitions unit is dealing with special situations. This involves such matters as negotiating credits or refunds for items not wanted or received in unacceptable condition, notifying requesters that their materials have arrived, arranging for the rush purchase and receipt of items required immediately, solving dilemmas related to poor vendor performance, and making adjustments in the budget as the fiscal year nears its end.

Developing and Analyzing Performance Statistics

A last responsibility of an acquisitions unit, developing and analyzing performance statistics, involves collecting a variety of statistical information on such numbers as orders placed, received, canceled, etc.; length of time required by vendors to fill orders; time spent by staff in establishing bibliographic information for ordering purposes; number of unwanted duplicates and items ordered by mistake; accuracy of preliminary price information or estimates, compared with final cost; rate of utilization of budget; and ratio of current materials' costs to costs in previous years. Many of these statistics can be routinely collected, analyzed, and reported by the computer in an automated acquisitions system, often as a by-product of other operations.

VARIATIONS IN ACQUISITIONS WORK

The following discussions will suggest some of the acquisitions variations associated with the type, size, and governance structure of a library. These variations, while common, are not necessarily found in all libraries of the types described.

Effect of Type of Library

The clientele that a library serves is the ultimate beneficiary of the work of the acquisitions unit. Thus it is not surprising that the emphasis of acquisitions activities varies somewhat according to type of library.

PUBLIC LIBRARIES. One of the major emphases of the typical public library is rapid acquisition of current trade publications, that is, those books, periodicals, and audio-visual materials released by commercial publishers and usually made available to retail stores in sufficient quantities to meet customer demand. Such items need to be purchased quickly, not only to satisfy the library's clientele, but also to obtain them before the publishers' stock is exhausted. The acquisitions unit must therefore be geared to speed in ordering trade materials. In fact, the acquisitions staff may work closely with selection staff to determine, from review copies or items provided by arrangements such as the Greenaway Plan, which materials will be needed in multiple copies so that the orders may be placed rapidly and the maximum discounts can be obtained. Especially in large public library systems and often in school districts, it is highly desirable to coordinate orders for the large number of duplicates required to meet the needs of the libraries' clientele at their various service outlets.

Again, because of the high proportion of trade publication purchases, the public library's acquisitions unit may rely more heavily upon jobbers as vendors, since typically a jobber is better able to supply those materials that can be secured in mass quantity from publishers. While large public libraries undoubtedly use as wide a range of vendors as the university library does, smaller systems are likely to rely upon as few as three or four vendors for 90 to 95 percent of their purchases.

COLLEGE AND UNIVERSITY LIBRARIES. Libraries that serve institutions of higher education tend to purchase fewer duplicates than do public libraries of comparable size and, thus, must place a higher number of separate orders than would be the case in a public library.

In recent decades, college and university libraries have attempted to find ways of reducing the time lag in obtaining materials that embody the scholarship and research findings fundamental to the curricular emphases of their institutions. In particular, blanket order and approval plans have proved useful in gaining better control over such materials. This development has, in turn, caused the acquisitions procedures to change. The typical sequence of receipt of request followed by placement of order has given way to receipt of material followed by creation of a bibliographic record. Even with blanket order and approval plans, however, some materials will be acquired in the old way. This situation prescribes a more complex set of acquisitions practices than would be needed if everything were ordered using one method.

SCHOOL LIBRARY MEDIA CENTERS. The creation of large, sometimes multi-county school districts has led to the development of processing centers designed to serve all of their media centers at the building level. In these centers, the purchases for each school are often coordinated so that multiple copies can be ordered at one time in order to secure the maximum discount offered by a jobber. It is not unusual for a processing center to establish specified dates, each term, for the receipt of requests from the library media staff in individual schools. The acquisitions activity in the center may thus be concentrated into two or three short periods each year so that the processing center can focus upon cataloging and related procedures at other times.

SPECIAL LIBRARIES. A peculiar characteristic of acquisitions management in a number of special libraries is the lack of a specific budgetary figure for the purchase of materials. In such cases, authorization of library purchases may be at the discretion of a corporate officer who diverts available funds to acquiring materials believed to be important to the work of the firm. In many instances, purchasing routines for library materials are dictated by established corporate procedures for ordering general supplies of all types. Thus the library's control over its acquisitions might be somewhat minimized, so that the company's regular purchasing staff can be utilized to secure library as well as all other materials needed in the organization.

Effect of Size of Library

Perhaps equally important as type of library in determining the scope and intensity of the acquisitions function is the size of the library. Indeed, it could be argued that the characteristics of orders in the small school library media center are not significantly different from those in a small public library or in an information center of a modest-sized corporation. The requirements of a large public library system, on the other hand, tend to be similar to those of the university research library.

SMALL LIBRARIES. The small library, if not incorporated into a library system, usually operates with a limited budget for both materials and staff. Its acquisitions structure is therefore quite simple and is often attached to the work of the library director's office. Order files are manually prepared and maintained, and the chief source of supply may be a local bookstore.

In many instances, the small library may rely quite heavily upon donations of money and materials to augment its collection. One exception to this pattern, however, is found in the small corporate library that is part of a sizable company. In this instance, staff time for acquisitions work may be minimal, but record keeping is often quite sophisticated as a result of the library's link to the computerized systems of the parent organization. In such instances, budgets may be more generous and sources of supply more numerous than in most libraries of comparable size.

LARGE LIBRARIES. In some respects, the acquisitions structure in the largest libraries appears to have little in common with the work that takes place in the smallest ones. Certainly the dimensions of the order activities in a research library, especially one with holdings of two million or more volumes, are often quite similar to those of a medium-sized business. Each acquisitions function in such a setting may have a staff larger than the total staff of many small libraries. Workers in the large acquisitions unit are likely to be employed for their skills and knowledge related to special types of materials such as serials, foreign-language works, and documents, to special aspects of purchasing such as the rare and out-of-print book markets and approval plans, or to fiscal and records management such as computer-based accounting and file management.

The financial complexities of the large library in particular demand sophisticated controls. Such organizations may have to establish and manipulate several hundred different fund accounts, administer dozens of grants and gift monies, monitor the performance of vendors who hold blanket orders and approval contracts, and pay for materials that cost well over a million dollars each year.

Also, acquisitions work in the large library may be organized into separate units along type-of-material lines. For example, one unit might handle monograph or book acquisitions, while another unit might handle serials. These units may be further subdivided into smaller units according to the way materials are acquired. For example, the monographic acquisitions unit may be subdivided into separate and smaller units for handling firm orders, blanket orders, and approval plans, and the serials unit may be subdivided into smaller units for periodicals and journals, standing orders, and continuations. Each unit and subunit would have a manager assigned to supervise its activities.

Effect of Governance Structure

Differences in acquisitions procedures may also vary according to the governance structure of the library. Public institutions, whether they be city libraries or state university libraries, are often bound by legal and administrative regulations that are not operative in private institutions. Such public institutions, however, may have access to a better discount structure by virtue of their ties with large governmental agencies.

PUBLIC INSTITUTIONS. Typically, libraries that operate primarily with public financing are bound by contractual relationships established by the funding agency. For example, many state libraries and state college and university libraries are expected to direct their purchase orders to one or more vendors who have been awarded contracts to provide library materials to state-supported institutions. While such constraints are not necessarily inhibiting, they may require that the vendor on contract be given what amounts to a first-refusal opportunity on all library purchases. This privilege means that the vendor may accept or reject an order, but the order may not be placed with another vendor until the contract holder has had a chance to see it.

Libraries in a school district and some public libraries are often either bound to contractual purchasing agreements or expected to seek bids on purchase orders over a stated amount. For example, a library that buys both books and audio-visual materials might be expected to direct its book orders to a jobber on state or municipal contract, while orders for its audio-visual materials must be accumulated and periodically put out for bids.

Financial accounting procedures in public institutions are regularly prescribed by their governing agency. In some instances, the library benefits from the relationship, since the agency, by virtue of its size and importance to the taxpayers, may be able to afford more elaborate equipment, especially computer equipment, than would be available in a private institution. In other cases, however, the library that serves a public agency might be required to use inappropriate order forms and cumbersome payment routines because they are standard for the governing agency.

PRIVATE INSTITUTIONS. Libraries that serve institutions that are financed largely by private funds are likely to have more flexibility and, generally, more autonomy in designing and operating acquisitions procedures. This does not mean, however, that all privately supported libraries are free to adopt new systems at any desired time or that they have open-ended budgets for acquiring new equipment to support their acquisitions work. In many cases, especially when the general economy is poor, private institutions must delay improvements until the institution's administration is convinced of the need and is ready to divert funds to a new system.

While many private institutions have eliminated bidding as a means of purchasing library materials, some still have such constraints. Also, it is not unusual for purchases to be paid for through the institution's business office, although, as these libraries grow, they often are entrusted with a greater proportion of their fiscal management.

AUTOMATION OF ACQUISITIONS ACTIVITIES

Libraries, for several decades, have relied on computers to improve and enhance their acquisitions activities. Indeed, some of the first applications of computers in libraries were for purchase order preparation and the maintenance of order files. While it is true that until recently there were few reliable automated acquisitions systems available for the average library, a variety of well-designed systems are available today for most sizes of libraries.

Automated Acquisitions System Options

Libraries today have several options from which to choose when selecting an automated acquisitions system. The option chosen will depend upon the volume of acquisitions work, the nature of the acquisitions activities, the extent and nature of other automation in the library, the funds available for automation, and the philosophy of library and acquisitions managers.

MICROCOMPUTER-BASED ACQUISITIONS SYSTEMS. The smallest automated acquisitions system operates on a microcomputer. The software, developed locally from scratch or supplied by a library automation vendor, might operate on an off-the-shelf microcomputer or on one especially modified by the vendor. The availability of these microcomputer-based systems has given many small to medium-sized libraries the opportunity that they otherwise might not have had to automate their acquisitions activities.

Most microcomputer-based acquisitions systems are stand-alone systems, not sharing their files or having electronic links to other automated systems, while others are integrated with other systems such as a circulation, acquisitions, or online catalog, and possibly linked with systems outside the library, such as vendor and utility systems. The microcomputer-based systems offer reasonable cost, ease of operation and management, and the ability to have the system located in the acquisitions department rather than in a remote computer center. Their limitations could include a limit on access to the system to only one or a few users at a time, the lack of some features available on larger systems, a limit to the size of records and files which can be maintained, and limits on the sharing of their files with other automated systems such as circulation and an online catalog.

MINICOMPUTER-BASED ACQUISITIONS SYSTEMS. Libraries having a large volume of acquisitions work or requiring more sophisticated features can use a minicomputer-based acquisitions system. The software for this size of system also is developed locally from scratch or, most likely, supplied by a library automation vendor.

These systems will offer automation of all acquisitions activities, an integration with other automated functions such as serials, circulation, and online catalog systems, an ability to accommodate many users simultaneously, and almost unlimited record and file sizes. Their limitations might include their relatively high initial and operating costs and their complexity.

MAINFRAME-BASED ACQUISITIONS SYSTEMS. Mainframe-based acquisitions systems may have no additional features than the smaller systems, but they can accommodate larger files, a high volume of processing activity, and more users simultaneously. Usually, the acquisitions function is well integrated with other automated systems in the library, such as serials, circulation, cataloging, and an online catalog so that data and features can be shared among them.

The mainframe-based acquisitions system can accommodate medium- to large-sized libraries well, and is particularly well-suited to support a number of independent libraries sharing the use of the system through a consortium or a network. The software is developed locally from scratch or supplied by a library automation vendor. These systems have relatively high initial and operating costs and can be very complex.

Capabilities of Automated Acquisitions Systems

A well-designed automated acquisitions system will perform all the tasks found in a manual system, and more. It will provide speed, accuracy, and consistency of work which many manual systems cannot offer. Also, an automated system may have many features not available in a manual system; for example, Boolean searching of order files, automatic updating of fund accounting files upon receipt of orders, and so on. A wide range of management reports can be provided automatically by an automated system that are not possible in a manual system, due to the cost and time required for their production.

Acquiring an Automated Acquisitions System

Acquiring an automated acquisitions system requires careful and detailed planning, a thorough comparison of the library's needs with the systems available, and an objective selection of the best option which should fill the library's acquisitions needs for from five to ten years into the future. This process has several steps, briefly described below.

NEEDS ASSESSMENT. A first step in acquiring an automated acquisitions system is to conduct a study or assessment to determine the library's needs for a system. This assessment will include the number of monographic and serial titles acquired annually and the expected growth rate for the next five to ten years, the way in which materials are acquired, the nature of the library's fund accounting activities and the number of fund categories needed, the number of vendors used in acquiring materials, the way acquisitions work is organized in the library, and other pertinent information.

NEW SYSTEM REQUIREMENTS. The needs which have been assessed can be translated next into a set of specifications or requirements for an automated acquisitions system. These requirements will define the desirable features of the system to be acquired, specify what the system must do and how it must perform, and describe how it is to be operated and maintained.

SYSTEM EVALUATION. The library should systematically compare the available options for an automated acquisitions system against the set of requirements developed in the previous step. This comparison can be done formally during a purchasing process required by the library's fiscal officers or through an informal process. The requirements also can form the basis of a Request for Proposal (RFP) or a Request for Quotation (RFQ) or other bidding documents which might be required by the library's fiscal officers.

SYSTEM SELECTION. Once the automated acquisitions systems available have been evaluated and compared against the library's set of requirements, the best option can be selected. This decision can be made on the basis of a combination of factors such as the highest number of requirements satisfied by a system, the greatest number of desirable features available, the best cost, the assessed potential for success with a system, the professionalism of the vendor's staff, and so on.

CONTRACT NEGOTIATIONS. After the selection of the automated acquisitions system which seems to best suit the library's needs has been made, contracts for the system must be negotiated and signed. Purchase, hardware maintenance, and software maintenance contracts are typically required by a library.

SYSTEM INSTALLATION AND IMPLEMENTATION. The last, and usually most difficult step, of acquiring an automated acquisitions system is its installation and implementation. The site for the hardware must be constructed or renovated; the hardware and software must be delivered, installed, and tested; the acquisitions workflow must be reworked to accommodate the new system; jobs within acquisitions must be reviewed and revised; the quarters for the acquisitions unit must be redesigned to accommodate the new workflow and the computer terminals; the library's vendor and fund accounting files must be converted to a machine-readable form; and staff must be trained to operate and manage the new system.

BIBLIOGRAPHY

Acquisitions Work

Alessi, Dana L., and Kathleen Goforth. "Standing Orders and Approval Plans: Are They Compatible?" *Serials Librarian* 13(October-November 1987): 21-41.

American Library Association. Bookdealer-Library Relations Committee. *Guidelines for Handling Orders for In-Print Monograph Publications.* 2nd ed. (Acquisition Guidelines, no. 4). Chicago: American Library Assn., 1984.

Cargill, Jennifer S., and Brian Alley. *Practical Approval Plan Management.* Phoenix, Ariz.: Oryx Press, 1979.

Ford, Stephen. *The Acquisition of Library Materials.* Rev. ed. Chicago: American Library Assn., 1978.

Grieder, Ted. *Acquisitions: Where, What, and How: A Guide to Orientation and Procedures for Students in Librarianship, Libraries, and Academic Faculty.* Westport, Conn.: Greenwood Press, 1978.

Library Acquisition Policies and Procedures. Ed. by Elizabeth Futas. 2d ed. Phoenix, Ariz.: Oryx Press, 1984.

Magrill, Rose Mary, and Doralyn J. Hickey. *Acquisitions Management and Collection Development in Libraries.* Chicago: American Library Assn., 1984.

Wulfekoetter, Gertrude. *Acquisition Work: Processes Involved in Building Library Collections.* Seattle: University of Washington Press, 1961.

Automation of Acquisitions Work

Aveney, Brian, and Luba Heinemann. "Acquisitions and Collection Development Automation." *Library Hi Tech* 1(Summer 1983): 4-53.

Boss, Richard W. *Automating Library Acquisitions: Issues and Outlook.* White Plains, N.Y.: Knowledge Industry Publications, 1982.

_____. "The Ideal Acquisitions System." In *Issues in Library Management: A Reader for the Professional Librarian*, pp. 52-63 (Professional Librarian Series). White Plains, N.Y.: Knowledge Industry Publications, 1984.

_____. "Issues in Automating Acquisitions." In *Issues in Library Management: A Reader for the Professional Librarian*, pp. 40-51. (Professional Librarian Series). White Plains, N.Y.: Knowledge Industry Publications.

_____. *The Library Manager's Guide to Automation.* 2d ed. White Plains, N.Y.: Knowledge Industry Publications, 1984.

_____, Susan Harrison, and Hal Espo. "Automating Acquisitions." *Library Technology Reports* 22 (September-October 1986): 479-634.

Clayton, Marlene. *Managing Library Automation.* Brookfield, Vt.: Grower, 1987.

Corbin, John. *Managing the Library Automation Project.* Phoenix, Ariz.: Oryx Press, 1985.

Matthews, Joseph R. *A Reader on Choosing an Automated Library System.* Chicago: American Library Assn., 1983.

Reynolds, Dennis. *Library Automation: Issues and Applications.* New York: Bowker, 1986.

Saffady, William. *Introduction to Automation for Librarians.* 2d ed. Chicago: American Library Assn., 1989.

FIVE

Bibliographic Searching

T HE BIBLIOGRAPHIC SEARCH is designed to serve two basic functions: to determine that a requested item is not already in the library collection or on order and to locate sufficient information about the item to be able to select an appropriate vendor and place a purchase order. To speed the processing of materials once they are received, a third function has been added in recent years: to obtain reliable cataloging information so that the library's bibliographic record of each item may be initiated with the placement of the purchase order. Also, the library wanting its order records to be accessible in its online public access catalog will want the bibliographic information to be as complete and accurate as possible.

Part of the bibliographic search is called "verification." While verification is not usually performed as a separate operation, it is important for the acquisitions staff member to be aware that not all requests for library materials are complete enough even to determine that the items have actually been published. It is thus presupposed that the search process will also isolate requests that appear to relate to unpublished or unrecognizable materials. For example, a request may be for an item that was announced prior to publication and has not yet been released, or it may be for the next volume in a series that has been delayed. In a few cases, a citation may appear to refer to nothing that has ever been published or anticipated. Experienced bibliographers are often needed to decipher garbled information and identify references to "ghosts" that have been listed in seemingly reputable sources.

Once the existence of an item has been established, the searcher can usually locate information for placement of a purchase order.

THE SEARCH STRATEGY

One of the interesting and challenging aspects of preorder searching is that so many requests are either incomplete or incorrect when received by the acquisitions unit. Also, the acquisitions librarian must become skilled in recognizing requests that are atypical so that routine search procedures will not be applied to materials for which they are likely to be ineffective. In general, however, the purpose of search procedure design is to minimize the time spent in searching requests while maximizing the information located. This purpose, in turn, implies making search strategy as routine as possible and reducing the number of examined sources to those that can be expected to yield useful results in the shortest possible time.

Since preorder searching is one of the costliest aspects of acquisitions work, considerable investigation and analysis have been applied to this task. Particularly in the 1960s, when libraries were often able to purchase more materials than they could process, efforts were initiated to determine the least-cost path to order information. For example, Fristoe, in his article, "The Bitter End," compared the effectiveness of searching various bibliographic sources, such as the *National Union Catalog*, *Cumulative Book Index*, and *American Book Publishing Record*, to determine which ones should be examined and in what order.[1] Groot, in "A Comparison of Library Tools for Monograph Verification," updated Fristoe's analysis of search strategy in locating bibliographic information.[2]

Increasingly, acquisitions staff, particularly in large libraries and in those that are members of bibliographic utilities, have attempted to reduce manual searching by using computerized databases. Thus searchers must develop skills in locating items listed in the machine-readable files of bibliographic utilities such as OCLC and RLIN, as well as in other online databases such as that created for *Books in Print*. While large research libraries may participate in several of these systems, many smaller libraries will have at best access to the files of the bibliographic utility in which they hold membership or to an inhouse bibliographic file stored on optical disc and searched by microcomputer. Even in large libraries, but especially in smaller ones, search strategy will involve a blending of manual and machine techniques to locate needed information.

As bibliographic services become computerized, their manual counterparts in book form or microform often are eliminated. The acquisitions staff, as a result, is continually pushed to reevaluate the use of these computerized services to determine whether they yield enough valuable information to justify their cost. Often, determination of the cost effectiveness of a bibliographic service will have to take into account the needs of other divisions of the library, since cataloging and reference staff may rely on the bibliographic information contained in them, even though its value is found to be marginal to the acquisitions unit.

Ideally, decisions about search strategy for locating bibliographic information for requested items should be based upon the previous record of success and failure in using certain services. Techniques from the discipline known as operations research are sometimes helpful in setting a path for routine searching of requests. It is not sufficient, however, to devise a search path and expect it to serve indefinitely. Changes in bibliographic services, in acquisitions policies, and in collection management goals require reassessment of the strategy and, in most cases, continuing adjustment of the search system.

When an order request appears to be complete and the expected cost of the material is not unreasonable, the acquisitions staff may decide to initiate the purchase of the item without further verification. In the long run, the cost of searching to fill the request may be as great as paying for a duplicate. In large libraries, particularly those that collect research materials, the likelihood that a new request represents a duplicate is greater than in the small institution. In such settings, verification of all requests may be handled routinely, even though the supplied bibliographic information is apparently accurate and complete.

SEARCH PROCEDURES

The process of bibliographic searching can have many detailed steps, as described below.

Receiving Requests

To encourage requesters to supply as much information as possible about materials to be acquired, libraries usually distribute a form that requests such information as author, title, publisher, place and date of publication, series relationship, price, standard number such as International Standard Book Number (ISBN), source of citation, and requester's name.

Sometimes the requester also can supply a copy of the original citation such as a publisher's announcement, a review, or a listing from a bibliography or dealer's catalog. Having at least the location of the citation enables the searcher to determine whether the material requested is current, old and possibly out of print, or not yet published. Unfortunately, bibliographic information in publishers' and dealers' catalogs is often incomplete, particularly with regard to date of publication. In such instances, the library staff will have to search further to verify the existence and bibliographic characteristics of the item.

In small libraries that operate as part of a public or school library system, order requests are commonly made by checking a list supplied by a processing center serving them. However, the center may, in effect, have already searched the items before placing them on the list, thus bypassing the need for further search. In large research libraries, in contrast, requests may be made in many ways: by checking dealers' lists, marking photocopies of published bibliographies, or supplying separate forms. When requests are received in list form rather than on separate slips or cards, the searcher often fills out a new form for each item, showing the bibliographic and source information in their appropriate places.

Typically, a request form or search record includes the following information:

Full title of item
Statement of persons or corporate bodies responsible for the item
Edition information
Information about format
Place of publication
Name of publisher, distributor, etc.
Date of publication, copyright, etc.
Series of which item is a part
Standard number for item (ISBN or ISSN—International Standard
  Serials Number)
Price of item
Library of Congress Card Number (LCCN)
Call number for any related item (e.g., previous copy or earlier edition
  already owned by library)
Notation(s) on sources to verify item's existence and to obtain catalog-
  ing information
Date of request and date of search
Name of requester
Fund to which item is to be charged

Often the requests have not been verified or searched before submission. It is thus highly desirable to standardize the sequence of recording the bibliographic information for each request by having the searcher follow some kind of form.

Presorting Requests

Because search techniques vary with the type of material requested, most acquisitions units institute some kind of presearch sorting to allow an effective grouping of requests.

This sorting may take into account such factors as the age of the material, that is, whether a title is likely or unlikely to be in print; language and country of publication, that is, whether a search is likely to be difficult because of the scarcity of bibliographies in the language or for the country; and format, that is, the form of the requested material for which bibliographies may be scarce, highly specialized, or complex.

Sorting may also take into account the completeness, or lack thereof, of the citation that accompanies the request, so that easy searches are separated from harder ones. Further, some monographs may be searched separately because of their series relationships, since such materials usually must be investigated from both the monographic and the series standpoint.

Checking the Library's Records

If a search accomplishes nothing else, it must reveal whether the library already owns, or has placed an order for, an item being requested. This seems relatively simple, but it can have hidden difficulties.

In the simplest case, the request may be too incomplete or inaccurate to permit the searcher to compare it with the library's catalog and order file. In this instance, verification must precede the check of the library's records. Checking bibliographic sources is described in the next section.

If the request is apparently complete bibliographically, the searcher can check the library's records to discover duplicates. This investigation is relatively routine, but problems can arise if the searcher is unskilled, unimaginative, or careless. Especially important is the searcher's understanding of the various types of entries for personal and corporate names, titles, and series in the catalog. A request may show a personal name as author of the work, but that name could be misspelled, incompletely represented by initials instead of the full form, or misrepresented as author when the person is actually an editor, compiler, or contributor. The searcher must be careful to check under the title, if no listing as author is found under the personal name. Further, a check of the series title, if one is provided, and of organizational names associated with the work may be needed to determine that the library does not have the item.

The check of the library's order or in-process file, while simpler, can be misleading as well. Many such files provide only a single access point, usually title. However, sometimes the name is chosen as the chief access point, so there is only one chance to find a duplicate order in the file. Particularly in order files arranged by main entry, the searcher must be careful to check for variant listings under title, corporate name, and series to be sure that the item is not already being acquired.

Even the fullest request forms may omit vital information necessary to identify of an item as a duplicate. Often, the series connection is obscurely indicated, if at all. But if the library's records emphasize the series and make little or no reference to the title or author of individual monographs, the duplication may go unnoticed. In such cases, the search may proceed beyond the library's records, only to be returned for a further check when missing information of this type is discovered.

Checking Bibliographic Sources

In some libraries, particularly small ones, an internal check of the order file and public catalog may be all that is required before placing the order. In such cases, all that the acquisitions staff needs to know is that the item has not yet been ordered or otherwise secured. Only if the bibliographic information supplied by the requester is found to be incomplete will the staff look further.

Such brief procedures are especially likely if the library orders through very few vendors and primarily acquires current materials that are distributed in the United States. Libraries that have a contractual relationship with a jobber, for example, sometimes expect the jobber to supply any further bibliographic information needed to obtain the requested materials. The jobber, in such instances, will often specify through the terms of its contract with the library how much information the library must submit, or will indicate the standard sources in which the materials should be listed. For libraries that purchase from a number of different vendors, the acquisitions search is expected to amass as much information as possible so that an appropriate vendor can be chosen and the material obtained with minimal delay.

The problems of finding complete bibliographic information tend to increase with the difficulty of the material that is requested. Items that are old, in an exotic language, or in an unusual format can be expected to require a more complex search. It is likely, as well, that more care will be taken in securing complete information about materials that are expensive.

The searcher, using what information is provided, will try to locate a citation to the item in some standard source: a CD-ROM bibliographic database used inhouse, a bibliographic utility such as OCLC or RLIN, a national bibliography such as the *British National Bibliography*, a national catalog such as the *National Union Catalog*, a publisher's catalog, or a dealer's list.[3] If full information for title, author, edition, place of publication, publisher, publication date, series connection, and standard numbers are found, the searcher may proceed to examine the library's records to determine whether the request duplicates material already acquired or on order.

A number of the bibliographic sources used in searching provide cataloging information of the type produced by the Library of Congress. Such sources as the *National Union Catalog*, the *Cumulative Book Index*, the *Weekly Record*, and the *American Book Publishing Record* include Library of Congress cataloging information, when available. Many libraries find it desirable to rework information on the request form to match Library of Congress cataloging standards. However, since these standards have changed over the years, particularly with adoption of the provisions of the second edition of the *Anglo-American Cataloguing Rules*, it is difficult for acquisitions staff to be certain that the older styles of cataloging are still acceptable.

Some bibliographic sources list the price of the material. Again, this type of information goes out of date quickly, and many large libraries have begun to use cost estimates, rather than searching for list prices that may no longer be valid. When requested items, especially rare materials, are likely to be expensive, cost verification may become extremely important. It is not unusual, in such cases, for a check to be made in appropriate dealers' catalogs and in the records of auction sales so that reliable price estimates can be made.

Recording the Search

In many libraries, the request form is also used as the medium for recording the results of searches. As new or corrected bibliographic information is located, it is incorporated into the request form until a final, reliable copy is produced. In addition, some forms have a line on which to record the sources in which the material was found. Others have a preprinted list of such sources beside which notations of the search results can be placed.

Returning Requests

If a request for acquisition of materials is submitted without a supporting citation, the searcher proceeds according to the library's policies. In some instances, especially if the acquisitions unit has only one or two staff members, incomplete requests may be returned to their initiator with a form requesting the needed information. If this procedure is followed, the searcher should be careful not to return a request merely because it lacks a technical detail not likely to be available to its initiator. Many footnotes and bibliographies that include the citation do not provide such information as the standard numbering, price, or series relationship of an item. In most instances, asking requesters to supply such information is futile, since they are not skilled in identifying or using the sources that provide it.

SPECIAL PROBLEMS

There are a number of special problems related to the bibliographic searching process, including unlocated requests and duplicates.

Unlocated Requests

Many problems associated with verification have been minimized by the use of online bibliographic databases provided by a utility such as OCLC or RLIN. Even though these systems are usually up to date, the entry of new bibliographic information is, to a great extent, dependent upon the contributions of member libraries; thus it is possible that certain types of materials, especially nonbook formats and books published prior to the advent of the utilities, will not be represented in these online sources. The fact that an item is not listed in the database does not necessarily mean that it has not been published or is not available. It is usually desirable that an experienced acquisitions staff member review requests that cannot be verified, to determine whether they have been inadequately searched or should be returned to their initiators for further investigation.

Duplicates

Since some libraries utilize standing order, blanket, and approval plans in addition to placing individual purchase orders, the search process must, in such instances, allow for the possibility that the requested item arrive automatically as a result of one or more of these plans. The checking that is necessary in this situation can vary according to the precision of the plan. For example, if the library has a standing order for a monographic series, the staff member who handles a request for one of the monographs can note it as a potential duplicate as soon as its series connection is established. Similarly, blanket orders with certain publishers are clearly delineated, and requests for current materials issued by such publishers can usually be identified as duplicates rather quickly.

Recognition of duplicates resulting from an approval plan is more difficult, since often there is no precise knowledge about what the vendor will send or from which publisher materials will be acquired. To combat this problem, some approval-plan vendors have developed microfiche-reporting services which give information about forthcoming publications, thereby allowing the library staff to predict which titles a library may receive. The library's profile or characteristics it uses to set up the approval plan may be specific enough to help in spotting possible duplicates, but it is likely that the acquisitions unit will need to maintain a list of potential duplicates to check against actual receipts from the approval-plan vendor.

Even the most effective search procedures cannot uncover every bit of information that is needed to make certain that unwanted duplicates are not ordered. If material being purchased is not particularly expensive, it may be cheaper to risk getting a duplicate than to search extensively in obscure sources. Unless the item represents a series, an expensive set, or a rare work, it is unlikely that the searcher will be encouraged to investigate the item in more than routine fashion.

SEARCH PRIORITIES

Although acquisitions searchers are usually assigned items according to their expertise in certain types of materials, there is a need to establish priorities among requests. Even the Library of Congress establishes priorities, giving particular attention, for example, to materials requested by members of the Senate and House of Representatives.

In the academic setting, materials needed for class use, such as reserve and parallel reading, may be identified as "rush" so that they will be searched and ordered quickly. Similarly, materials expected to be in high demand in the public library need to be searched rapidly. In most libraries, items needed for reference or for special research will be given fast processing. Certain types of out-of-print materials also need to be searched quickly so that they may be ordered before they are sold to someone else.

Ideally, the search process should be conducted so speedily that no item would have to be rushed through it. It is difficult, however, in some libraries to control the searchers' workload so that it will be even, never to exceed by more than a day or two the time available to finish it. Some school libraries, for instance, order only two or three times each year, thus placing a high demand on the search staff at infrequent intervals.

Acquisitions supervisors must work with their staff to develop plans for making sure that important materials are not delayed while, at the same time, not overburdening the searchers with many difficult searches on a rush basis. If search staff members are put under too much pressure, they may make too many mistakes or be tempted to lay aside some of the time-consuming requests so that they can dispose of the easier ones.

TRAINING AND EVALUATING SEARCH STAFF

In large libraries, particularly those that serve research functions, acquisitions search staffs are relatively numerous. In such a setting, each searcher may be assigned particular types of materials, categorized by the items' age, language, subject area, or format, as appropriate to the searcher's capabilities. Searchers usually are trained in a kind of apprenticeship, in which the new staff member is led through the process by someone who is experienced with the same or similar type of material. At the outset, the new searcher may be monitored at every step; later, the search record may simply be revised or checked to be sure that it appears to be complete and correct and, if necessary, redone in order to identify and eliminate mistakes.

The training process can be quite brief in libraries that acquire relatively uncomplicated materials, and quite lengthy in those where the search process is highly variable and the judgment of the searcher is utilized frequently. After a level of expertise has been attained, the searcher may be spot-checked, or even allowed to work unrevised so long as the quality of the search does not appear to deteriorate. Searchers' errors, unlike those made by some other staff members, are usually discovered eventually, often when an unwanted duplicate appears or a purchase order is returned by a vendor because of its inadequacy.

Searching is considered by some staff members to be routine and uninteresting, although others find it challenging and demanding. The repetitive nature of searching does suggest that it can be handled in most libraries by nonprofessional staff. Development of a searchers' manual can be helpful in training new staff, particularly when an established strategy is to be taught. However, the searcher should usually be allowed some latitude in choosing how far to carry the search. This kind of expertise appears to be attained best by a searcher working under an experienced search supervisor.

Although searching may lack the challenges offered by other library jobs, it is crucial to the smooth functioning of the acquisitions unit. Poorly verified requests, misplaced forms, and inaccurately transcribed information can cause materials to be delayed or even lost to the library's clientele. For this reason, searchers must be well trained, carefully monitored, and recognized for the vital work they perform in making it possible for the library to obtain the materials that its users need.

BIBLIOGRAPHY

Bloomberg, Marty, and G. Edward Evans. "Bibliographic Verification—
General Principles and Manual Systems." In *Introduction to Technical
Services for Library Technicians*. 4th ed., pp. 10-16. Littleton, Colo.:
Libraries Unlimited, 1981.

Flowers, Janet L. "Time Logs for Searchers: How Useful?" *Library Acquisitions: Practice and Theory*, 2(1978):77-83.

Fristoe, Ashby J. "The Bitter End." *Library Resources & Technical
Services*, 10(Winter 1966):91-95.

Futas, Elizabeth. "A Searching Sequence for College Libraries." *Collection Building*, 1(1979):77–80.

Groot, Elizabeth H. "A Comparison of Library Tools for Monograph
Verification." *Library Resources & Technical Services*, 25(April/June
1981):149-161.

Hobert, Collin B., and Dilys E. Morris. "Cataloging and Searching
Combined." *Journal of Academic Librarianship*, 10(March 1984):
10-16.

Lazorick, Gerald J., and Thomas L. Minder. "A Least Cost Searching
Sequence." *College & Research Libraries*, 25(March 1964):126-128.

Neikirk, Harold D. "Less Does More: Adapting Pre-Order Searching to
On-Line Cataloging." *Library Acquisitions: Practice and Theory*, 5
(1981):89-94.

Raouf, Abdul, Feroz Ahmed, and Syed M. Asad. "A Performance Prediction Model for Bibliographic Search for Monographs Using Multiple
Regression Technique." *Journal of Library Automation*, 9(September
1976):210-221.

Reid, Marion T. "Effectiveness of the OCLC Data Base for Acquisitions
Verification." *Journal of Academic Librarianship*, 2(January 1977):
303-326.

_____. "Searching and Verification: How Much Is Enough?" *RTSD
News*, 10(1985): 52-54.

SIX

Purchasing Individual Items

Once the decision has been made to acquire a particular item for the library's collection, consideration must be given to the means by which it is to be obtained. Although many items are ordered individually, a number of libraries, particularly the larger ones, have attempted to minimize the time-consuming procedures associated with item-by-item ordering by placing standing, blanket, and approval orders with reliable vendors. Libraries are also involved, in many instances, in programs of soliciting materials through gift and exchange arrangements. Occasionally, depository agreements are established so that some materials are obtained on a long-term loan basis.

This chapter deals with the procedures and problems associated with purchasing items individually. Succeeding chapters treat group purchasing, special types of book materials, nonbook materials, serials subscriptions, and gifts and exchanges.

SELECTING A VENDOR

Three types of purchasing agents may be utilized when the library acquisitions unit decides to order an item: jobber, dealer, or publisher. Depending on the arrangements negotiated in advance with these agents, each may serve as the best source for certain kinds of purchases.

Jobbers

The jobber performs the role of wholesaler of books and other library materials by trying to anticipate what its customers, usually schools, bookstores, and libraries, are going to buy and stocking those items in quantity in advance. Most jobbers set up headquarters in a low-rent area, using a large warehouse for storing the materials and simple functional office space in which order records are processed. By buying large stocks from publishers, the jobber obtains a maximum discount—often as large as 40 to 50 percent of the list price, which is the price charged to the general public. Part of this discount then can be passed on to its customers. If the purchasing library were to order these materials directly from the publisher, it is likely that its discount would be less because it costs the publisher more to ship materials item-by-item than to send them in bulk to a jobber.

In theory, the jobber's function can be clearly distinguished from that of the publisher and the dealer. The publisher is directly responsible for getting the material into marketable form, while the dealer may handle many types of materials, whether recently published or issued many years earlier. The jobber, in contrast, concentrates on current materials from two to five years old and usually on those published in one country and in the major language or languages of that country. For example, an American jobber will not ordinarily be able to supply German-language materials, although a Canadian jobber may very well handle both English- and French-language items.

Unfortunately, these theoretical distinctions become blurred in reality. Publishers may also serve as jobbers or dealers for particular types of materials. In the last two decades, some major publishers have merged with larger communications organizations and have found it valuable to extend their vending functions. Similarly, dealers that once concentrated on the out-of-print market have begun to assume jobbing functions. Whatever the business structure, however, the jobber's role is usually distinguishable as limited to supplying current titles easily available from publishers and at a high discount.

Since jobbers make a profit by a rapid turnover of stock, they generally are not interested in trying to supply materials that are difficult to identify or obtain. In most cases, their staff is not large in comparison with the workload, and they are not able to spend much time solving bibliographic problems. They specialize in processing orders quickly and can be expected, depending on the types of materials ordered, to supply perhaps 75 to 80 percent of them within six to eight weeks after a purchase request is received. Often the jobber will contractually agree with the library either to ship all items requested or to report on their status within 60 to 90 days of receipt of an order.

The basic purpose of all jobbers may be considered the same, but some are more effective than others in meeting certain types of library needs. One jobber may be better at handling multicopy orders for school and public library systems, while another may prefer to deal with single-copy purchases of academic, special, or small public libraries. Some jobbers include university press materials in their stock, while others avoid such sources because of the small discounts that these publishers offer.

As a library's acquisition staff decides where to place an order, a jobber may be its first choice for several reasons: high discounts, rapid service, and ease of payment. In such cases, the acquisitions staff must be certain that no time is wasted by ordering titles that the jobber is not equipped to supply.

Jobber performance needs to be monitored to determine whether materials are supplied promptly and correctly and whether the record keeping and payment procedures are managed well. Without clear and documented evidence, the library will be hard pressed to argue for a change of jobbers when a new contract or agreement is negotiated. Fortunately, many automated acquisitions systems available or being developed include a statistical subsystem that will help the library analyze vendor performance.

Dealers

The usual characteristic of dealers as vending agents is that they handle a wider range of materials than the jobber. In general, the dealer is less likely to limit stock because of the age of the material, the language in which it is written, or the discount given by the publisher. However, dealers often limit their stock in other ways, either by subject field, format, or quantity of copies maintained in stock. Selecting an appropriate dealer is therefore contingent upon knowing the dealer's specialties.

Because many dealers' emphases overlap, the acquisitions staff has to become familiar with dealers' specialties to avoid selecting an inappropriate vendor. Some limitations and preferences are fairly obvious. It is not wise, for example, to place, as one library accidentally did, an order for Israeli materials with an Arab dealer. Nor is it desirable to ask a vendor of general, secondhand books to assist in acquiring antiquarian maps, unless the dealer is known to have a sideline in cartographic collections. Successful dealer-library relationships are usually cultivated over a number of years and thrive on mutual respect and trust. Dealers' personnel change, however, and long-time arrangements can deteriorate, sometimes quite suddenly. The library must monitor its dealer relationships as regularly as those with jobbers and be prepared to terminate them if they no longer meet the library's needs.

Discount rates of dealers are usually lower than those offered by jobbers. Dealers, however, often give more personalized service to the library, seeking materials that are hard to find and providing advance quotes on items the library wants. A library may even place its desiderata or want list with a dealer and, in essence, use the dealer as an extension of the acquisitions staff.

Because of the small discounts obtained by dealers from publishers, the library may not receive a discount at all on some items. If the dealer has to scour the secondhand market to find a particular item or receives no discount from the publisher, a service fee may be attached to the price of the material. Acquisitions librarians need to know the discount and fee policies of the various dealers, as well as their reputation for good service. Few vendors can be selected merely on the basis of their prices, since the money saved through a discount can be paid back to the dealer in time-consuming correspondence and telephone calls about confused orders and billing practices.

Publishers

In recent years, libraries have tended to reduce the number of orders placed directly with the publisher and to increase those put into the hands of jobbers and dealers, but there are still advantages in ordering direct. If the publisher has an efficient sales division, the material may be supplied more promptly than from a jobber or dealer, and billing and payment may be simple and straightforward. On the other hand, many publishers prefer to sell through a middleman such as a jobber or dealer who will buy in quantity, thus reducing their paperwork. In fact, some publishers will not sell directly to libraries; others, especially small or private presses, will not sell to jobbers or dealers, but only to individual customers.

From the standpoint of attaining maximum reward with minimum effort, the acquisitions staff will usually find that ordering individual items through jobbers or dealers is more economical. There will always be materials, however, that can be obtained only by direct order, and procedures for such purchases will have to be established. Experience often teaches the acquisitions staff which items cannot be effectively acquired through a jobber or dealer, and unless contractual arrangements prohibit, these items can be routed directly to the publisher.

PURCHASING PROCESSES AND RECORD KEEPING

After a vendor has been selected, the purchase process is initiated. As part of this process, records of the purchase are established and a variety of routines performed for keeping track of each item until it is either received or its purchase order is canceled.

The procedures for preparing an order, transmitting it to a vendor, and maintaining appropriate records on its status are often among the earliest to be placed under computer control. Ideally, there should be no more than one keyboarding of the bibliographic information to identify a particular item that the library wants to purchase. Once that is done, a well-designed automated acquisitions system can generate copies of the orders to be transmitted to a vendor, as well as retain a record that can be consulted and updated during the time that the material is in process through the routines associated with receipt, cataloging, and physical preparation for use. The same computer-controlled information may eventually become the basis for the permanent cataloging record and for circulation control.

Computers are also useful in maintaining budgetary information and financial accounting records. Encumbrances and payments are frequently entered into an institution's computer even when the library has not yet developed procedures for generating orders or keeping individual purchase records by computer.

During the decade of the 1970s and in the early part of the 1980s, a number of libraries that previously had for various reasons been unable to automate their acquisitions procedures began to transfer significant parts of their routine record keeping functions to computer control.

Preparing the Purchase Order

The purchase order is the means of letting the vendor know that the library wishes to buy materials. The order may be transmitted in a variety of ways such as by letter, printed form, magnetic tape, or electronic signal. While the first two methods have been the more common, computerized or computer-assisted order transmission is becoming increasingly popular. For some time to come, nonetheless, acquisitions staff can expect to deliver an order in whatever form the vendor can interpret. If the vendor's equipment cannot process machine-readable orders, the library will have to continue to prepare them in traditional ways.

In whatever form it is transmitted, the order must carry, in recognizable sequence, the required information about each item. This information must include, in most instances, the bibliographic details of the work such as title, statement of responsibility, edition, imprint, series, and standard numbering, and the terms of purchase such as where it is to be sent, what records to include with it, and under what conditions it should not be sent without the library's agreement. The order will also specify the date of transmission and may include other information to assist the acquisitions staff in identifying and processing it. For example, the name of the requester, the fund to which the item is to be charged, and the estimated price may be included as part of an order.

If the library prepares its orders by computer and transmits them by direct electronic connection with the vendor, it is desirable to minimize the amount of information sent, since both computer and communication times are costly. In theory at least, only three pieces of information are required for a purchase: the standard number of the ordered material, the standard number of the library, and the standard number of the vendor. Behind each of these numbers, however, is a pre-established file of information to link the standard number of the material to its bibliographic characteristics, the standard number of the library to its address and specification of terms of purchase, and the standard number of the vendor to the name and location of the seller. The computer, through appropriate programming, can supply the order date for each day's transmissions. However, since not all materials, libraries, and vendors have yet been assigned standard numbers, transmission of orders with full information will probably continue for some time.

One of the most popular means of transmitting orders is the multiple-copy order form. Its chief advantage is that it provides, with one typing or keyboarding, a group of identical forms that can be separated and distributed for various record keeping purposes. One copy can go to the vendor, as the purchase order; another can be sent to, then be returned by, the vendor with the material or the invoice; others can be placed in the library's order file. The latter are used in sending the received item to be cataloged, are forwarded to the requester as notification, are mailed to the vendor to claim the item if it fails to appear, and are held as a record of the commitment to pay or encumbrance. Some libraries put a copy of the form in the public catalog to let the staff and library users know that the item has been ordered; others use it to order catalog cards or to develop lists of new acquisitions for distribution to staff and users.

Libraries that use automated acquisitions procedures often create a unit record that can be duplicated as many times as needed to serve the purposes which the multiple order form once fulfilled. The computer has the advantage not only of requiring merely one keyboarding of the information, but also of being able to rearrange and shorten the information, if appropriately programmed, to feature certain elements in particular situations; for example, placing the author's name first on an acquisitions list, while featuring a short title, standard number, and price on the encumbrance record.

As a fundamental part of most automated acquisitions systems, the library can input the basic bibliographic information about the item that is ordered and the name of the vendor. Then according to preprogrammed instructions, the computer prepares the purchase order and such other records as the library arranges to have made. A record of the order also can be displayed through the library's public online access catalog.

Encumbering the Funds

While it is possible to order a number of materials, particularly in a small library, without encumbering the funds, there is always danger that, because of delay in the vendor's response, not enough money will remain in the budget to pay for the items when they finally arrive. The purpose, then, of encumbering is to place a hold on the funds needed to pay for the materials so that the library will not be embarrassed by receiving more items than it can finance.

Basically, encumbering is part of the accounting process. Notification must be given to the library's financial staff that newly purchased items are expected to consume a certain amount of the materials funds. As the budget year nears its end, this staff examines the remaining encumbrances to determine whether the materials are likely to be received and paid for before the new budget year begins. If not, the encumbered funds may be released to pay for items that can be purchased quickly and paid for out of the current budget.

Since an encumbrance is usually only an estimate of the final cost of the material, adjustments can be made continually to the budget's balance. When an item is paid for, its encumbrance is eliminated and the actual cost deducted. If the cost exceeds the amount encumbered, the unexpended balance will be less than anticipated and the budget may become seriously out of adjustment. The library may thus prefer to err on over- rather than under-encumbering so that the budget will not be under spent. Overencumbering can be a problem too, however, since it can prevent allocation of funds for other materials until quite late in the budget year, thereby making it difficult to spend available monies by year's end.

Estimating the cost of materials is not always easy. While some vendors offer a consistent discount on all materials, others vary the discount according to the rate given by publishers. If the library purchases from a number of vendors, the acquisitions staff may be unable to make more than an educated guess about the cost of each item. For this reason, some assign a cost based on the expected price of various types of materials. Published price indexes are very helpful in suggesting the average cost of materials in subject categories, and the library staff may use them to determine price estimates for a given budget year.

In addition to encumbering monies from the overall materials budget, the staff may encumber particular materials against special funds. Depending upon the size and complexity of the library, the budget may be divided into a number of categories. Each item must then be allocated to one of these categories, and its encumbrance will be made both within the category and against the materials budget in general.

Automated acquisitions systems normally include provisions for a number of such subaccounts. When the expected cost of an item is entered into one of these, the amount is also encumbered against the total budget without separate action on the part of the staff. Similarly, the item, when it is received, can be disencumbered and its cost assigned to both general and subaccount funds by a single transaction.

Without such machine control, each item must be encumbered manually against its subaccount as well as against the general materials budget. The awkwardness of such complex accounting procedures demonstrates the primary reason for computerizing financial record keeping in the library. The computer also has the advantage of making fewer arithmetical errors, if the proper figure is entered by the operator in the first place.

Maintaining Library Order Files

During the time material is on order, that is, the time between sending the purchase request and receipt of the material, some record of the expected transaction needs to be maintained in the library. Traditionally, the library acquisitions unit establishes a manual file, often of cards or order slips approximately the same size as a catalog card (12.5 × 7.5 cm.), in which records for each ordered item are arranged alphabetically by the expected main entry or the anticipated final catalog entry. This type of manual file offers considerable flexibility and is a distinct improvement over earlier record keeping systems that relied upon lists of items compiled according to date of order and vendor and posted in a ledger or inserted in a loose-leaf notebook.

Recently, however, this file has been analyzed for effectiveness. A number of libraries have substituted title entry for main entry arrangement, since the selection of an appropriate main entry heading is often difficult for the acquisitions staff. The title is frequently the most reliable piece of information about a new item and can be more easily located in a file that contains, as most manual order files do, only one copy of the purchase request for each item.

For the past two decades, increasing emphasis has been placed on the development of computer-based order files. In such systems, the purchase request is entered into the computer as soon as it is ready to be forwarded to the vendor. Depending on the sophistication of the system, the record can subsequently be located by one or more search patterns, thus obviating the need for deciding on the arrangement of the file by either main entry or title entry, since both approaches are possible.

Computerization of order records can also solve the problem of making the order file responsive to a wide variety of staff needs. Typically, during the time an item is on order, questions arise concerning a variety of issues:

whether a newly requested item has been authorized for purchase; when particular items were ordered and which orders have remained too long unfilled; from what vendor the item was ordered; against what fund the item will be charged and how many items have been authorized under a fund; which items in a series have been ordered; whether an item has been received and transmitted to the cataloging unit; and what problems, if any, are associated with a particular item such as, for example, if it should be rushed when it arrives, if it has been reported out of stock, or if it was ordered prepublication and has not yet been published.

If a manual file is maintained, especially one which contains only one entry point for each item, some of these typical questions cannot be easily answered without developing supplementary files of one kind or another. To find out quickly which items have been on order for more than three months, for example, the acquisitions unit will usually establish an additional file arranged by date of order. Otherwise, the entire alphabetical file would have to be checked, item by item, for the date of each order. Similarly, to locate what has been ordered within particular series, a supplementary file may be set up by series. To determine what is charged to particular funds, a fund file may emerge.

The special advantage of the computer-based order record is that it can, if the system is appropriately programmed, answer all normal questions without the difficulties associated with maintaining manual files. If records are properly entered and coded and the computer program is correctly written, the system should be able to generate on demand or at regular intervals lists of items that have not arrived within a prescribed length of time, items to be charged against a particular fund, items associated with a particular series, and orders placed with a particular vendor, with information concerning the rate of order fulfillment of the vendor. If desired, although a programming and program maintenance cost is always associated with such additional features, the system might be able to generate lists of items to be rushed, those that are out of stock, those with prices over a specified amount, and so on. Indeed, one of the major problems with the design or purchase of an automated acquisitions system is determining which of the many features are essential and which can be omitted, given the additional expense associated with each special requirement.

Large manual order files may generally be described as error prone and labor intensive. Even though the filing staff is well trained and conscientious, it is easy for anyone to misfile a thin slip of paper. In many research libraries, literally thousands of items are on order at any given moment, and the likelihood of filing errors is thus very great. Unlike the library's public catalog, however, the manual order file usually offers its users only one chance to find the record. If that record is misplaced, the error can result in a duplicate order and unwanted expense for the library. For this and other reasons, computerization of the on-order record is highly desirable, especially in large libraries.

Paying for Materials

One of the most difficult procedures about which to generalize is the method of payment for materials purchased by libraries. Payment systems are sometimes controlled by the library itself, but at other times by the library's parent organization which may be a governmental body that operates under fiscal regulations that are imposed upon the library in the same way they are imposed upon other governmental purchasing units.

If the library is fortunate enough to establish its own system for payment and bookkeeping, the acquisitions unit will devise procedures for verifying that the material received from the vendor is indeed the item ordered, determining whether the price is fair under the terms of the contract or agreement negotiated with the vendor, recording the price paid for the item, preparing the check or other form of payment, and sending the payment to the vendor according to prior arrangement. Some vendors prefer to have the payments grouped and sent at regular intervals, while others want payment immediately for each item shipped.

For libraries that must rely upon a unit within the parent body to make payments for their materials, procedures will still be established for verifying the correctness of the material and its price; however, in order to have the payment drawn, the acquisitions unit must send to the payment unit all appropriate documentation. Such documentation varies widely. Some payment units accept the word of the library staff and merely draw up the checks and mail them, while others demand a list showing the name and cost of each item or copies of the vendors' invoices for the materials, with the library's indication of receipt.

There obviously is greater risk of delay or erroneous payment when the library does not write its own checks, but many parent bodies are regulated or audited in such a way as to make delegation of the payment responsibility to the library either impossible or very difficult. If the library is not permitted to make its own payments, the acquisitions staff is likely to spend considerable time straightening out problems with the payment unit and explaining to vendors the reasons for payment delays. Good communication between the library and the payment unit, on the one hand, and the library and the vendor, on the other, is essential if this complex system is to function effectively.

Despite the best staffs and systems, disagreements between a vendor and the acquisitions unit can emerge. Prices for materials may be unexpectedly high, discounts can be unexplainedly absent or short, materials may be incorrect or defective, and items, supposedly sent, can go astray. All of these snags occasion extra work for the acquisitions staff in that they generally require a letter or telephone call to resolve the difficulty. Excessive errors on the part of either the acquisitions or the vendor's staff reduce the effectiveness of the acquisitions program and should be eliminated wherever possible.

Libraries that make their own payments will undoubtedly be subjected to periodic audits. It is particularly important that the acquisitions staff establish a proper audit trail so that examination of its records will be uneventful. In designing or purchasing an automated system, the staff will want to study the system's characteristics for generating payment records acceptable to the library's auditors.

Once payment has been sent, the encumbrance against the budget needs to be released and the actual cost of the item entered as a debit. While some small libraries may not have a large enough budget to warrant a formal encumbering process, it is very important that payment be debited as quickly as possible so that accidental overspending will be minimized. In some systems, overspending is a violation of municipal, county, state, or other governmental laws or regulations and can result in severe consequences for the library if it is not corrected.

Clearing Order Records

Since the purchase order serves a limited function, namely to cause a particular item or group of items to be acquired for the library collection, it may be considered temporary rather than permanent. Although, technically, the record may become expendable once an item has been received and its payment sent, there are a number of reasons for retaining it for an extended period. Perhaps the foremost reason is the time required for the item to be cataloged and then processed, and the fact that no public record of the item will normally be available until the cataloging and processing are finished. While this time can be shortened by using catalog records prepared by other agencies such as the Library of Congress, a commercial vendor, or a bibliographic utility such as OCLC or RLIN, there is likely to be at least a short period during which the material is in the library but not yet available to the public. To prevent unwanted duplication of the item during this interval, the record of the purchase is usually retained in the order file until the item is released to the shelves and its catalog record made available to the public.

In some libraries, the order record, although cleared from the on-order file, may be retained in manual or machine-readable form to allow the acquisitions staff to compile information about the number of items received, vendor performance in supplying materials, cost of the items bought with certain funds, and the like. In addition, certain libraries, particularly those that receive special grants for the purchase of special kinds of materials, use the order records to report those purchases to the funding agency. For this and other reasons, many libraries never destroy their order records; some have committed older records to microform, while others indefinitely store the computer tapes or disks on which the records are stored.

In libraries that use a manual system for maintaining order records, clearing the files involves removing the order record from every location to which it was sent initially and establishing a received file for longer retention. Since there may be a number of files (alphabetic, date, fund, etc.) to be cleared, the process of removing records is often complex and subject to error. Removing the record from a computer file is simpler. However, if an error is made and the wrong record is deleted, the consequences can be more severe, since the deletion affects all of the associated files at once.

Once the order record is cleared from the current files, it may be desirable to alert a staff member or library user that the material has arrived and is available for use. A manual order record has the advantage of providing multiple copies of the purchase order for notification when they are no longer needed in the current files. Computerized systems can be designed to generate such notices, once the purchase record is cleared, but the price for a special service of this type can be higher than some libraries wish to pay. Another means for providing notification may have to be created if the automated system cannot accommodate the requirement economically.

Dealing with Special Problems

The variety of special problems that arise in purchasing library materials is great—so great that it almost defies categorization. A few of the common difficulties are mentioned below.

ITEMS NOT SUPPLIED. If an item fails to appear after a reasonable length of time, the library must claim the item; that is, the staff must query the vendor about the status of the order and the likelihood of its being filled in the near future.

Sometimes the vendor fails to report, even after a claim has been sent, and correspondence or telephone conversations are needed to find out what has happened. Because of the time and expense in such transactions, some libraries, in keeping with a contractual clause, specify that orders for all items that are not supplied within a stated period of time such as 60 or 90 days or six or twelve months are automatically canceled.

WRONG ITEM SUPPLIED. If the wrong item is supplied, the library may need to check its records to discover whether misleading information was supplied to the vendor.

Depending on whose fault it was that the item was missent, the library may either accept the loss or return the item for credit. All such instances are, of course, costly in staff time and delay the availability of the material to its potential users.

DEFECTIVE ITEM SUPPLIED. If an item is physically defective, the acquisitions staff must return it to the vendor for replacement.

An item may be improperly bound or packaged or have a defect that would inhibit its use. Complications can arise if the vendor does not have access to another copy or if the vendor's staff misunderstands the reasons for an item's return.

INCOMPLETE ORDER. On checking the vendor's invoice against the materials received, the acquisitions staff may discover that some items were not supplied.

This problem is particularly annoying because the staff often has no way of knowing whether another package has been sent but has been delayed, whether the vendor is still trying to locate the missing items, or whether an error was made in packing the materials for shipment. Again, this type of difficulty is likely to occasion written or oral communication with the vendor, sometimes over an extended period of time.

MISSING ORDER RECORD. Sometimes the order record for the material supplied by the vendor cannot be located.

In such cases, the staff often has reason to believe that the item has been correctly supplied by the vendor, but the purchase order has been misplaced or was never properly recorded in the system. Sometimes a manual record, lost from one file, can be found in another. In the machine-based file, however, loss of the record can be almost impossible to overcome, unless a backup file on magnetic tape, disk, or paper has been maintained.

DUPLICATE ITEM ORDERED OR RECEIVED. An item may be discovered to be a duplicate.

Depending on the reason for the duplication, the library may have to accept the item and absorb the loss, or return the material for credit. Some vendors permit an item to be returned even if the duplication turns out to be the library's fault, so long as the material has not been marked or otherwise damaged. For this reason, some libraries are careful not to place ownership stamps on new materials until the staff has verified the item against the purchase order.

Occasionally, duplication of an order will be detected before the item arrives, and in such cases the second order can be canceled or the duplicate can be returned before it is channeled into the cataloging and processing systems.

Even in the best of libraries, however, some materials will not be determined to be duplicates until they have reached the final stages of processing or are placed on the bookstack shelves. In these instances, the library may simply keep the duplicate in the hope that it will be useful to library users, or it may place the duplicate in storage to be used as an exchange item with another library or as stock for a library book sale.

There is a particular situation in which the library may be permitted to receive credit for a duplicate even though it is not discovered until the item reaches the shelves. If the vendor has supplied an item that is part of a series which the library did not know was in series at the time of the order and if the vendor's agreement with the library specifies that the library be notified of this situation before the material is sent, then the vendor is at fault, and the library will usually not be charged for the material. It is important to note, however, that any item that is associated with a series which was not identified before it was ordered should be tagged immediately as a potential duplicate and appropriately checked before it is released for cataloging and processing. Libraries often insert in the vendor's contract a clause about items in series because these materials may already be on order as a result of a subscription or standing order that the library has placed for the series as a whole.

INCORRECT ITEM CHECKED IN. Sometimes, an item is received but incorrectly checked in by the acquisitions staff.

This type of mistake is hard to identify and sometimes even harder to correct. Usually, an assistant related the received material to the wrong purchase order, marking the order manually or sending a message to the computer that it has been received, when actually it has not yet arrived. When the correct material comes, it appears to be a duplicate, although in fact it is not.

Frequently, there is no easy means to discover what has happened. Often the mistake is not located until a claim is entered for the material which was erroneously checked in and the vendor reports that it was sent. Unfortunately, by this time, the item that was thought to be a duplicate may have been returned, further confusing the vendor's staff, and will have to be reordered. Such mix-ups are time consuming and wasteful, but almost inevitable in any sizable acquisitions unit. The likelihood of such confusion can be minimized by properly training the checking staff and helping them understand how much trouble is caused by mishandled orders.

UNAVAILABLE ITEMS. An item can be reported as not available and the order canceled.

Many disagreements between libraries and vendors center on materials reported as unavailable for various reasons. Depending on their interests and capacity, the vendor's staff may decide that one or more items will be more trouble to secure than they will be worth in profit to the vendor. In such cases, a responsible vendor will report the situation accurately; but others, not so careful, may report the item to the library as out of stock or, even more inaccurately, out of print to avoid having to pursue the item beyond their inventory.

Acquisitions librarians rightly object to a vendor's careless out-of-print designation for any item that is not in the vendor's warehouse, since the material may be easily available from other sources. When the library staff suspects that a vendor is using an out-of-print designation for "not in stock and not expected," it will be wise to initiate further checks on the status of the material and confront the vendor with evidence of incorrect reporting. Repeated out-of-print reports that are wrong can justify terminating the relationship with a vendor if the situation is not immediately corrected.

UNEXPECTED COSTS OF ITEMS. An item may be priced far higher than the library expected, and payment either cannot be made or will severely unbalance the budget if it is made.

To avoid this problem, libraries often write into the vendor's contract a provision that the material should not be sent or should be sent only on approval if the price is more than a specified percentage over the amount in the purchase order. Other libraries simply indicate a dollar figure as the upper limit and require that the vendor not send the material until agreement is reached concerning fair payment, if the price exceeds that upper limit.

Libraries with low budgets and those in which overspending is not permitted need to develop such precautionary techniques. Affluent libraries may simply accept the discrepancy between estimated and actual price, but many are sufficiently cost conscious to avoid the problem by taking precautionary measures.

INVOICE ERRORS. The vendor's invoice may contain errors. There are several mistakes that are commonly made. One mistake is that one or more items on the invoice are in disagreement with the materials sent, although the materials are the ones that were ordered. This leaves the library in doubt whether the prices charged are correct. A second common mistake is that the discount applied to the publisher's list price is incorrectly calculated, computed at the wrong rate, or erroneously omitted. A third mistake is that the invoice total is not in agreement with the sum of the prices listed on it. A fourth mistake is that the number of copies for which the library is billed is incorrect.

Since payment is commonly based upon the invoice total, mistakes of these types ordinarily need to be corrected before the library or its fiscal agency pays the bill, although, if the vendor has a reliable bookkeeping staff, it may be possible to make the corrections after payment is received. If the library's fiscal unit demands that all errors be cleared before payment, the acquisitions staff may be involved in a tedious series of telephone conversations or correspondence to discover the proper total with minimal delay.

IMPROPER PAYMENT MADE. Improper payment may have been made by the library, or the vendor may have incorrectly credited a payment.

Resolution of this problem must usually be handled by the library's fiscal unit. Unless the errors are corrected promptly, the budget balance may become unreliable, a situation that is particularly intolerable toward the end of the fiscal year.

INCORRECT ACCOUNTING RECORDS. The acquisitions or fiscal staff may make mistakes in keeping the financial records.

These problems involve such errors as failing to deduct a payment from the budget, deducting the wrong amount, deducting the amount from the general budget but not from the fund against which the item is to be charged, debiting payment against the fund account but not against the general budget, and failing to remove the encumbered price when the actual cost is entered.

To some extent, this type of error can be reduced, although probably not completely eliminated, by using an automated system for bookkeeping. The software for such systems ordinarily prescribe that, for example, entry of a debit against a particular fund will cause it automatically to be deducted from the budget total as well. Even the most sophisticated automated system cannot, however, prevent staff from entering figures incorrectly or failing to enter them at all.

Reporting to Other Libraries and Bibliographic Systems

One procedure sometimes overlooked in the delineation of acquisitions routines is the need to report purchases to other libraries or bibliographic agencies for cooperative purposes. Such cooperation may exist on a national, state, regional, or local level, and the reporting mechanisms can vary according to the intent and responsibilities of the cooperative system.

The National Program for Acquisitions and Cataloging or NPAC, initiated by funds from the Higher Education Act of 1965, was established to identify libraries that purchase materials, especially libraries of research interest, from a variety of sources at home and abroad. Libraries selected by the Library of Congress (LC) for participation in NPAC are expected to notify LC of any purchase orders for materials of recent publication that do not have catalog records prepared by LC at the time of the order. To facilitate verification of this situation, LC supplies to participating libraries one copy of each catalog card printed by LC. These cards are supplied in batches, arranged according to the titles of the works. Initially the cards were arranged in main entry order, but the change to title occurred as more and more acquisitions process files were sequenced by title rather than by main entry.

The advantage of participation in NPAC is primarily that of assuming prompt cataloging of foreign publications by the Library of Congress so that local libraries will be relieved of costly original cataloging. The plan also assures that backup copies of research materials will be in the LC collection, complementing those in the local libraries.

Several of the bibliographic utilities that capture library cataloging information in machine-readable form and display it online for the use of all participants are adding order record information to their databases. Members of a particular utility may enter their purchase information on the interactive terminal so that the basic bibliographic information will be usable by all members. Local purchase orders can be generated from the entries according to library specifications, and budget and statistical reports can be obtained periodically from most of these systems. While bibliographic information related to the orders is displayed for all users, purchasing information is restricted to viewing by staff from the local library.

In addition to participation in NPAC and in bibliographic utilities, libraries may be members of regional, state, or local cooperative systems that require interchange of order information. Some of these systems are organized around library subject specialties such as medicine, population studies, etc., while others exist to stimulate cooperative collection development in a particular locale. Whatever the purpose and mode of operation, these systems require the acquisitions staff of their member libraries to report to a central source the expected purchases for the local collections. Reporting may be in the form of a paper record sent by mail or messenger, or as is increasingly likely an electronic message to a centralized, computerized database.

Participation in a cooperative acquisitions system entails extra work for the acquisitions staff. The benefits to the library, however, often far outweigh the costs of the added record keeping and reporting activities, since the local library may avoid making costly purchases in duplication of available materials that are sometimes as little as a mile or two away.

ORDERING STANDARDS

Few standards for ordering library materials existed before the use of automated acquisitions systems became widespread. The Book Industry Systems Advisory Committee (BISAC) of the Book Industry Study Group (BISG) has been active in promulgating standards for the electronic transmission of orders, invoice information, and status information about orders between libraries and other organizations and materials vendors. These standards have been adopted and are being used to some extent in automated acquisitions systems.

The International Standard Book Number (ISBN) and the International Standard Serial Number (ISSN) are being used universally. The Standard Address Number (SAN) is now being used by some vendors, but the movement has not yet been widespread.

With the advent of automation, particularly systems which have several library functions integrated together, there has been a need for bibliographic records to be captured in a machine-readable form as soon as a library contemplates acquiring material. To this end, many automation vendors now use the MARC (Machine-Readable Cataloging) format in the systems which they sell to libraries. As acquisition departments begin to download bibliographic records electronically from bibliographic utilities and other online bibliographic databases, the use of the MARC format will become commonplace.

BIBLIOGRAPHY

American Library Association. Library Administration Division. Library Organization and Management Section. Budgeting, Accounting, and Cost Committee. "Primer of Business Terms and Phrases Related to Libraries." *Information Reports and Bibliographies*, 9(1980):15-25.

Berkner, Dimity S. "Communication Between Vendors and Librarians." *Library Acquisitions: Practice and Theory*, 3 (1979):85-90.

Borlase, Rod. "A Nonlinear, Bimodal Model for Monitoring the Flow of Materials Fund Allocations." *Journal of Academic Librarianship*, 5 (November 1979):274-276.

Bullard, Scott R. "The Language of the Marketplace." *American Libraries*, 9(June 1978):365-366.

Cenzer, Pamela S. "Decentralized Acquisitions—A Future Trend?" *Library Acquisitions*, 9(1985):37-40.

Eaglen, Audrey B. "Book Wholesalers: Pros and Cons." *School Library Journal*, 25(October 1978):116-119.

Ford, Stephen. *The Acquisition of Library Materials*. Rev. Ed. Chicago: American Library Assn., 1978.

Goodyear, Mary Lou. "Acquisitions and Records Management: Help Where It Is Needed." *Library Acquisitions: Practice and Theory*, 1 (1977):157-161.

Grieder, Ted. *Acquisitions: Where, What, and How.* Westport, Conn.: Greenwood Press, 1978.

Hensel, Evelyn, and Peter D. Veillette. *Purchasing Library Materials in Public and School Libraries: A Study of Purchasing Procedures and the Relationships Between Libraries and Purchasing Agencies and Dealers.* Chicago: American Library Assn., 1969.

Long, James K. "Electronic Order Transmission." *Journal of Library Automation,* 14(December 1981):295-297.

Mastejulia, Robert. "Publisher Policies and Their Impact on the Market." *Library Acquisitions,* 11 (1987):139-144.

Melcher, Daniel. *Melcher on Acquisitions.* Chicago: American Library Assn., 1971.

Muro, Ernest A. "Standards and Interfaces." *Information Technology and Libraries,* 14(December 1982):315-317.

National Information Standards Organization. Subcommittee U. "Proposed Standard Purchase Order, Variable Format for the Computerized Ordering of Books." *Information Technology and Libraries,* 3(June 1984):184-207.

Paul, Sandra K. "Computer-to-Computer Communication in the Acquisition Process." *Journal of Library Automation,* 14(December 1981): 299-303.

Snowball, George J., and Martin S. Cohen. "Control of Book Fund Expenditures Under an Accrual Accounting System." *Collection Management,* 3 (Spring 1979): 5-20.

Somers, Sally. "Vendor/Library Relations: A Perspective." *Library Acquisitions,* 11(1987):135-138.

Stewart, Charles C. "Update on Ordering Standards." *Information Technology and Libraries,* 14(December 1982):341-343.

Thompson, James C. "Booksellers and the Acquisitions Librarian: A Two-Way Relationship." *Library Acquisitions: Practice and Theory,* 1(1977):187-191.

Wulfekoetter, Gertrude. *Acquisition Work: Processes Involved in Building Library Collections.* Seattle: University of Washington Press, 1961.

SEVEN

Vendor-controlled Order Plans

A WIDE VARIETY of vendor-controlled order plans is available. "Standing orders" are those in which a publisher or jobber is instructed to supply, until further notice, all monographs in a numbered series, all works published on a specified subject, all recordings on a particular label, all works by a particular author or composer, successive editions of an annual, all volumes of a work published over a period of years, etc. Standing orders are usually "firm" orders, meaning no returns are accepted, although some dealers allow exceptions to that rule.

The terms "blanket order," "approval plan," and "gathering plan" became common in discussion of acquisitions during the 1960s, but use of these terms was not consistent. All of them, however, referred to agreements between libraries and vendors that involved some degree of responsibility for selection given to the vendors and, in certain plans, some degree of return privileges allowed to the library.

Blanket orders are similar to standing orders, in that they may be arranged with individual publishers of printed materials and producers of nonprint materials, or with distributors or jobbers, and may involve something as specific as a publisher's series or as general as instructions to supply everything of a certain type or on a certain subject. A blanket order plan generally does not allow the buyer return privileges, but again there are exceptions, depending on the vendor. The term "gathering plan" has ordinarily been reserved for a blanket order arrangement with a foreign dealer, who is, in effect, given instructions to gather and ship whatever can be obtained in specified categories.

An approval plan may also be arranged with individual publishers or producers or with a jobber. The distinguishing feature of such a plan is that the materials are sent "on approval," and those not considered appropriate may be returned by the library. Approval plans with jobbers are usually agreements by which the jobber selects and sends to the library current imprints, based on a detailed "subject profile" of the library's collecting priorities. (The subject profile is a way of expressing the library's collection development policy, in a set of instructions to the jobber about what to send and what to withhold.) Approval plans may be limited to one subject or professional area (for example, medicine, architecture, music), one publisher's output (for example, a particular university press or academic publisher), one type of publication (for example, music scores, art exhibition catalogs, contemporary *belles lettres*), or they may cover the whole range of current publications from one country or in one language.

In conjunction with their approval plans, a number of dealers offer notification or current awareness service for new publications. Libraries that subscribe to such a service usually receive preprinted multiple-order forms for titles that match the library's profile. Some libraries use this service in place of an approval plan, while others use it to supplement the approval plan. In the latter case, a library would receive approval books for a basic profile and notification slips for books that fall just outside that profile or within an expanded version of the profile.

One other type of vendor-originated book supply plan is the lease or rental plan, designed to provide regularly changing collections of best-sellers. Although some books received through a lease or rental plan may eventually be purchased for addition to the permanent collection, these plans are not primarily acquisition channels. They make selected books of temporary interest available and provide an alternative to purchasing multiple copies of high-demand books.

DEVELOPMENT

Examples of mass purchasing or block buying can be found in most eras of library history. Entire personal libraries, or part or all of the holdings of a book dealer, have often been purchased by libraries without prior knowledge of all individual titles represented. However, large-scale block buying, with significant vendor control, began in the United States during World War II and spread shortly after the war ended. At that time, when the European book trade was still disorganized and systems for compiling national bibliographies were not operating efficiently, research libraries turned to purchasing methods that allowed dealers much discretion in deciding what to ship. The Library of Congress reported in 1942 that it had begun using "so-called 'blanket orders.'"[1]

Since the late 1950s, public libraries have had available a type of blanket order plan called the Greenaway Plan, named for Emerson

Greenaway, former director of the Free Library of Philadelphia. Beginning in 1958, he worked out a series of arrangements under which publishers sent all of their trade books to a library before publication, at the same time they sent out review copies. Greenaway Plan terms vary from one publisher to another, but, in general, discounts are higher than normal and returns are not allowed. This type of blanket order plan is attractive to large public libraries because it allows staff members to review books early enough so that multiple copies can be ordered and processed by the time the public begins to demand them.

Most academic libraries in the United States experienced budget increases in the late 1950s and early 1960s. Since many of them were not able to add staff commensurate with their increased acquisitions budgets, a number turned to blanket order or approval plans as the best way to gather their materials. Some libraries had as many as 30 or 40 separate plans operating at once, covering both foreign and domestic publications. In some cases, large percentages of the book funds were spent through this method, although other libraries were very selective in their choice of plans. Librarians were encouraged to consider blanket order plans when their selection procedures reached the point at which decisions on individual titles had become perfunctory, when they were already acquiring almost all new publications in specified subject areas, or when the regularly appropriated budget seemed to be covering the purchase of current imprints easily.

Although library materials budgets have not remained as generous as they briefly were in the 1960s, blanket orders of one type or another still constitute a major acquisitions channel in many libraries. As budgets became tighter in the 1970s, some libraries retreated from vendor-designed systems for supplying new imprints and turned to more careful local selection. However, staff reductions, due to decreasing budgets, concern about changing inventory policies of publishers, and inefficient local acquisitions systems, leading to slow arrival of needed materials, have led some librarians to reinstitute their blanket order or approval plans. These revived plans are usually based on more sophisticated profiling techniques and computer-controlled subject matching—a fact that has contributed to their resurgence.

A 1977 survey of 482 libraries of various types found that 37 percent of the libraries used approval plans, 20 percent used blanket orders, and 70 percent used standing orders of one type or another.[2] Although some public libraries and special libraries use blanket order arrangements, the practice is much more widespread in academic and large research libraries. Results published in 1977 for a survey of 101 academic libraries of various sizes showed that 70 percent had used or were currently using an approval plan.[3] The same survey found that the larger the materials budget, the more likely the library used approval plans.[4] Fifty percent of academic libraries surveyed in 1987 by a joint committee of the American Library Association's Resources and Technical Services Division and the Association of American Publishers reported participating in approval plans, but the largest libraries were all involved in approval or blanket order plans.[5] A 1981 survey of 101 large research libraries (members of the Association of Research Libraries) found that 85 percent of the respondents were using approval plans.[6] These libraries were spending a median of $80,500 for domestic approval plans and a median of $35,000 per year for foreign plans.[7]

The importance of approval plans in large libraries continues to be apparent. The Association of Research Libraries (ARL) conducted another survey of its members in 1987, which found that the number of respondents using approval plans had increased to 93.6 percent of the total.[8] Among these ARL libraries, 86.2 percent had both foreign and domestic plans. Amounts spent on domestic plans ranged from $800 per year to $500,000; amounts for foreign plans started at $1,300 and ran to $750,000. The scope of the plans being used by these large research libraries varied from comprehensive to specific subject or special format. The report noted: "It is evident from use patterns and comments that while some libraries view approval plans primarily as a method of mass acquisition, others find value in smaller plans focusing on specific geographical areas, subjects, or formats."[9]

STRENGTHS AND WEAKNESSES

Librarians disagree in their assessments of the strengths and weaknesses of using vendor-controlled order plans, which some view primarily as a way to streamline acquisitions procedures and others see as collection development tools. There are those who believe the only way to build a high-quality library collection is through individual, expert selection of each item that goes in it. Others argue that there is a place in collection development for acquisitions based on objective or quantitative criteria. Brownson, for example, calls this "mechanical selection" and defines it as a system "driven by criteria that do not require unusual knowledge or training to apply."[10] Examples of such criteria include price, format, publisher, publication date, etc. "Mechanical systems emphasize group rather than individual characteristics, tending to be statistical in nature."[11] In other words, if the collection development librarian notices that the library, through expert selection, regularly acquires a large percentage of a particular publisher's output, he or she may decide to buy, automatically or mechanically, all the new publications of that publisher, without consideration of the differences among the individual titles. Vendor-controlled ordering plans are one way to exercise this mechanical selection.

Standing orders, because they are usually firm orders for a narrow category of materials, are usually less controversial than blanket order or approval plans. Placing standing orders for publishers' monographic series, for example, appears to be an automatic and easy way to provide at least a few substantive monographs for certain parts of the collection. However, the purpose of each series, the publisher's ability to maintain that purpose, the quality of the individual publications, and the frequency and cost of the publications need to be reviewed regularly. A series in which the first titles are appropriate for the library's collection may eventually move out of scope or become duplicative of materials already acquired.

Proponents of other, broader vendor-controlled plans point out that the carefully designed blanket order or approval plan can provide systematic coverage of current publishing in fields of interest to the library. Such plans may be of great value in identifying materials, such as publications from small presses or foreign sources, that are not advertised widely in the United States—although some librarians have found that their blanket-plan vendors tend not to supply nontrade titles of importance for research, probably because such publications are outside their regular book trade connections. Approval plans present special problems in regard to this tendency not to supply certain titles. Any publications that are not returnable to the publisher by the dealer or that carry little or no discounts are very unlikely to be included in approval plans.

When items which would have been routinely selected are supplied automatically, collection development personnel can concentrate on nonroutine decisions, collection evaluation, and retrospective purchasing. On the other hand, if the dealer's coverage of current publishing is unpredictable and unreliable, with unexpected gaps, collection development staff may spend a great deal of time monitoring what dealers do and do not send. A library without the staff to scan many bibliographies and reviewing tools in order to maintain a collection in certain specialized areas can usually, through a blanket order plan, at least ensure a basic collection of materials.

One of the major advantages of any dealer-originated ordering plan is that the materials arrive early, before they are requested and before they go out of print. Some libraries have canceled their plans because of slow delivery of materials, but others have started (or resumed) plans because of the developing tendency for books to go out of print quickly (some within a few months of publication). Economic pressures and reinterpretations of tax regulations have encouraged specialized and academic publishers to order short print runs and keep their inventories low. A standing order, blanket order, or approval plan may be the best way to ensure receipt of important works from these publishers.

Among the strengths of vendor-controlled ordering is the fact that initiation of a large-scale general approval-plan forces a library to review collection policies and procedures. The exercise of developing a profile which accurately reflects collection priorities helps all staff members involved arrive at a better understanding of their collection development efforts. One approval-plan vendor suggests that collection development librarians must make three important decisions in regard to the library's profile: (1) whether to emphasize the subject or publisher approach; (2) whether to focus on essential or nonessential needs; and (3) whether to receive notification slips on the books themselves.[12] All three decisions have implications for how quality and quantity will be balanced in relationship to all of the library's constituencies. The profile as a relatively precise expression of policy is also useful in planning cooperative collection development projects with other libraries. Monitoring the approval-plan dealer's performance can encourage regular review and necessary revision of the profile and other policies.

Another of the often cited advantages of approval plans is that selectors—whether librarians, faculty members, or others—can select with the item in hand. Balanced against this advantage is the fact that most approval-plan materials arrive before their reviews become available. Another negative collection development aspect of approval plans is the tendency of some librarians to accept marginal material because returns are so costly in staff time and postage. Of course, a poorly conceived profile generally produces inappropriate selections. The dealer's operating procedures, quality of staff, and preconceptions of what a particular type of library should collect affect the interpretation of the profile. Avoiding unwanted duplication—caused by monographs in series or works simultaneously published in two countries—is also a problem with some blanket plans.

It is difficult to say whether vendor-controlled ordering is advantageous to the library from a financial point of view. Reports on costs of operating these plans vary widely from one library to another. Some librarians report that their average discounts are higher for blanket order or approval plans than for the firm orders they place for individual titles, but other librarians have had the opposite experience. Since the library usually pays postage on approval items returned, libraries with high return rates may have considerable expense associated with that activity. It is true, of course, that libraries that use these plans are limited in their ability to take advantage of prepublication discount offers. On the other hand, some libraries use standing and blanket orders on the assumption that materials, on average, are least expensive when they are first published.

Budgeting for standing orders, blanket orders, or approval plans can be a problem. It is difficult to anticipate the cost of these plans, and it may also be difficult to integrate the plans into the library's regular accounting system. Items received on a blanket-order plan could be charged to specific departmental accounts within the materials budget, or all receipts on the blanket-order plan might be covered by one fund. If separate accounts are used, problems arise with accounts in which receipts on the blanket plan either far exceed or do not approach the amount budgeted. Not every departmental library in a university, for example, will receive the same number of books from a general blanket-order plan, because amount of publication varies across subjects and from year to year. If all blanket orders are charged against a single fund and departments are allowed small individual accounts for discretionary and retrospective buying, inconsistencies will still arise. The departmental library, receiving the blanket-order-plan copy of a book, does not give up any of its allocation, but the unit that buys the second or third copy loses much of its ability to buy other materials.

One of the areas in which librarians hope to save money with vendor-controlled plans is processing costs. Some libraries have initiated these plans and experienced reduction in the amount of bibliographic verification needed, since preorder searching is eliminated. In other libraries, both professional and clerical staffs spend a great deal of time monitoring the plan. Separate files and routines are usually needed for blanket orders or approval plans; if the library has several plans, it may need several different routines. When the library attempts to integrate standing, blanket, or approval plan order routines with those for materials acquired through individual orders, exchanges, gifts, etc., the system becomes increasingly complex. Some librarians suspect that the staff time saved at one point in the work flow of vendor-controlled order plan processing is merely transferred to a later step in the process.

Although the 1987 survey of ARL libraries noted that "the effect of automation on approval plans is not yet very great," advances in the automation of acquisition processes may change the way approval plans are handled in the future.[13] Direct electronic transmission of bibliographic files from the vendor to the library may make it possible for librarians to do title-by-title review and authorize proposed shipments before they are sent. Libraries with large approval plans and librarians with a concern for controlling expenditure rates may also find that automated systems providing accounting data will make it easier to handle those approval plans effectively.

ESTABLISHING AND ADMINISTERING APPROVAL PLANS

Constructing the profile is one of the most important steps in instituting a general approval plan. A poorly designed profile guarantees that the coverage of the plan will be inadequate. (A 1977 survey of academic libraries found that inadequate coverage by dealers or unhappiness with the profile were the most common criticisms made by respondents who had discontinued approval plans.[14]) The typical profile for a general approval plan, covering all subject areas, may represent selections from as many as 5,000 subject descriptors provided by the dealer's thesaurus, combined with a variety of nonsubject modifiers. Nonsubject modifiers may include academic level, publisher, country of origin, language of publication, geographic and time limitations, subject treatment, physical format, price, etc. Most general plans automatically exclude unrevised new editions, reprints, government publications, dissertations, translations, periodicals, textbooks below college level, juvenile books, and popular, mass-market publications. Librarians may negotiate profiles with different nonsubject modifiers for different parts of the collection. Some dealers make their thesauri available in both hierarchical and alphabetical arrangements. Development of the profile is a joint responsibility of the library staff and the dealer. For profile preparation to work, the dealer must offer adequate profile components and know how to apply them. The library staff has an equal responsibility to reach an understanding about collection priorities and budget restrictions before trying to make an agreement with the dealer.

When profiles have been carefully developed and conscientiously followed, the number of items that have to be returned should be low. One foreign dealer has reported an average rejection rate of less than 6 percent.[15] Thirty-seven percent of the academic librarians who participated in a 1977 survey reported rejection rates of 5 percent or less.[16] More than half had rejection rates under 10 percent. In general, a rejection rate of less than 10 percent seems to be considered characteristic of a satisfactory approval plan arrangement.

When the volume of receipts on an approval plan is large, physical and staffing problems may be associated with displaying the materials, scheduling their removal, packing returns, etc. If approval plan receipts are to be reviewed, they must be displayed in a convenient location for a specified period of time. Choosing a display period that will allow sufficient time for review, yet will not delay processing, may be difficult, but getting all the people involved in selection to inspect the items on schedule may be even harder.

One of the most persistent problems for librarians who use blanket orders or approval plans is determining whether an item requested by a user can be expected to arrive on the blanket order. Decisions must be made about how long requests for specific titles will be held before individual purchase orders are placed. "Claiming" for approval plan books also presents unusual problems. Establishing when a book is released by the publisher is difficult and makes the timing of claims difficult. Claims sent in too early make unnecessary work, but waiting too long may result in the book's being unavailable. Some dealers provide regular status reports, so that librarians who use their plans can have advance notice of which titles will be shipped to them. These status reports are usually transmitted on microfiche, but this is likely to be done more often in the future by downloading machine-readable files.

Large, decentralized libraries sometimes have more trouble accommodating blanket order or approval plans than do physically centralized libraries. These problems arise from the fact that most blanket order plans are designed to provide only one copy of each title. In a decentralized library system, there may be a dispute about which library unit will get the copy that arrives on the blanket order, who will make that judgment, who will order added copies for other units, and how the departmental or branch librarians will be involved in these decisions.

Collection development librarians are increasingly conscious of the costs of the materials they acquire for the library. In the administration of approval plans, this has meant use of price limits as a part of the profile, a narrowing of subject profiles, careful review, and more frequent return of titles received, and greater reliance on notification slips. Budget problems and unexpected receipts under the approval plan have forced some libraries to suspend their plans in the middle of the fiscal year.

CHOOSING AN APPROVAL PLAN

A 1981 survey of 101 large research libraries found that they used over 200 different dealers for their various approval plan arrangements.[17] Fifty-three of the dealers were actually publishers, but the others included eight American or Canadian companies that provided general approval plans and an assortment of foreign and domestic dealers that offered plans for specific subjects or types of materials, such as music scores or art exhibition catalogs. A 1987 survey of the same group of libraries found that more than 300 different plans were being used.[18]

The selection of an approval-plan dealer must be made with care. The advantages expected from an approval plan can be completely nullified if the distinctive features of a particular plan do not match the library's particular requirements and operating procedures. The type of library, its purposes, the size and characteristics of its clientele, the materials budget and allocation requirements, size and quality of staff, service priorities, holdings, collection development goals, and current acquisitions procedures are considerations in choosing to accept or reject a particular approval plan. For example, it has been suggested that an approval plan is unlikely to work well in any library in which final authority to reject materials, sent on approval, rests outside the library staff, because selection by faculty members or researchers often results in either a high number of rejections or none at all. Joint selection, by librarians and other interested parties, tends to work well, especially if one librarian has authority for reviewing decisions about approval-plan materials and for communicating with the dealer. When a library staff depends heavily on reviews for selection, the approval plan, which provides books before reviews are available, may not be an appropriate or welcome arrangement. Of course, if the library staff is unable to articulate a clear subject profile for a particular part of the collection, the approval plan is unlikely to work well in that area.

After analyzing the library's needs, resources, and current procedures, the library staff may be ready to gather information about the various approval plans available. Checklists have been developed for comparing the strengths and weaknesses of various dealers vis-a-vis the library's requirements. A good example, by Berkner, provides for analysis of type of plans offered by a dealer, formats covered, stability and reputation of the dealer, caliber of the dealer's staff, level of profile differentiation offered, treatment of special formats, sources used for title selection, method used for matching titles with profiles, bibliographic information provided with shipments, timing of shipments, treatment of claims, arrangements for returns, billing procedures, profile monitoring, statistical reports available, cost, and special options.[19] The 1988 SPEC Kit on approval plans published by the Association of Research Libraries also has examples of questions and criteria for evaluating vendors. One of the special services, provided by at least one dealer, is computerized matching of a library's profile against a magnetic tape listing noncurrent titles, in order to provide suggestions for retrospective purchasing.

EVALUATING AN APPROVAL PLAN

Questions about the degree to which approval plans meet their objectives have caused many librarians to undertake studies of their plans. Most studies have been informal and have tended to compare vendors with each other on the basis of bibliographic accuracy, discount, speed of delivery, return rates, and various operating procedures, such as profiling techniques or notification arrangements. Studies seldom attempt to measure effects of these plans on organization of staff or on costs of processing. A number of approval plan studies have compared approval plan receipts with order requests generated through traditional procedures; some have compared approval plan receipts with staff members' perceptions of what should have been received; and others have compared library circulation of approval plan materials with items specifically requested by librarians, faculty, etc.

Whether an approval plan produces a group of new acquisitions, different from those that would have been selected through different procedures, is a key question for collection development personnel. To check this, some libraries, after initiating an approval plan, have continued to use all their traditional selection techniques for several months. Each nonrush request through traditional channels, from librarians and faculty who use review journals or publishers' announcements, is held for a specified time and eventually checked against approval plan receipts. If a large number of internal requests fail to arrive on the approval plan, revision of the profile, or at least the vendor's interpretation of it, may be necessary.

Librarians who want to avoid operating a dual system of selection have checked their approval plans in another way. A sample may be drawn from trade bibliographies or reviewing journals and that sample evaluated by the library staff in terms of the profile constructed for the approval plan. The staff's interpretation of the profile, reflected in the items from the sample that they judge to match the profile, is then checked against approval plan receipts. In this way, discrepancies in interpretation and weak areas of the profile can usually be identified. Perrault found that the microfiche database service offered by a major approval plan vendor was a useful tool for monitoring the vendor's interpretation of the library's profile.[20]

Finding ways to refine profiles in order to ensure low return rates is another area of research interest. Pasterczyk reported on a study at one university involving both approval plan receipts and notification slips. This was an attempt to identify vendor-assigned subject codes or publishers that would differentiate rejected from accepted books. In the areas studied—computer science, mathematics, and geology—vendor-supplied codes were not found to be adequately precise for this purpose.[21] This study also found that limiting profile selections to the scientific and technical parts of the thesaurus would eliminate many desirable titles.

Addressing the question of whether vendor-originated orders really match local collection needs, Evans attempted to determine if there were differences in the first-year circulation of books selected by librarians, requested by faculty members, from those supplied through approval plans in academic libraries. Using data from four university libraries, he found that, for English-language publications, books that arrive through an approval plan were the least likely new acquisitions to circulate.[22] In a replication of this study, Evans and Argyres found that the difference in circulation between materials selected by librarians and those provided by approval plans was greater in the sciences and humanities than in the social sciences, and that, on the whole, approval plans tended to be least satisfactory in the sciences.[23]

Although many articles have been published describing how one library or another has attempted to evaluate an approval plan, more systematic study is needed. Shirk, in his list of nine specifications for a vendor evaluation model, makes the point that the library's behavior has a great influence on the approval-plan vendor's performance. "The library must acknowledge its impact on observed measures of overall approval plan performances."[24] Knowing what the approval plan is expected to contribute to the library's collection development program is essential to an effective evaluation of the plan. "The design should include steps which identify the library's needs, the performance required of the plan to satisfy those needs, and the performance the library must require of itself."[25] Another important criterion for an evaluation project is an adequate duration. Shirk suggests five stages of evaluation, beginning with the vendor-selection process. Another assessment should be made at the time the agreement is formulated. Feedback during the course of the plan's operation should be monitored, and formal measurement and analysis should be started as soon as the plan reaches its assumed optimum level of performance. After that, a decision must be made to continue the agreement with additional evaluation or to terminate the agreement.

ACQUIRING FOREIGN MATERIALS

Materials from many parts of the world are difficult for libraries in the United States to acquire on a title-by-title basis. One of the major reasons is that many countries lack effective bibliographic control of new publications. Because editions are often small and sometimes not handled through the usual book trade of the country in which they are published, American librarians may not learn about these publications until they are out of print. Even when new publications can be identified, each order must survive the usual barriers of language difficulties, monetary exchange regulations, trade restrictions, and shipping problems. A typical reaction by the acquisitions librarian to these conditions—although not a perfect solution—is to arrange blanket or standing orders with vendors in the various countries affected.

Foreign blanket orders have disadvantages beyond those of domestic plans. Many of the foreign dealers do not include government or university publications, and books in series—an important part of European publication—are also sometimes omitted. Duplication is a problem unless multinational publishers are identified and omitted from the plan, and, of course, returns are expensive. In some cases, books acquired through a blanket plan may actually be foreign-language translations of United States publications. Schmidt, in an article dealing with the differences between publisher-based and subject-based plans, recommends the subject-based plan for foreign agreements.[26]

Finding a knowledgeable, reliable, and efficient exporter is the essential first step in making a foreign blanket-order plan work. The best source for identifying such dealers is likely to be the experienced recommendations of librarians who have worked with dealers in the country of interest. When a competent foreign vendor can be found, most librarians prefer to use that dealer year after year. The continuing business relationship, which may become almost a personal relationship, contributes to better communication between librarian and vendor. Successful communication is very important, because postage costs and transportation delays generally make returns impractical. Of course, exporting firms change ownership from time to time, and must be monitored for adequate performance.

English-language foreign publications, particularly British publications, offer a possible exception to the above comments. Many British titles are published simultaneously in the United States and will probably be available through U.S. dealers. The decision of whether to use an import dealer or an export dealer may depend on such factors as relative values of the pound and the dollar at a particular time, breadth of coverage, timeliness of delivery, and the ready availability of cataloging data. The collection development goals of the library and the amount of money available to pursue those goals will determine how these factors are weighted.

NATIONAL PLANS

The Farmington Plan, first discussed during World War II and begun in 1948, was designed to ensure that at least one copy of every book important for research, published anywhere in the world, would be available in at least one American library. The need for such a plan was recognized during the war, when it was discovered that many important foreign publications were not owned by any library in the United States. Libraries that participated in the plan agreed to accept shipments of materials in chosen subject categories—selection of the materials to be done by dealers in the country or region of origin. The Farmington Plan (discontinued in 1972) was not only the first national project for cooperative acquisitions, it was also a national blanket-order plan. Dealers who worked with the Farmington Plan refined their techniques and offered blanket-order arrangements to other libraries. Some of the plans operated today by foreign dealers are based on their Farmington Plan experiences.

Another national plan, also discontinued, grew out of the Seminar on the Acquisition of Latin American Library Materials (SALALM). SALALM, formed in 1956 as a forum for exchange of information on publishing in individual Latin American countries and on acquisitions problems, has been involved in a variety of cooperative projects. One of the most important results of SALALM meetings was the organization of the Latin American Cooperative Acquisition Project (LACAP) in 1960. Through LACAP, Stechert-Hafner Inc. employed agents to gather published materials throughout Latin America and ship them to libraries that participated in blanket-order arrangements. LACAP was discontinued early in 1973; but by that time the profitability of the North American market had been demonstrated, and a number of Latin American dealers had begun to specialize in exporting books to the United States through both blanket-order plans and individual orders.

In 1962 the Library of Congress opened overseas offices in Cairo, New Delhi, and Karachi under a special foreign-currency program referred to as Public Law 480 (PL-480). This program allowed part of the foreign currencies obtained by the U.S. government through the sale of agricultural products in developing countries to be spent on books, journals, and newspapers in those countries. The Library of Congress received much foreign material under this program, but other libraries in the United States were also given the opportunity to receive materials on a blanket order basis. Participating libraries agreed to accept, retain, and service whatever publications the Library of Congress agents shipped to them under the PL-480 program. Within ten years, PL-480 offices operated in

India, Ceylon, Israel, Pakistan, Egypt, Yugoslavia, Poland, Tunisia, and Iran. Some of these offices were incorporated into the National Program for Acquisitions and Cataloging, and others were phased out when surplus currency ceased to be available in a particular country.

Library of Congress overseas offices provide a type of blanket-order service to libraries that participate in their various cooperative acquisitions programs. When the National Program for Acquisitions and Cataloging originated with Title IIC of the Higher Education Act of 1965, it provided for acquisition by the Library of Congress of library materials of scholarly and research value published throughout the world. To carry out that mandate, the Library has established overseas offices in Cairo, New Delhi, Karachi, Jakarta, Nairobi, and Rio de Janeiro. All of LC's offices gather and ship materials to the Library of Congress, and all (except the one in Rio de Janeiro) have provided materials to other participating libraries.

The overseas offices are expected to review and gather as many appropriate current publications as possible from the countries for which each is responsible. Where practical, blanket order arrangements are made with local dealers, but staff members also go on buying trips and cultivate personal contacts in the book trade of these countries. Participating libraries have little choice about which titles they will receive, although some programs allow for preselection of languages, geographic areas, or subjects. Most of the cooperative acquisition programs administered by the overseas offices are directed to the needs of university research programs, but three—the English-language programs operating through the New Delhi and Karachi offices and the Arabic Reading Collection Program (begun in 1981)—have been of potential benefit to public libraries. In 1987 the Library of Congress reported "a new wave of interest" in its cooperative acquisition programs "after several years of declining membership."[27]

Beginning in 1978, the Library of Congress New Delhi office operated a microform reproduction center for the materials collected through the Cairo, Karachi, Jakarta, and New Delhi centers. When copyright permission could be obtained, books and journals on poor-quality paper, or available in limited quantities, or priced unusually high were copied onto microfiche. Standing orders for sets of these fiche have been made through the Photoduplication Services of the Library of Congress.

BIBLIOGRAPHY

Alessi, Dana L., and Kathleen Goforth. "Standing Orders and Approval

Plans: Are They Compatible?" *Serials Librarian*, 13(October-November 1987):21-41.

Association of Research Libraries. Office of Management Studies. Systems and Procedures Exchange Center. *Approval Plans in ARL Libraries*. Washington, D.C.: Assn. of Research Libs., 1982. 109p. (SPEC Kit no. 83)

_____. *Approval Plans*. Washington, D.C.: Assn. of Research Libs., 1988. 124p. (SPEC Kit no. 141)

Axford, H. William. "The Economics of a Domestic Approval Plan." *College & Research Libraries*, 32(September 1971):368-375.

Brownson, Charles W. "Mechanical Selection." *Library Resources & Technical Services*, 32(January 1988):17-29.

Cargill, Jennifer S., and Brian Alley. *Practical Approval Plan Management*. Phoenix, Ariz.: Oryx Pr., 1979. 95p.

Cushman, Ruth Carol. "Lease Plans—A New Lease on Life for Libraries?" *Journal of Academic Librarianship*, 2(March 1976):15-19.

Devilbiss, Mary Lee. "The Approval-Built Collection in the Medium-Sized Academic Library." *College & Research Libraries*, 36(November 1975):487-492.

Dobbyn, Margaret. "Approval Plan Purchasing in Perspective." *College & Research Libraries*, 33(November 1972):480-484.

Evans, G. Edward. "Book Selection and Book Collection Usage in Academic Libraries." *Library Quarterly*, 40(July 1970):297-308.

_____, and Claudia White Argyres. "Approval Plans and Collection Development in Academic Libraries." *Library Resources & Technical Services*, 18(Winter 1974):35-50.

Ferguson, Anthony W. "British Approval Plan Books: American or British Vendor?" *Collection Building*, 8(1987):18-22.

Grant, Joan, and Susan Perelmuter. "Vendor Performance Evaluation." *Journal of Academic Librarianship*, 4(November 1978):366-367.

Gregor, Jan, and Wendy Carol Fraser. "A University of Windsor Experience with an Approval Plan in Three Subjects and Three Vendors." *Canadian Library Journal*, 38(August 1981):227-231.

Heroux, Marlene, and Marlene Fleishauer. "Cancellation Decisions: Evaluating Standing Orders." *Library Resources & Technical Services*, 22(Fall 1978):368-379.

Hulbert, Linda Ann, and David Steward Curry. "Evaluation of an Approval Plan." *College & Research Libraries*, 39(November 1978):485-491.

International Conference on Approval Plans and Collection Development (4th; Milwaukee, 1979). *Shaping Library Collections for the 1980's*. Edited by Peter Spyers-Duran and Thomas Mann, Jr. Phoenix, Ariz.: Oryx Pr., 1980. 235p.

International Seminar on Approval and Gathering Plans in Large and Medium Size Academic Libraries (1st; Western Michigan University, 1968). *Proceedings*. Edited by Peter Spyers-Duran. Kalamazoo: Western Michigan Univ. Libraries, 1969. 142p.

_____. (2nd; Western Michigan University, 1969). *Advances in Understanding Approval and Gathering Plans in Academic Libraries.* Edited by Peter Spyers-Duran and Daniel Gore. Westport, Conn.: Greenwood, 1972. 220p.

_____. (3rd; West Palm Beach, Fla., 1971). *Economics of Approval Plans.* Edited by Peter Spyers-Duran and Daniel Gore. Westport, Conn.: Greenwood, 1972. 134p.

Issues in Acquisitions: Programs & Evaluation. Edited by Sul H. Lee. Ann Arbor, Mich.: Pierian Pr., 1984. 133p.

Kevil, L. Hunter. "The Approval Plan of Smaller Scope." *Library Acquisitions: Practice and Theory*, 9(1985):13-20.

Kniskern, Alice L. "Library of Congress Overseas Offices: Acquisition Programs in the Third World." *Library Acquisitions: Practice and Theory*, 6(1982):87-110.

McCullough, Kathleen. "Approval Plans: Vendor Responsibility and Library Research: A Literature Survey and Discussion." *College & Research Libraries*, 33(September 1972):368-381.

_____, Edwin D. Posey, and Doyle C. Pickett. *Approval Plans and Academic Libraries: An Interpretive Survey.* Phoenix, Ariz.: Oryx Pr., 1977. 154p.

McDonald, David R., Margaret W. Maxfield, and Virginia G. F. Friesner. "Sequential Analysis: A Methodology for Monitoring Approval Plans." *College & Research Libraries*, 40(July 1979):329-334.

Martin, Murray S. "The Series Standing Order and the Library." *Choice*, 10(October 1973):1152–1155.

Newborn, Dennis E., and Irene P. Godden. "Improving Approval Plan Performance: A Case Study." *Library Acquisitions: Practice and Theory*, 4(1980):145-155.

Pasterczyk, Catherine E. "Quantitative Methodology for Evaluating Approval Plan Performance." *Collection Management*, 10(1988):25-38.

Perrault, Anna H. "A New Dimension in Approval Plan Service." *Library Acquisitions: Practice and Theory*, 7(1983):35-40.

Posey, Edwin D., and Kathleen McCullough. "Approval Plans One Year Later: The Purdue Experience with Separate School Plans." In Association of College and Research Libraries. *New Horizons for Academic Libraries*, pp. 483-489. New York: K.G. Saur, 1979.

Rebuldela, Harriet K. "Some Administrative Aspects of Blanket Ordering: A Response." *Library Resources & Technical Services,* 13(Summer 1969):342–345.

Reidelbach, John H., and Gary M. Shirk. "Selecting an Approval Plan Vendor: A Step-by-Step Process." *Library Acquisitions: Practice and Theory*, 7(1983):115–122.

_____. "Selecting an Approval Plan Vendor II: Comparative Vendor Data." *Library Acquisitions: Practice and Theory*, 8(1984):157-202.

_____. "Selecting an Approval Plan III: Academic Librarians' Evaluation of Eight United States Approval Plan Vendors." *Library Acquisitions: Practice & Theory*, 9(1985):177-260.

Rossi, Gary J. "Library Approval Plans: A Selected, Annotated Bibliography." *Library Acquisitions: Practice & Theory*, 11(1987):3-34.

Savary, M. J. *The Latin American Cooperative Acquisitions Program: An Imaginative Venture*. New York: Hafner, 1968. 144p.

Schmidt, Karen A. "Capturing the Mainstream: Publisher-Based and Subject-Based Approval Plans in Academic Libraries." *College & Research Libraries*, 47(July 1986):365-369.

Sewell, Robert G. "Managing European Automatic Acquisitions." *Library Resources & Technical Services*, 27(October/December 1983): 397-405.

Shepard, Marietta Daniels. "Cooperative Acquisitions of Latin American Materials." *Library Resources & Technical Services*, 13(Summer 1969):347-360.

Snoke, Helen Lloyd, and Jean L. Loup. *Comparison of Approval Plan Profiles and Supplementary Collection Development Activities in Selected ARL Libraries*. A Report to the Council on Library Resources. 1986. 54p. (ED 278 412)

Stave, Don. "Art Books on Approval: Why Not?" *Library Acquisitions: Practice & Theory*, 7(1983):5-6.

Stueart, Robert D. "Mass Buying Programs in the Development Process." In *Collection Development in Libraries*, pp. 203-217. Greenwich, Conn.: JAI Pr., 1980.

Thom, Ian W. "Some Administrative Aspects of Blanket Ordering." *Library Resources & Technical Services*, 13(Summer 1969):338-342.

Walters, Mary D. "Approval Program Timing Study: Baker & Taylor *vs* Blackwell North America." *Collection Building*, 7(Spring 1985):14-18.

EIGHT

Purchasing Special Types of Book Materials

OLDER MATERIALS

Rᴇᴛʀᴏsᴘᴇᴄᴛɪᴠᴇ ᴄᴏʟʟᴇᴄᴛɪᴏɴ ᴅᴇᴠᴇʟᴏᴘᴍᴇɴᴛ involves deciding which titles, not currently in print, should be added to the collection. For a variety of reasons—many of them financial—librarians have put less emphasis on this aspect of collection development since the 1970s. When budgets are tight and staff is inadequate, the natural tendency is to buy new, easily acquired materials first. The growth of microform publishing and the availability of reprographic copies of some types of older materials have also made the purchase of out-of-print books less urgent.

One of the most interesting and challenging aspects of acquisitions work is the pursuit of out-of-print materials. The sense of accomplishment can be great when one has found an elusive title or built a weak section of the library to breadth and depth over a period of months or years. The search for out-of-print materials is particularly important for college and university libraries where new programs and courses, or new faculty members teaching existing courses with new emphases, require the extension of library holdings. Public libraries also need out-of-print services for replacement of lost, worn-out, or damaged materials; to meet changes in demand for materials; and occasionally to make up for years of poor financial support.

All too frequently, librarians set aside their work on out-of-print materials until work on in-print materials, subscription renewals, and other acquisitions is done, only to discover one day that such work is *never* done and that, by postponing the out-of-print effort, they have built hopelessly large files of records for these items. When materials budgets are not generous, librarians may believe that they must concentrate on the purchase of in-print materials. Under strained circumstances, it may be necessary to narrow attention to in-print titles, but this will be a disservice to library users who need materials that are not in print. The effect may be cumulative, so that, after several years of neglect of its out-of-print needs, a library will be weakened.

Most libraries build, in one way or another, desiderata files—that is, files on out-of-print materials that the library wants. In the past, these files were usually in card form, frequently utilizing the original order request or a part of the set of order forms. By use of standard copying equipment, along with forms incorporating templates, these cards could be transformed into slips to be sent to dealers as desiderata lists. However, libraries putting great emphasis on retrospective collection development often use microcomputer database management packages to build and maintain their desiderata files. Each record in the desiderata file should show what has happened to the item listed: when it was reported out of print; how and who reviewed it; whether it has been searched again to determine if it has been reprinted; and what action has been taken to obtain it as an out-of-print item.

Desiderata files are ordinarily indexed or arranged by author entry, sometimes by title, and occasionally by language or country of origin, if there are significant numbers of titles within these categories. Some librarians arrange these files by broad disciplines—social sciences, humanities, sciences—or by special subjects for which the trade has specialist dealers or for which catalogs appear, such as economics, German language and literature, and art history.

There are two ways by which librarians discover materials are out of print. First, the preorder search may reveal that a book is not listed in *Books in Print*, or in one of the other tools that list materials in print or about to be published. Second, a wholesaler, dealer, or publisher may report a book as out of print. A third route to the desiderata file is from reports of antiquarian and out-of-print dealers that titles selected from their catalogs or lists were sold to other customers before the library's order was received. Some of the titles reported sold may have come from the desiderata file; others may have been selected from the catalog or list without reference to specific desiderata files.

In any of these cases, titles should not go automatically to a desiderata file; they always should be reviewed to determine whether they ought to be sought as out-of-print titles. The need for a book that was presumed to be in print when it was selected, and consequently easy and perhaps inexpensive to purchase, may be questioned, since as an out-of-print title it will cost more in staff time to secure and probably more to buy. Other items may have gone out of print for good reasons: a new edition is to be published, or the contents are so out of date that the item could only be of historical interest. Still other titles are so difficult to obtain on the out-of-print market (examples are pamphlets and the publications of local governments, schools, university bureaus, institutes, etc.) that listing them in the desiderata file would be a waste of time, both for the library and for the dealers who would be approached to find the titles. If there is a strong need for the content of these items, the acquisitions department should try to obtain a microform or full-size photographic copy.

Desiderata files should be reviewed periodically to be sure that the titles are still being sought, and they should be searched annually against *Books in Print* (or comparable foreign bibliographies) to discover if they have been reprinted. In a large library, a desiderata file may contain thousands of titles. At some point in the life of an item in the desiderata file, its acquisition in microform or in a photocopied version should be considered. Some libraries have an "automatic point" at which this is done. This may be after lists have been circulated to three dealers, or advertised and then placed with a dealer for two years, or some combination of these or similar steps.

Dealers

Dealers in these older materials may call themselves out-of-print (OP), antiquarian, or secondhand-book dealers. They may even call themselves bookstores, for many businesses deal in both in-print and out-of-print materials. In the United States and Great Britain, there are five chief sources of out-of-print books. First are the rare book dealers who work primarily with special libraries and special collections in large libraries and with private collectors. Frequently their catalogs are extremely informative, and some of them list items that are moderately priced and may be of interest to other than rare-book collectors.

Second, there are general out-of-print dealers with large, diversified stocks. They also deal in rare books, have specialties, and issue special subject catalogs, but the bulk of their business is in general out-of-print books. Third are specialist dealers who concentrate on particular subjects or geographic areas. Their offerings may be broad in scope (books in all of the social sciences, for example) or narrow (books, say, on Alaska). Many of them do not maintain retail stores, working instead from their homes or from offices not open to the public and doing their business entirely by mail.

The fourth major source is the scout—a book dealer who keeps no stock. This person buys from a shop or private party and resells immediately, usually on consignment. Scouts often work for bookstores, but some libraries have had success with "our buyer in Paris" or an equivalent elsewhere. Local used bookstores may be important sources for local history material, and they may be useful for other out-of-print material as well. There are also junk shops, where old books, sheet music, etc., from house sales mix with odd issues of old magazines and other unwanted items. Searching for materials for libraries in junk shops, however, is seldom rewarding.

Exchanges are a fifth possible source of out-of-print materials. Exchange lists, published by institutions with collections similar to one's own, may be valuable, and some groups of libraries pool their duplicates for mutual benefit. For most libraries, however, the chief sources for out-of-print materials are general out-of-print dealers and specialists.

In general, the out-of-print trade on the continent of Europe is organized the same as in the United States, Canada, and Great Britain. Most dealers will accept correspondence in English, but they may reply in English or in their native language. Bills that are not stated in American dollars can be paid in dollars by getting the exchange rate through a bank or business office. Many foreign dealers have bank addresses in the United States to which a library's checks may be sent. Many American and British dealers handle out-of-print books published on the European continent and elsewhere in the world. In general, those with offices abroad will be able to do a better job, but specialist dealers in the United States may have out-of-print foreign stock in some fields.

Dealers in out-of-print books in the United States are listed in the *AB Bookman's Yearbook* (including some outside the United States), the *American Book Trade Directory* (biennial, Bowker), and *Bookdealers in North America* (8th ed., Sheppard, 1980). There are also foreign and international directories, but the best information about out-of-print dealers may be obtained from experienced acquisitions librarians.

Catalogs

Catalogs of out-of-print or secondhand books arrive on the desk of the acquisitions librarian in every shape, size, and condition, and acquaintance with them and the world of books they represent is for many acquisitions librarians one of the most rewarding aspects of their work. Some of the catalogs are crowded, poorly mimeographed, and on bad paper; others are handsome printings on good paper; but all may be useful to the library. Arrangements of entry can vary: geographically, by subject, by catchword titles, by no apparent classification, or by whatever the dealer thinks will catch the customer's eye and sell books. The main entry may be informally established, and not be one a librarian would select, although some catalogs present excellent bibliographic descriptions. The makers of catalogs often regard series information as inconsequential, and this omission can cause unwanted duplication in the library in which the offered item is handled as part of a series, rather than as a monograph.

With few exceptions, the out-of-print dealer's catalog refers to only one copy of each item listed. Consequently, these catalogs must be handled with great speed in the library. Although a catalog from a typical dealer has a life as long as two months, and some dealers include items in their catalogs that they usually carry in stock, most of the best items in a catalog will be gone within two weeks, or in a few days for a particularly interesting catalog.

Money invested in selection, searching, and ordering is wasted on an old catalog. Some librarians will not work on a catalog that has been in the library more than twenty-four hours; and when delays in mail handling and delivery (which make most catalogs old when they are received) are considered, this stricture may not be excessive. In some libraries, where preorder searching and order writing cannot be completed within a day or two, the dealer is contacted by telephone, telegram, cablegram, or air letter and asked to reserve the items selected. Reserving before searching should be done only when the acquisitions librarian is confident that the library will have few of the items being held. Otherwise, the dealer may be put to unnecessary work and lose other sales for the items.

Many librarians telephone, telegraph, cable, or even transmit purchase orders by computer to try to get ahead of other customers for wanted items. The complexities of ordering and invoicing imposed upon some libraries may force the acquisitions staff to inquire of a dealer whether a wanted item is still available before they write a firm order. Another way to speed action on dealers' catalogs is to work out means of moving them in the mail more quickly. Some dealers send catalogs first class, or even offer advance proof copies. Many dealers in Western Europe automatically send catalogs airmail, at their own expense. Special arrangements of this nature are worked out individually between dealers and libraries, and librarians should be willing to pay for unusual service.

Librarians use out-of-print catalogs in two ways: to check against their desiderata files in the search for specific titles already identified as needed, and to read and select items for the library without reference to needs for specific titles, with general collection development in mind. The latter requires the same judgments as are made in the selection of newly published materials. When out-of-print catalogs are read for selection without reference to a desiderata file, the work is usually done by the same people who ordinarily participate in the selection process.

Lists

A frequently used technique for obtaining out-of-print books is to make lists of wanted books and send them to appropriate dealers. This is done in two ways. First, a list is sent to several (even many) dealers, asking them to quote prices for items they have; and second, a list is sent to one dealer at a time, giving each organization an exclusive opportunity to work on the list. In recent years, dealer resistance has reduced the use of the former method. Many dealers believe that they waste time working on lists which other dealers are also considering and that the practice encourages unfair competition. Some dealers will not work on lists that are not exclusive. Distribution of a list to more than one dealer has a distinct advantage for libraries; it permits access to more than one stock of books, and the library gets more books in a shorter time than if exclusive lists are used. Libraries may obtain materials more cheaply, but if acquisitions staff members are working with reputable dealers (as they should be) and place value on service and size of stock, price advantages may not be very great. Lists of desiderata should represent fields in which the dealer can do a good job, which usually means basing the lists on subject or language specialties.

A modification of both types of lists is sent to a number of dealers in turn, asking them to quote on items they have in stock within a short time limit—not holding the list for search outside of stock. This allows the library to move a list to five or six dealers in as many months, and is often used to obtain books that are needed quickly. In the most frequently used dealer listing technique, the list is turned over to a dealer exclusively—for six, twelve, eighteen months, or perhaps indefinitely. With time and exclusive listing, dealers can look for specific items for a library, using all their acquisitions sources and confident that if they find the requested materials, they will very likely make a sale. Libraries that place indefinite orders with established dealers continue to receive offers four, six, even ten years later. There is evidence, however, that most dealers quickly lose interest in a list and turn their talents and energies to newly received lists that will be more productive for them. Consequently, most libraries that send out lists establish time limits, forwarding the lists to other dealers at the end of the specified time.

When one is selecting the first dealer to whom a title is to be sent, it is a good practice to identify the second, third, and perhaps additional dealers, in the event the item is not obtained from the first dealer or from subsequent ones. Dealer selection is time consuming, requiring the attention of an experienced staff member. Three dealers can be identified less expensively at one time than at three widely separated times. In the first case, the transfer of a search from one dealer to another becomes automatic and can be done by a clerk. Lists that have been through one or two dealers should also have new titles added to them; otherwise, the later dealers may be working on only the titles most difficult to find, with the result that enthusiasm and performance may decline.

Most libraries require price quotations on offers before they can place firm orders. Under a modification of this practice, a dealer is authorized to send anything on a library's list that costs under a specified amount per volume. For instance, a librarian may tell a dealer to ship and send a bill for any title on the list that will be priced at $30 or less per volume, and to supply price quotations on items that cost more. This saves paper work for both the library and the dealer, and gives the dealer even greater confidence of a guaranteed sale. Some libraries make similar arrangements, agreeing to accept, without quotation, any book for a set amount over the original list price. This has the advantage of keeping prices in proportion to value, but does not consider variations in scarcity, and requires the library to search out the original list price (an extra step in many cases). Dealers like these arrangements, and many of them perform very well.

Advertising

Many librarians use advertising, in all or part of their efforts, in securing out-of-print materials. Those who use it exclusively believe they reach the stocks of more dealers and consequently get more materials more quickly than with other means. Supporters of advertising also point out that library costs are lower because no time is spent checking catalogs against desiderata files, making special lists, or corresponding with dealers.

It is clear that advertising works well for some libraries. These appear to be small or medium-sized libraries, without large desiderata files or highly specialized needs. Most of the books they want are in English. Critics say that the flood of quotes a library receives after each advertisement creates an in-house clerical burden that lessens the advantages of advertising. Large libraries with sizeable desiderata lists tend to use advertising only for quickly needed materials or for titles not obtainable elsewhere.

Two advertising media are available to librarians in the United States: *The Library Bookseller* and *AB Bookman's Weekly*. *The Library Bookseller* is exclusively an advertising service for libraries, to which they must subscribe—as must the several hundred book dealers who give quotes on the library lists. Librarians pay for advertisements by the line in *AB Bookman's Weekly*, which is seen by more book dealers. Lists in *The*

Library Bookseller cannot be very long, or their publication will be delayed. It is often more productive to arrange lists by subject. In *The Library Bookseller*, these special lists bring more quotations than miscellaneous lists, probably because the specialist dealer's attention is drawn to them.

Although librarians should wait to place orders until a reasonable number of dealers have had a chance to quote on an advertised list, they should not attempt to get the lowest possible price by delaying until all returns are in. If they wait too long, many of the books on which there were early quotations may already have been sold. Quotes that should be accepted the day they are received include those from dealers who are known by experience to offer good stock at reasonable prices or from a dealer who, as a result of specialized stock and high turnover, may report uncommon titles as sold. Materials not obtained from initial advertising may be readvertised at a later date, before the list is sent to a dealer or purchase of a microform or photocopied version is considered.

Prices

Although there are wide variations, the out-of-print trade, in general, works on a markup of 100 percent. Determining how much a library should pay for an out-of-print book is not an easy task. The chief considerations are how much the item is worth on the market and how important it is for the library. One rule of thumb that some librarians use for scholarly out-of-print books (not rare books or collectors' editions) is that if the book costs more than a copy enlarged from microfilm, it is too expensive. In most cases, the copy is as usable as the original edition, and it will probably be on better paper and last much longer.

In deciding value, some librarians check recorded prices, such as the annual auction records in *American Book-Prices Current* or the compilations from dealers' catalogs such as *Bookman's Price Index* (Gale). These prices can be helpful but they can also be very misleading, since they represent the cost of other copies of different origins and physical condition.

Rare Books

Purchasing rare books is outside the financial limitations of many libraries, but even the smallest may seek out *some* rare items, especially materials on local history. Librarians may also find it suitable, and within collection development policy and budget, to buy early or fine printings, fine bindings, and illustrated editions for demonstration and exhibit purposes. The special rare-book collection can make a library more visible to its community and offer a unique educational opportunity for its users to learn about the book arts.

Rare books are acquired by libraries in several ways other than direct purchase. Many rare materials are identified by acquisitions staff when they screen purchases moving through the receiving steps and gifts that are being considered for addition to the collections. It is in this way that librarians find limited editions, important first editions, association copies, fine printings and bindings, and items that are rare by virtue of their age and place of publication. The development of gifts is of course important in the acquisition of rare books. Collectors should be cultivated not only as potential donors of their collections but also with a view to purchasing their collections. The benefit gained from their work in gathering the collections (probably when the items were easier to obtain) may be considerable.

Buying is done by selection from catalogs, at auctions, through visits from dealers, and by library staff visits to dealers. In contrast to general out-of-print buying, want lists are not often used because the percentage of positive responses from dealers would be very small. Materials are usually ordered on approval to give the librarian an opportunity to confirm the dealer's description and to make sure there is no unintentional duplication of these usually expensive items. Works received on approval should either be paid for or returned promptly.

Bibliographic work in acquiring rare books often must be in the hands of skilled specialists, because, in addition to knowledge of the materials, subject areas, or languages, knowledge of uncommon bibliographic tools is needed. In many cases, this work is done in the rare-book or special collections department, or in close coordination with members of that department.

Auctions and Buying Trips

American librarians do not make extensive use of auctions for acquisition. While some may appear at an auction and place their bids, most librarians who buy at auctions do so through dealers. A dealer charges a commission on purchases made through this service, representing payment for the time and expertise put into the bidding for all the items of interest to the library—those that are *not* obtained as well as those on which the library is the high bidder. Determining the amount to be bid requires the assistance of a librarian or dealer who is thoroughly familiar with the material wanted. The auctioneer may be asked for an opinion on what a successful bid will be, but most librarians seek the advice of the dealer and, together, they arrive at the maximum amount that the library is willing to pay.

The value of sending staff members on buying trips for out-of-print materials is usually not great. Negotiations to purchase out-of-print materials can often be made more successfully and inexpensively by mail than in person. However, a buying trip can have the distinct advantage of bringing the librarian and dealer to a closer understanding of each other's needs and methods of operation, resulting in establishment of a mutually beneficial business relationship.

MATERIALS FROM FOREIGN SOURCES

The amount of material purchased by U.S. libraries from foreign sources— at least material published in foreign languages—has been declining since the 1970s. Typically, foreign-language materials are purchased by academic libraries to meet the research needs of faculty and the course-related needs of students and by public libraries to meet the general reading needs of ethnic groups within the community. The decrease in foreign acquisitions is attributed to several factors: declining enrollment in foreign-language classes at all educational levels, library-use studies that show small-circulation counts for foreign-language materials, inflation of book prices in many countries, the weakness of the U.S. dollar, and smaller library materials budgets in the United States. Another problem has been the tendency for serial costs to consume a larger and larger share of the materials budget, leaving less money for books in any language. (Academic libraries do still purchase many serials from foreign countries, but many of these titles are published in English.)

The current approach to collection of foreign-language materials involves careful planning and great selectivity. Public libraries survey the community to identify the groups for whom materials should be purchased in languages other than English. Country of origin, social and political attitudes, economic and educational levels, general interests and reasons for reading are all points to be considered when developing this part of the collection development plan. Public libraries tend to limit their collections of foreign-language materials to contemporary fiction, children's books, and some books of general interest, although foreign-language materials may be acquired in a variety of formats.

Libraries in educational settings rely heavily on faculty requests to guide their acquisition of foreign materials. Except where colleges or universities offer area studies programs or have other reasons for collecting a wide range of foreign materials, most purchasing by academic libraries is concentrated in language and literature. A favored technique for building a collection with a literary emphasis is the author list, which is used to identify the specific authors for whom original and critical works will be collected. Such a list may be used to establish standing orders or to place orders for individual items. In a study of 21 medium-sized university libraries, Schreiner-Robles found heavy reliance on faculty requests, domestic approval plans, and U.S. reviewing sources to identify foreign materials for purchase. Only four libraries in that group used reviews from foreign literary journals and order slips from foreign book dealers.[1]

The organization of the book trade varies widely around the world. In general, better-organized book trades are characterized by adequate bibliographical control of new publications, a tradition of publishers distributing their materials through booksellers or wholesalers, and initial printings of sufficient size to enable books to stay in print a reasonable length of time. Because many countries lack these characteristics, purchasing of materials published in other countries differs in several important ways from domestic purchasing. For example, librarians ordinarily do not order books from foreign publishers, except in instances in which dealers or booksellers are also publishers or when materials must be purchased from a government agency. Foreign dealers offer a complete in-print and out-of-print procurement service more often than do suppliers of works published in the United States. Because bibliographical sources (if they exist at all) are often delayed in publication and because materials stay in print so short a time, it may be necessary to place orders without having complete bibliographic information and prices. Discounts are not usually available to libraries, although the acquisitions librarian is wise to inquire about them, especially for quantities of trade books.

The chief decision facing an acquisitions librarian is whether to order foreign materials from importers in the United States or from exporters in the country or region of publication. The decision should be based upon the size of the business a library does in materials published abroad. It is true that some large libraries buy foreign works in the United States because of convenience and service, and some small libraries have successful contacts in Western Europe for their purchasing. For the most part, however, the larger a library's acquisitions from outside the United States, the more probable that some of its purchasing will be done abroad.

Importers

Importers may supply all kinds of works from throughout the world, or they may have specialties. The latter is more common. Examples of specialization might be dealers in books published in Spain, or in French and German literary works, or in art books from many countries. Prices charged by importers usually will be somewhat higher than those of exporters. Importers must use expensive American staff and charge for the service of selecting, importing, and stocking materials that they expect will be purchased by American libraries.

These dealers usually give good value for their slightly higher prices. Their stock selections and catalogs are tailored to the needs of many American libraries; language of transaction is always English; claims and correspondence are easily understood; they can perform the special order and invoice procedures required by some libraries; they are paid in the same way as any other American vendor; they can be reached easily by telephone; and their representatives attend many library conferences.

A good importer provides a total service for in-print and out-of-print books, continuations or standing orders, and subscriptions. Some importers have offices in Europe and other parts of the world to help them provide services comparable to those of exporters. Libraries with inflexible business procedures imposed upon them may find dealing with an importer much easier than with an exporter.

Smaller libraries, without complete bibliographic apparatus, will also find an importer helpful. Acquisitions staff in such institutions may not be able to know whether a book is in print because the library cannot afford to purchase (or keep up to date) the relevant tools, because it does not have the language competence on its staff, or because the country of origin produces no record of which books are still in print. A good importer can provide the information these librarians need and will sometimes try to get books, whether they are in print or not.

Exporters

Exporters usually deal in materials from the country in which they have their offices, but some offer publications from several countries. There are many dealers in Western Europe, and librarians can choose an exporter who will let them develop arrangements that best suit their needs. In other parts of the world, one dealer may serve a large part of a continent. For instance, in parts of the Middle East one or two dealers can best supply acquisitions from several nations. Most librarians who buy materials published in Great Britain will want at least to experiment with buying from one of the excellent exporters there. Exporters do not always charge for mailing, and may offer lower prices if they have lower overhead costs. If an item is not in stock in the warehouse of an importer in the United States, a library usually can get it more quickly with a direct order to an exporter, avoiding the delay that is almost inevitable with a middleman. Exporters usually will invoice in American dollars, if asked to do so.

In negotiating with exporters, the language barrier is not so serious as might be imagined. Most dealers in Western Europe correspond in

English. When one does not, and a librarian learns by letter that the library's *Abbonement* has expired or a *factura* remains unpaid, dictionaries usually suffice. Among the most useful are Jerrold Orne's *Language of the Foreign Book Trade* (3rd ed., American Library Assn., 1976) and *Bookman's Glossary*, edited by Jean Peters (6th ed., Bowker, 1983). A reply in English, however, may not be entirely satisfactory, and some librarians answer such letters by the expensive practice of having them written in the appropriate language by a specialist.

In comparing a library's use of an exporter with that of an importer, the careful librarian will watch for differences in the currency rate of exchange and whether a dealer charges for packing and mailing. Nurturing relations with a dealer helps to solve problems, for a dealer who can make a profit is more likely to handle difficult orders; but profit can usually be realized only on regular orders. Sometimes ownership of exporting firms changes, and service may deteriorate. Librarians should, if possible, visit both domestic and foreign dealers to gain firsthand knowledge of the people with whom they are going to be working.

Purchasing from Developing Countries

Large libraries must purchase books and other library materials from all over the world, including developing countries that have a weak or poorly organized book trade. These countries may also have export restrictions and other trade limitations that make purchasing from them very difficult. Except for Latin America and parts of Africa, most of these countries have languages with non-Latin alphabets. The various cooperative arrangements of the Library of Congress' National Program for Acquisitions and Cataloging (mentioned in the chapter on vendor-controlled purchasing) have been of assistance in acquiring materials from the countries covered.

In most research libraries, acquisition of materials from non-European countries is linked with their selection, cataloging, and sometimes reference service, because of the language knowledge required. Helpful as this may be, the performance and management of acquisitions from these countries require specific skills, whether in these specialized units or in the central acquisitions department.

Selecting Dealers

As with dealer selection for other library materials, no sure rules can be advanced and no fully reliable list can be consulted. Importers advertise in American library journals, are listed in directories, have representatives at library association conferences, and issue catalogs. Many importers are selected on the basis of their specialties. Colleagues in other libraries can provide preliminary evaluations of these dealers, and in college and university libraries faculty members may have recommendations (since dealers visit professional conferences in addition to those for librarians). Exporters also advertise, are listed in directories, and some have representatives who appear at American conferences and call at American libraries. The advice from staff at libraries with similar collecting interests is important in making a choice. Among the more useful approaches is to refer to lists of dealers used by several of the large research libraries in the United States.

Dealers of foreign materials and importers are listed in the *American Book Trade Directory* (biennial, Bowker). *International Library Market Place* (annual, Bowker), a directory of publishers, booksellers, and related agencies in countries outside the United States and Canada, includes export-import information. A possible source for names and addresses of foreign dealers, most of whom handle books as well as subscriptions, is *International Subscription Agents* (4th ed., American Library Assn., 1978). Another useful source of information to support the purchasing of foreign materials is *The Book Trade of the World* (Verlag fur Buchmarkt-Forschung, 1972–83; distributed by Bowker in the United States). The four volumes of this work provide a country-by-country survey of bookselling practices, along with importing and exporting information. The Seminar on the Acquisition of Latin American Library Materials (SAL-ALM) has published *Acquisitions Manual: Guidelines for Librarians, Bookdealers, and Publishers* (1988), which attempts to communicate to Latin American dealers a series of norms for the preparation of their lists and catalogs and does the same for libraries with regard to preparation of order forms. The text is in English, Spanish, and Portuguese.

GOVERNMENT PUBLICATIONS

The challenges that librarians face in selection of government documents are similar to those experienced in selecting other types of library materials, but obtaining the publications of government offices offers special problems for acquisitions or documents librarians. A large percentage of the materials published throughout the world emanates from local, state or provincial, national, and international agencies and governments. Their publications vanish, or reappear with new titles and frequencies, making acquisitions as much a matter of luck as the application of specialized training, experience, and diligence. Publications may merge and change character or coverage, sometimes with excellent effect, but usually provoking confusion for the user and the librarian.

For acquisitions purposes, some governmental publications are never in print, because the complete stock is distributed upon publication. For example, the report of a city treasurer may be released in thousands of copies to residents or taxpayers, with no extras retained for selling or giving to libraries. Other government publications, never intended for distribution, were seen by their originators as of little interest beyond narrow agency confines; but librarians or researchers have learned of them, listed them, and determined to acquire them. Many government publications are mimeographed or are otherwise ephemeral in nature, but they may contain information important to library collections and users.

Government publications are rarely available through regular commercial channels. Their bibliographic control is sometimes different from that accorded other publications, and in many cases less satisfactory. Catalog entries for government publications are time consuming to use because of the high proportion of titles without unique or even uncommon features.

Training acquisitions staff to do bibliographic searching for government publications is more difficult than training for other searching. The "United States" section in any library catalog of size is testimony to the skill required to find a government document. Many librarians catalog and classify government publications in ways different from the systems used for other publications. For example, United States and United Nations publications, which are collected in depth by many North American libraries, have their own classification schemes and published indexes. When separate bibliographic treatment is used, acquisitions staff members may require special training for preorder searching, unless it is done by documents specialists. Clearly, government publications present more complex problems for libraries than regular commercial publications, and consequently are more expensive to acquire, unless depository collections are used.

Libraries with separate documents collections have staff members with expert knowledge. They may be part of the general public services staff or they may constitute a separate documents unit. Frequently in such libraries, these specialized staff members do all or most of the work in acquiring government publications. They may send purchase requests to the acquisitions department that are completely researched, with all of the information needed to place an order. In these cases the acquisitions department is required only to prepare and transmit the order. The specialized staff may work in a similar way with a gift and exchange unit, or they may bypass such a unit and work directly with gift sources. It sometimes is good practice to use the skills already held by the documents staff, rather than try to duplicate them in the acquisitions department. On the other hand, where documents acquisitions is a large enterprise, and especially where there is no separate documents service staff, the best use of staff may be in the provision of a documents specialist in the acquisitions department. Such a position requires, of course, careful coordination with other work being done with documents in the library.

Several journals, among them *Government Publications Review*, *RQ*, *Serials Librarian*, and *Microform Review*, provide current information on documents, including their distribution and bibliographic control. The Government Documents Round Table (GODORT) of the American Library Association compiles an annual list of notable documents, published in *Library Journal*, which includes federal, state, and international documents.

U.S. Government Publications

The U.S. federal government, acting through its many departments and agencies, has been described as the world's largest publisher. From the librarian's point of view, the two most important publishing agencies are the Government Printing Office (GPO) and the National Technical Information Service (NTIS). The number of titles held in the GPO's active stock was reported to be more than 15,000 in 1988, with an average of 3,000 new titles being added to the sales inventory each year. NTIS, a self-supporting agency of the U.S. Department of Commerce, is the major supplier of unclassified U.S. government-sponsored research and development reports and translations of foreign technical reports. NTIS adds approximately 70,000 new technical reports to the *NTIS Bibliographic Database* each year and carries approximately 80,000 titles in its shelf stock.

Several publishers have produced guides designed to make U.S. government publications easier for the average librarian to use. *Guide to Popular U.S. Government Publications* (Libraries Unlimited, 1986) by LeRoy C. Schwarzkopf describes approximately 2,800 federal publications of popular interest. It also attempts to provide what the generalist librarian in a small library would need to know in order to acquire the documents. The same publisher distributes Joe Morehead's *Introduction to U.S. Public Documents* (3rd ed., 1983), a standard text on the subject, and Judith Schiek Robinson's *Subject Guide to U.S. Government Reference Sources* (1985). A recent publication from Oryx Press, *Tapping the Government Grapevine: The User-Friendly Guide to U.S. Government Information Sources* (1988) by Judith Schiek Robinson, is also aimed at the generalist.

Two recent trends in the distribution of federal documents have required adjustments by librarians responsible for building and maintaining documents collections. These trends have also made acquiring and using government information more expensive. Whereas government documents were once distributed exclusively in printed form, government information is now likely to be in microform or a machine-readable format. NTIS is the primary vendor for electronic products, but GPO sells some CD-ROM products and microcomputer software, when the paper version is already part of the GPO sales program. In 1988, the Federal Depository Library Program of the GPO started distributing selected census data in CD-ROM format. The variety of formats in which government information may now be provided requires an equal variety of readers, printers, microcomputers, CD-ROM drives, etc., in order to access the content.

Another concern of government documents librarians in recent years has been the pressure exerted on government agencies to cut costs by reducing paperwork. "More and more government information is being made available, and will continue to be made available through the private sector as the government adapts to the ground rules set forth in OMB circulars A-76 (reliance on the private sector) and A-130 (information resource management)."[2] The basic message of Circular A-130 (1986) is that federal agencies should only collect and distribute the information necessary for the proper functioning of each agency. As a result, the GPO is receiving a smaller portion of federally sponsored publications for its depository and sales program. Those items that can be classified as "cooperatively" published with an outside agency must be sold through other channels.

Depository Collections

Approximately 1,400 libraries function as depositories for U.S. government publications. (Names, addresses, and telephone numbers of these libraries are available in *Federal Depository Libraries*, published by the Office of the Public Printer.) Congress has been passing laws concerning the distribution and deposit of government documents since the early 1800s; the most recent comprehensive legislation on the subject is the Depository Library Act of 1962. The authority for operation of the depository library program is Title 44 of the United States Code. Except for a limited number of regional libraries, which must select all depository items, depository libraries choose only those publications that they wish to receive from the GPO. Selections are made by series and groups of publications in advance of printing, rather than title by title as they are published.

In general, there may be two depository libraries in each congressional district, designated by the representative from the district, and two depositories designated by each senator. State libraries and the libraries of land-grant colleges and universities, independent agencies of the U.S. government, and major bureaus and divisions of departments and agencies of the government are depositories. Some congressional districts have more than two depository libraries because of redistricting, which occurs decennially. Once a depository library is designated, it cannot lose its privilege unless it so chooses or it goes out of existence. However, the depository relationship can be discontinued if the library does not abide by the laws governing the program.

Ordering Government Documents

The basic tool for identifying current federal documents has traditionally been the *Monthly Catalog of United States Government Publications* (GPO), which attempts to list all publications for sale by the Superintendent of Documents or available from the issuing agencies. In its online version, the *Monthly Catalog* supplies a complete record of GPO monograph and serial titles produced since July 1976. All the titles still available from GPO may be identified through a microfiche service, the *GPO Publications Reference File* (PRF), which consists of quarterly mailings of a complete master file. PRF is also available online through one of the major database vendors. *Government Periodicals and Subscription Services (Price List 36)* is a partially annotated list of all subscriptions sold by the GPO and is revised quarterly. The approximately 225 free bibliographies of government publications produced by the GPO are listed in *Subject Bibliography Index (SB-599)*.

In fall 1982, the GPO released the first issue of *U.S. Government Books*, a quarterly illustrated and annotated description of approximately 1,000 books, magazines, and posters per issue, designed to promote documents with appeal to a general audience. *New Books*, also started by the GPO in 1982 and directed toward "those who use government books in a professional capacity," appears every two months, each issue listing all publications that have been added to the Superintendent of Documents' sales inventory since the last issue. A useful handbook for identifying agencies and changes in name and organization, and for finding addresses is the *United States Government Organization Manual* (annual, GPO). Libraries Unlimited publishes *Government Reference Books: A Biennial Guide to U.S. Government Publications*, which describes atlases, bibliographies, catalogs, directories, indexes, and other reference tools issued by U.S. government agencies, and also *Government Reference Serials* (1988), which describes reference periodicals and serials distributed by the GPO to depository libraries.

Libraries that are not depositories and depository libraries requiring more than one copy of a government publication may place orders through the distribution center of the Government Printing Office. Because of the cost of acquiring and processing documents, nondepository libraries are usually highly discriminating in their selection of documents. Regular checking of the *Monthly Catalog of United States Government Publications*, as well as catalogs and bibliographies from individual departments and agencies, will be necessary. Small libraries may find the listings in *U.S. Government Books* adequate for their needs.

Since government documents are often printed in a limited number of copies, orders must be placed as soon after publication as possible. The GPO does not ship and bill; payment, in the form of a check or money order, must accompany orders for publications. Libraries may establish a deposit account by sending money, against which their purchases are charged (the minimum deposit is $50). The deposit account is especially useful for libraries that have difficulties with payment-in-advance orders, and works well for inexpensive publications when the business office is unable or unwilling to write checks for small sums, especially under one dollar.

Orders that include GPO stock numbers are processed more quickly than other orders. Libraries should also use GPO catalog numbers with the complete title and price of each item. Orders for periodicals or subscription services should be submitted separately from orders for individual publications. Renewal notices are sent 90 days ahead of expiration, and prompt return of subscription payments is required if periodical receipt is to continue uninterrupted. Claims for missing issues should be made promptly, since the GPO has a limited supply of back issues.

Many free mailings of government publications are available to libraries, some from the GPO and others from departments and branches. There are also publications of general interest and value that come to libraries on special mailing lists but are not available as depository items. Some libraries obtain priced and unpriced publications through their congressional representatives. They would generally save time by corresponding directly with the issuing agency for free publications. Some priced publications are available from the agency without cost, because it has a special supply for free distribution. It may be less expensive in terms of library staff time to purchase all documents, rather than solicit them from several sources and end up having to purchase some of them, perhaps after their season of greatest demand in the library is over.

For large libraries, the special problems relating to U.S. government publications concern the extent of completeness of their acquisitions. Most large libraries are depositories, but, as previously noted, the Superintendent of Documents controls and distributes to depositories only a small portion of the total publications of the government. Libraries must secure the balance of publications outside the depository privilege. NTIS is a major source for nondepository items.

Many important U.S. government publications of the past have been reprinted or made available in microform. In some instances, more than one reprint or microform is available. The GPO reissues some documents, but most reprinting is done by commercial publishers, especially reprint publishers. When a title is available from more than one publisher or in more than one form, the acquisitions librarian should compare prices and other features, such as paper and binding, ease of storage, and convenience to the user. Antiquarian and out-of-print dealers are also an important source of backfiles and out-of-print government titles.

The freedom with which government documents may be reprinted by commercial publishers presents occasional problems. Some publishers announce reprinted government publications under popular title or without reference to the original issuing body. While this may have been done unintentionally, the effect for many libraries has been the purchase of expensive sets that were already in the documents collection.

State and Local Documents

There are almost as many methods of issuing the publications of states as there are states. Obtaining information about these publications is difficult because the issuing agencies are not full-time, profit-making publishers and are not usually synchronized with library procedures. Many of their publications go out of print rapidly and permanently. However, since the information in state and local documents is official and presumably important, libraries have the responsibility to do the best job possible of identifying and acquiring them.

Some states issue checklists of their documents, and many have a central agency for the distribution of some or, occasionally, all state publications. Some states have legislation providing for depository libraries for their documents. In 1975, the American Library Association adopted recommendations for a state document program called "Guidelines for Minimum State Servicing of State Documents." These guidelines outline the basic elements of a full state program for depository libraries, out-of-state exchange, and complete publication lists.

The principal bibliography of current state publications is the Library of Congress' *Monthly Checklist of State Publications*. Important as this is, it is not complete. The chief interest of most libraries is in the publications of their own state, and the checklists from the individual states must be used if acquisitions are to be comprehensive. Some of these checklists are inclusive bibliographies, while others are incomplete or selective. A few states issue no lists at all.

State Publications and Depository Libraries: A Reference Handbook, by Margaret T. Lane (Greenwood, 1981), cites documents and newsletters by state and provides a state-by-state compilation of state laws relating to document distribution, state rules and regulations, and a bibliography of items pertaining to that state's documents. The same author has written *Selecting and Organizing State Government Publications* (American Library Assn., 1987). Another, related publication from the ALA is *Guide to the Publications of Interstate Agencies and Authorities* (1986) by Jack Sulzer and Roberta Palen.

Most state publications are available free to libraries in the state, and frequently to libraries outside the state as well. When prices are given in the checklists, acquisitions librarians should send checks or money orders with their orders, rather than expect shipment and invoicing. Once a library has been placed on a publications mailing list, it should maintain a special procedure for claiming those publications, as lists may be considered temporary by some agencies or be subject to changes in budget support. The *Book of the States* (biennial, Council of State Governments) lists state offices and officials, and is a good source for addresses. Manuals or bluebooks are published for most states, and these are useful for identifying agencies that have publications and for securing their addresses, as well as providing basic information about the states themselves. *State Bluebooks and Reference Publications: A Selected Bibliography* (Council of State Governments, 1983) is a useful guide.

Local documents, including the materials issued by local governmental agencies and their subunits, municipalities, counties, townships, villages, special districts, school boards, park districts, port authorities, transportation boards, etc., are perhaps even harder to acquire than state documents. The acquisition of local documents generally costs more in library staff time than the documents themselves. Most of these publications are free, but to obtain them requires constant vigilance in discovering which city and county agencies have publications and in getting and remaining on their mailing lists. Watching local newspapers is one of the best ways to learn of new local publications, but their bibliographic coverage is extremely poor. References in the Public Affairs Information Service *Bulletin* and notices, reviews, and news notes in journals concerned with local governments are sometimes useful.

Documents of International Organizations

Acquisition of the publications of the United Nations (U.N.) and its related agencies each year ranges from a dozen or so titles from the U.N. and UNESCO in almost every library to the thousands that will be acquired by a research library with a special interest in international intergovernmental publications. The U.N. and its special agencies (UNESCO, ILO, WHO, FAO, and others) are independent of one another and publish separately. There are also other international organizations that publish useful material. The *Yearbook of International Organizations* (3v., K.G. Saur, 1988–89) provides information on more than 24,000 organizations.

Of materials from the United Nations, publications are for public consumption and are offered for sale, while documents are not intended for public use. *NDOC: The United Nations Document Index*, one of the products of the United Nations Bibliographic Information System (UNBIS), a computer-based online system, provides a monthly listing of U.N. documents and publications received by the U.N. library, along with instructions for placing orders. UNESCO and the other specialized agencies have their own publication services or deal through distributors, whose addresses may be obtained by writing to the appropriate agency. Several agencies offer comprehensive lists of their publications, and almost all of them issue sales catalogs periodically. *International Bibliography, Information, Documentation* (IBID), a quarterly publication of Unipub, provides current coverage for priced publications of the United Nations and related international organizations.

TECHNICAL AND ANNUAL REPORTS

Technical reports are publications of government, commercial, and academic laboratories that report research, usually in science and technology. The research and the reports are often government sponsored. These reports represent a large field of publication, and their acquisition is necessary for many academic and special libraries. The importance of the technical report often arises from the fact that it can be published faster separately, rather than as a journal article, although it may later appear in a journal in an edited and shortened form. While many titles are published as technical reports, they usually appear in only a few copies, and acquiring them may be complex and frustrating. Their distribution is often limited. Many are available free, and some are deposited in selected libraries. Those that are widely available are usually priced.

Technical reports are not normally available from the usual book and periodical sources. They are seldom indexed in the conventional bibliographical tools used for acquisitions, and there is no union list of library holdings. However, bibliographic machine-readable data files (discussed later) are an important source for identifying technical reports. Many of the federal government data files are available through commercial vendors of online search services. Chief among the printed bibliographic sources is *Government Reports Announcements and Index*, published twice a month by the National Technical Information Service (NTIS) of the U.S. Department of Commerce. It announces research and development reports and technical publications, and listed items may be ordered from NTIS unless another source is indicated. The U.S. Department of Education has a clearinghouse system, called ERIC (Educational Resources Information Center), which produces *Resources in Education*, an abstracting service with information about educational research reports, including instructions for ordering.

Libraries may purchase technical reports from these government services in paper copy, on microform, and sometimes on magnetic tape or disks. Some technical report series are available on standing order for libraries with well-defined and continuing interests. NTIS offers such a standing order service on microfiche.

Although many reports that are not government generated are included in the previously listed titles, others are not. These are usually obtained directly from the corporation or institution that publishes them or from the author. The acquisitions librarian should not overlook the resources of other libraries, especially those with strong technical reports collections or those that specialize in areas that might encompass an elusive title. These resources usually can be tapped through interlibrary loan or photocopying services.

Other types of specialized technical documents include standards, specifications, and codes. "Engineering standards may be defined as rules for the quality, size, shape, performance, definition, and testing methodology of manufactured products."[3] Codes are statements of rules—some with statutory force—on one subject. Building codes, safety codes, etc., are examples. Specifications list requirements for materials to be purchased for official use by a governmental agency. Standards, codes, and specifications vary widely in format. Some are single sheets; others are multivolume sets. Some are printed; others are in microform or machine-readable form. Identifying and purchasing these materials requires persistence. The National Bureau of Standards' *KWIC (Keyword-in-Context) Index of U.S. Voluntary Engineering Standards* and the database of the National Standards Association are two possible sources of information. Since standards, codes, and specifications usually have to be acquired directly from their issuing organizations or agencies, libraries that have a heavy demand for these publications should hold membership in the major standards-issuing organizations and get on the regular mailing lists of other appropriate groups.

Corporate annual reports are important additions to business collections, because they provide primary source material on the history, financial status, products, personnel, and plans of individual companies. Thousands of companies distribute annual reports to their stockholders. Librarians can usually obtain these free on request, but deciding which ones to request involves professional judgment based on a thorough knowledge of how such reports may be used locally. Ordering reports indiscriminately serves little purpose, since making and monitoring requests takes staff time and storing the annual reports may require a great deal of space.

One of the solutions to these acquisition and storage problems is to order annual reports on microfiche from one of the vendors who assembles and distributes them in this form. In addition to being more expensive, the microfiche version is usually not as attractive as the original version, but it takes much less space. Some libraries, serving users who approach annual reports for a variety of reasons (to identify officers, to gather statistics, to study product design, etc.), acquire both print and microfiche versions and discard the print version after a few years.

BIBLIOGRAPHY

Older Materials

Cameron, Kenneth J., and Michael Roberts. "Desiderata File Maintenance: Purging and Its Politics." *Journal of Librarianship*, 14(April 1982):123-133.

Cook, Sarah A. "The Selective Purchase of Out of Print Books: A Survey of Practices." *Library Resources & Technical Services*, 10(Winter 1966):31-37.

Heinzkill, Richard. "Retrospective Collection Development in English Literature: An Overview." *Collection Management*, 9(Spring 1987): 55-65.

Heppell, Shirley G. "A Survey of OP Buying Practices." *Library Resources & Technical Services*, 10(Winter 1966):28-30.

Kaiser, Lillian S. "Searching for Out-of-Print Books." *School Library Journal*, 26:(May 1980):45.

Kilton, Thomas D. "Out-of-Print Procurement in Academic Libraries: Current Methods and Sources." *Collection Management*, 5(Fall/Winter 1983):113-134.

Kim, Ung Chon. "Comparison of Two Out-of-Print Book Buying Methods." *College & Research Libraries*, 34(September 1973):258-264.

Larsen, A. Dean. "The Role of Retrospective Materials in Collection Development." In *Collection Development in Libraries*, pp. 261-279. Edited by Robert D. Stueart and George B. Miller. Greenwich, Conn.: JAI Pr., 1980.

Mitchell, Betty J. "Methods Used in Out-of-Print Acquisition: A Survey of Out-of-Print Book Dealers." *Library Resources & Technical Services*, 17(Spring 1973):211-215.

_____, and Carol Bedoian. "A Systematic Approach to Performance Evaluation of Out-of-Print Book Dealers: The San Fernando Valley State College Experience." *Library Resources & Technical Services*, 15(Spring 1971):215-222.

Nuzzo, David J. "A Reasonable Approach to Out-of-Print Procurement Using dBase II or dBase III." *Library Acquisitions: Practice & Theory*, 11(1987):165-180.

Perez, Ernest R. "Acquisition of Out-of-Print Materials." *Library Resources & Technical Services*, 17(Winter 1973):42-59.

Perrault, Anna H. "Humanities Collection Management—An Impressionistic/Realistic/Optimistic Appraisal of the State of the Art." *Collection Management*, 5(Fall/Winter 1983):1-23.

Reichman, Felix. "Purchase of Out-of-Print Materials." *Library Trends*, 18(January 1970):328-353.

Smith, Eldred. "Out-of-Print Book Searching." *College & Research Libraries*, 29(July 1968):303-309.

Streit, Samuel A. "Acquiring Rare Books by Purchase: Recent Library Trends." *Library Trends*, 36(Summer 1987):189-213.

Materials from Foreign Sources

"Acquisitions from the Third World." Guest editors, Brian Kent Mulliner and Haw-Wei Lee. *Library Acquisitions: Practice and Theory*, 6(1982):79- 238.

Acquisitions of Foreign Materials for U.S. Libraries. 2nd ed. Edited by Theodore Samore. Metuchen, N.J.: Scarecrow, 1982. 218p.

Coscarelli, William F., and Peggy P. Chalaron. "Acquisition of French Language Monographic Materials." *Collection Management*, 8(Spring 1988):45-53.

Deal, Carl W. "Collecting Foreign Materials from Latin America." In *Collection Development in Libraries*, pp. 219-239. Edited by Robert E. Stueart and George B. Miller. Greenwich, Conn.: JAI Pr., 1980.

Downey, J. A. "The Acquisition of Social Science Literature from the Anglophone Caribbean: A British Perspective." *Library Acquisitions: Practice and Theory*, 9(1985):121-145.

Hacken, Richard D. "Current Trends in the Planning and Management of Northern European Collections." *Collection Management*, 5(Fall/ Winter 1983):69-87.

Karhanis, Sharad. "Acquisition of South Asian Material for the Libraries of North America and Europe: Problems, Prospects and Perspectives." *Library Acquisitions: Practice and Theory*, 8(1984):11-30.

Markwith, Michael. "Some Perspectives on Foreign Acquisitions." *Library Acquisitions: Practice and Theory*, 7(1983):255-260.

Rutledge, John. "Collecting Contemporary European Literature for a Research Library." *Collection Management*, 5(Spring/Summer 1983):1-13.

Schreiner-Robles, Rebecca. "Collection Development in Foreign Literatures at Medium-Sized Academic Libraries." *Library Resources & Technical Services*, 32(April 1988):139-147.

Sohn, Jeanne, and Russ Davidson. "Out of the Morass: Acquiring Spanish-Language Materials from Latin America." *Library Journal*, 107(July 1982):1290-1293.

"The State of Western European Studies: Implications for Collection Development." Guest editors, Anthony M. Angiletta et al. *Collection Management*, 6(Spring/Summer 1984):1-273.

Welsch, Erwin. "Collecting Foreign Materials from Western Europe." In *Collection Development in Libraries*, pp. 241-259. Edited by Robert D. Stueart and George B. Miller. Greenwich, Conn.: JAI Pr., 1980.

_____. "A Collection Development Model for Foreign Literatures." *Collection Management*, 7(Spring 1985):1-11.

_____. "Will American Libraries Continue to Have European Books?" *European Studies Newsletter*, 10(March 1981):1-8.

Wolcke-Renk, Irmtraus-D. "Acquisition of African Literature—Problem and Challenge for Bookdealer and Librarian." *IFLA Journal*, 10(1984):377-384.

Zielinska, Marie, and Irena Bell. "Selection and Acquisition of Library Materials in Languages Other than English: Some Guidelines for Public Libraries." *Collection Building*, 2(1980):7-28.

Government Publications

"Collection Development for Government Publications." Issue editors, Peter Hernon and Gary Purcell. *Government Publications Review*, 8A(1981):1-125.

Copeland, Nora S., Fred C. Schmidt, and James Strickland. "Fugitive U.S. Government Publications: Elements of Procurement and Bibliographic Control." *Government Publications Review*, 12(May-June 1985):227-237.

Eisenbeis, Kathleen. "An NTIS Case Study: A Skirmish in the Privatization Wars." *Government Publications Review*, 15(July/August 1988):355-369.

Gillispie, James. "Columns and Journals Reviewing Governmental Publications." *Serials Review*, 12(Spring 1986):9-15.

Hernon, Peter. "Publications and Information of the United States Government in an Electronic Age." *Serials Review*, 12(Summer and Fall 1986):133-147.

_____, and Charles R. McClure. *Academic Library Use of NTIS: Suggestions for Services and Core Collection*. Springfield, Va.: National Technical Information Service, 1986. 60p.

_____. "GPO's Depository Library Program: Building for the Future." *Library Journal*, 113(April 1, 1988):52-56.

_____. *Public Access to Government Information.* 2d ed. Norwood, N.J.: Ablex, 1988. 560p.

Kearley, Timothy. "The European Community Depository Library System in North America."*Government Publications Review*, 14(1987) :11-31.

Lane, Margaret T. *Selecting and Organizing State Government Publications.* Chicago: American Library Assn., 1987. 368p.

_____. *State Publications Depository Libraries: A Reference Handbook.* Westport, Conn.: Greenwood, 1981. 573p.

Levin, Marc A. "Government for Sale: The Privatization of Federal Information Services." *Special Libraries*, 79(Summer 1988):207-214.

Moody, Marilyn. "Developing Documents Collections for Non-Depository Libraries." *RQ*, 25(Winter 1985):185-189.

Morehead, Joe. *Introduction to United States Public Documents.* 3rd ed. Littleton, Colo.: Libraries Unlimited, 1983. 309p.

Morton, Bruce. "The Depository Library System: A Costly Anachronism." *Library Journal*, 112(September 15, 1987):52-54.

Nakata, Yuri. *From Press to People: Collecting and Using U.S. Government Publications.* Chicago: American Library Assn., 1979. 212p.

Nakata, Yuri, Susan J. Smith, and William B. Ernst, Jr. *Organizing a Local Government Documents Collection.* Chicago: American Library Assn., 1979. 61p.

Parish, David W. "Some Light on State Bibliographies." *Government Publications Review*, 12(January-February 1985):65-70.

Price-Wilkin, John. "OPTEXT: Government Publications on CD-ROM." *Reference Services Review*, 15(Summer 1987):9-14.

U.S. Government Printing Office. "The GPO's Library Programs Service: The Way It Is." *Government Publications Review*, 12(January-February 1985):25-44.

Weisman, Stuart M. "Computer Information Products at NTIS." *Reference Services Review*, 16(1-2)(1988):17-24.

Technical and Annual Reports

Bernstein, Judith R. "Corporate Annual Reports in Academic Business Libraries." *College & Research Libraries*, 47(May 1986):263-273.

_____. "Corporate Annual Reports: The Commercial Vendors." *College & Research Libraries News*, 47(March 1986):178-180.

Hamilton, Beth A. "Managing a Standards Collection in an Engineering Consulting Firm." *Special Libraries*, 74(January 1983):28-33.

Newman, Wilda B., and Michlean J. Amir. "Report Literature: Selecting versus Collecting." *Special Libraries*, 69(November 1978):415-424.

NINE

Purchasing Nonbook Materials

SINCE ALL RECORDED INFORMATION forms the universe from which the collections of libraries are built, librarians who have collection development responsibilities must be able to identify and obtain materials in any format. The information needs of any library's clientele are not limited by the type of package in which that information appears. The collection development librarian seeks the best materials available in terms of authority, accuracy, and presentation, and sometimes the most effective medium for presenting the chosen content is in an aural or graphic form.

For many years, libraries have collected music scores, pamphlets, pictures, maps, and other types of printed, nonbook materials. School library media centers have a long tradition of acquiring educational materials in whatever form they appear, printed or not. Large public library systems have traditionally built strong collections of films, and even small public libraries have had collections of phonograph records. Now college and university librarians are recognizing that much of the content available in nonbook formats is pertinent to the educational and research goals of their institutions. In recent years there has been growing emphasis on acquiring films, filmstrips, slides, video recordings, sound recordings, microforms, and machine-readable data files. These are sometimes referred to as "special materials," because they may require special adaptations of traditional library procedures.

The special formats, discussed in the following sections, are considered separately because bibliographic and evaluative information on them appears—when it appears at all—in a wide variety of sources. In addition, many are distributed in ways entirely distinct from the systems used for monographs and serials. On the other hand, selection of these special formats is based on the same considerations as any library material: the objectives of the library, the needs of the clientele, the materials already owned by the library or available to it through cooperative arrangements, as well as the authority, accuracy, treatment, cost, and general value of the item. A key question in selecting any material for the library is always whether the chosen format is the most effective medium for communicating that particular information.

In addition to the general principles applied in selecting all library materials, other matters are to be considered for some of these formats: technical matters involved in their production; the extraordinary expense of some and the need to preview before purchase; the requirement for expensive, well-maintained equipment in order to exploit some of the formats properly; and the fact that their bibliographic information is less readily available than information about monographs and serials.

The assignment of the responsibility for acquiring these materials depends upon the size and organization of each library. Frequently, the acquisitions unit is first involved late in the ordering process, because the preorder searching and verification has already been done by a competent and interested staff member in public services or by an expert in a departmental or divisional library. In some libraries, however, a specialist in acquisitions may handle all of the ordering, receiving, and precataloging for one or several of these forms, as well as participate in the selection process. For example, a library with a large collection of music may have a specialist in the acquisitions unit who is responsible for order work related to music scores, sound recordings, and books about music. In some cases, such a specialist might also have public service duties.

Careful coordination between acquisitions and public service or special materials units is necessary, under any acquisitions arrangement, to assure that there is no duplication of work, that orders move ahead without delay, and that all purchasing regulations are met. Budgetary control usually is retained in the acquisitions unit to guarantee that allocation or budgetary policies, such as rates of expenditure, are observed and that there is no overexpenditure. When acquisitions work is done outside the acquisitions unit, it is good practice to have it completed under the general supervision of the head of the acquisitions unit to be sure that the work is consistent with the library's policies and practices and to give the nonacquisitions unit the advantages of the acquisitions librarian's expertise in acquiring materials and managing order procedures.

ELECTRONIC DELIVERY OF INFORMATION

The development of electronic data transmission technology has provided libraries with rapid access to information and opportunities for new services, but the new technologies for recording and delivering information also present problems to collection development librarians. One of the problems is the speed with which electronic technologies—and the equipment required to exploit them—have been developed, improved, and (in some cases) abandoned. Not only must librarians struggle to keep up with what is new, but they must also decide when and where to incorporate electronic delivery into their library's services, knowing that the wrong decision may mean spending a great deal of money for equipment that will soon be obsolete.

Early versions of machine-readable data files—recorded electronically and/or read electronically—were purchased by some librarians as they became available. As defined in the *Anglo-American Cataloguing Rules* (2nd ed., American Library Assn., 1978, p. 567), a machine-readable data file (MRDF) is "a body of information coded by methods that require the use of a machine (typically but not always a computer) for processing. Examples include files stored on magnetic tape, punched cards, aperture cards, disk packs, etc." (The 1988 edition of *Anglo-American Cataloguing Rules* uses the term *computer file*, defined as "a file [data and/or programs] encoded for manipulation by computer" [p. 617].) Since their appearance, MRDFs of various types have been collected in special libraries and technical information centers, but their acceptance has now become general. During the latter part of the 1970s, academic libraries, many public libraries, and some school libraries began to obtain access to MRDFs through telephone connections with large computers in other parts of the country.

When electronic delivery of information by way of telecommunication with a central, remote computer became popular, collection development librarians became concerned with questions of ownership, access, and preservation. Some electronically available databases may be sold outright to libraries; others are provided in a format that is physically present in the library, but only on a lease or subscription basis; still others are available to libraries on a per-use basis through telecommunications lines. Microcomputer software is an example of the first kind of electronic product; many of the CD-ROM indexes fall into the second category; and online search services fit the third type. When information is only available through lease arrangements or on a per-use basis, questions arise concerning the preservation of that information for long-term or later use.

Librarians have, in most cases, developed procedures for incorporating the online databases into their operations. Vendors typically provide online searching of a number of different databases, and libraries using their services pay according to the cost of the databases searched and the search time required. Machine-readable data files with numeric data are less likely to be available through vendors; therefore, providing access to them can be more difficult and expensive, because libraries must buy, load, and service them locally. These operations have been carried out smoothly for some time in certain large research libraries or special libraries; smaller libraries may not have the expertise, or the need, to provide such services.

However, librarians are still struggling with some of the questions relating to the small magnetic disks used on microcomputers and the newer CD-ROM. Libraries of almost every size and type may need the information contained in these formats. The CD-ROM (compact disk— read-only memory) is a digitally encoded platter, 4 3/4 inches in diameter, which can be read through a CD-ROM drive attached to a microcomputer terminal. Although it offers slower data access than magnetic disks, it can store large amounts of data in a small area. Once a CD-ROM master has been produced, copies are relatively inexpensive. Databases available through online vendors provided the content for the earliest CD-ROM systems to be marketed to libraries.

Machine-readable data files that are available to libraries are sometimes classified as bibliographic or nonbibliographic. Among the bibliographic MRDFs are periodical indexes, library catalogs, newspaper databases, legal and patent databases, and some chemical, medical, and toxicological databases. The bibliographic database developers originally concentrated on scientific and technical fields, but they later moved into the social sciences and humanities. These are the types of files to which libraries are most likely to provide access. Nonbibliographic MRDFs have typically been numeric files, but full-text files are becoming more common. Most are designed to provide financial and marketing data to businesses, although a few cover such things as chemical properties and have scientific-technical applications. The remainder generally provide census data, focus on demographics, and are of particular interest to social scientists.

Decisions about which MRDFs or electronic formats to provide to users most often arise in connection with reference materials, because this is where information is more likely to be available both in print and electronically. In fact, a number of periodical indexes are available in a print version, in a CD-ROM version, and online by telecommunications from a central computer. Printed reference sources are less up to date than electronically delivered material, but they require little training of users and, in some cases, cost less. Online databases are likely to be the most current form of delivery, with constant and regular updating, and they only cost the library for the actual amount of use. However, hourly searching costs can add up rapidly with heavy use and/or untrained searchers. CD-ROM products, which are searched through a microcomputer work station, offer the advantage of predictable costs and more currency than printed sources. However, user access is limited by the number of work stations the library can afford, and initial costs of hardware and furniture for work stations can be substantial.

Choosing which MRDFs to make available through telecommunications usually means choosing which vendor (or vendors) with whom to establish an account. The number of databases available in this way runs into the thousands, and the typical vendor can supply at least hundreds of them. Information on new bibliographic MRDFs is usually available from the limited number of vendors who service them, and detailed descriptions of new databases appear regularly in the periodicals *Database* and *Online*. Information on nonbibliographic MRDFs appears in a variety of sources, and is sometimes harder to locate. Several printed database directories and indexes are available to guide the librarian in identification. One of the most comprehensive is *Database Directory* (4th ed., Knowledge Industry Publications, 1986). This directory lists approximately 3,000 databases accessible in North America and provides basic information about each, including size, subject, corresponding printed sources, producer and vendor information, and search aids. The *Directory of Online Databases* (quarterly, Cuadra/Elsevier) also contains information on more than 3,000 databases and is available online. It too has subject indexing, along with producer information. *North American Online Directory* (2nd ed., Bowker, 1987) contains descriptions of 2,600 databases and has a classified subject index. It also has sections on database producers, information brokers, consultants, and other related topics. Gale Research publishes the *Online Database Search Services Directory* (2nd ed., 1988), which includes information on more than 1,700 libraries, information firms, and other organizations that provide computerized information retrieval and related services.

The federal government is a major producer of machine-readable data files. Well-known examples include MARC (Library of Congress), MEDLINE (National Library of Medicine), AGRICOLA (Department of Agriculture), ERIC (Department of Education), and databases from NASA and the Department of Commerce. Since the early 1970s, various federal agencies have distributed information about their MRDFs, but format, scope, etc., of these directories vary widely from one agency to another. *Federal Database Finder: A Directory of Free and Fee-Based Databases and Files Available from the Federal Government* (2nd ed., Information USA, Inc., 1987) lists federal MRDFs, approximately 400 of which are online. It also includes information on computer tapes and disks available from the Census Bureau, the National Technical Information Service, and the National Archives. Oryx Press published in 1988 *Federal Statistical*

Data Bases: A Comprehensive Catalog of Current Machine-Readable and Online Files, which is an updated version of the *Directory of Federal Statistical Data Files*, originally published by the U.S Department of Commerce.

Another source of information about nonbibliographic MRDFs is the Inter-University Consortium for Political and Social Research (ICPSR). This is an international research repository for quantitative data, founded in 1962 and presently housed at the University of Michigan. Many academic institutions pay annual membership fees to support ICPSR and to ensure access for their users to the MRDFs contained in that collection. Some university systems have developed consortia in relation to ICPSR; some of these sets of MRDFs are housed in libraries. ICPSR publishes *Guide to Resources and Services*, and that, together with similar smaller catalogs or directories published by individual MRDF collections, plus a variety of newsletters and special reports, may cover most of the easily available public data files.

In addition to machine-readable data files with bibliographic or numeric data, many libraries now collect software packages, particularly for microcomputers. A survey conducted by the Association of Research Libraries in late 1985 found that 38 percent of the respondents were circulating microcomputer software among their users.[1] Almost all the respondents were purchasing microcomputer software for staff and administrative use. The amount of software available is growing rapidly. According to the statistics collected by R.R. Bowker, more than 22,000 microcomputer software titles were available in 1985 and 25,000 to 27,000 were expected the next year.[2] The advertisement for the 1988 version of the Bowker database claimed that 28,500 microcomputer software packages were listed.

Some librarians are beginning to see the need for specific collection development policy statements concerning microcomputer software. A report in *Choice* in 1986 noted that, although few libraries had such policies, those that did "basically extended their current acquisition policies by recognizing computer software as information in a different format, acquired with the same guidelines used for any format to be integrated into a library's existing collection."[3] One library that did develop specific guidelines for software included these factors as significant in the selection decision: subject scope (must be related to instructional and research interests of the institution); user need; uniqueness of data; authority of data; confidentiality of data; availability of online access; and documentation.[4] Other policies contain statements about machine compatibility, location of materials, and copyright. Most of the problems encountered by librarians with this form of material center around machine compatibility and copyright protection. Microcomputer software is generally designed to run on a specific type of machine with a specific operating system. The same software package may appear in a number of versions to accommodate this variation, and the librarian must always take availability of equipment into account when making a selection. Copyright protection is a particular problem if the collection is designed to circulate rather than be used in a special section of the library.

Fortunately for librarians, several sources of bibliographic and evaluative information on software packages now exist. *Microcomputer Software Sources* (Libraries Unlimited, 1988) attempts to list and evaluate these reference sources. More than 50 software publishers' catalogs are available in microfiche with a printed index in *Software Publishers' Catalogs Annual* (Meckler, 1988). *The Software Encyclopedia* (Bowker, 1988) provides annotated listings for 28,500 microcomputer programs, with subject indexing and arrangement designed to guide the user to compatible systems. For government-produced software, the *Directory of Computer Software* (National Technical Information Service, 1987) may be useful. It lists approximately 1,700 machine-readable items from more than 100 federal agencies. *Library Software Review*, a quarterly publication started by Meckler Publishing in 1982, is intended to provide current information on software packages with educational and library applications. *Choice* began reviewing microcomputer software in 1984. "Microcomputer Software and Hardware Guide Online" is marketed by Bowker through one of the major online vendors. It claims to provide ordering information on more than 30,000 software programs from 3,500 producers.

Selection of CD-ROM products ought to proceed on the basis of a library's collection and service goals. As the number of these products available increases, some librarians are recognizing the need for collection development statements to establish guidelines and criteria specifically for evaluating CD-ROM. Some of the points that may be considered include suitability of the content for the library's users, time span covered by an index, frequency of updating, whether or not a print or online version exists, compatibility with equipment already owned by the library, reliability and services offered by the vendor, existence of licensing restrictions, searching capabilities, and cost.

Because CD-ROM is newer on the market than the other forms of electronic delivery, the bibliographic and evaluative sources are not yet as extensive. *CD-ROM Review; the Magazine of Optical Publishing* (bimonthly, CW Communications) and *CD-ROM Librarian* (monthly, Meckler) provide some guidance in this area.

AUDIOVISUAL MATERIALS

Films, filmstrips, slides, video and sound recordings—although composed of various combinations of film, plastic, and magnetic tape—are usually categorized as audiovisual materials. Keeping up with new technology, new equipment, and new producers of audiovisual materials is difficult; the procedures and distributors form a complex pattern. As with monographs, commercially oriented producers for most of these media tend to focus on either the mass market or the educational market. The same bibliographic tools may not list materials for both markets. Many audiovisual materials are also produced by institutions, associations, and other noncommercial organizations. Complications arise because a large number of audiovisual materials are locally produced by educational institutions, from elementary schools to universities. In addition, most audiovisual producers distribute their own materials. This diversity of producers and distributors makes it very difficult for librarians to identify what exists. Bibliographic control of most types of audiovisual materials is still less complete than the coverage of print materials. There is no general in-print list for audiovisual materials. For this reason, libraries usually maintain collections of producer/distributor catalogs.

There are a few general guides to sources of information about audiovisual materials, such as *Aids to Media Selection for Students and Teachers*, an annotated list by Yvonne B. Carter and Barbara Spriestersbach (rev. ed., National Association of State Educational Media Professionals, 1985). Mary Robinson Sive's *Media Selection Handbook* (Libraries Unlimited, 1983) describes the most essential selection tools for nonprint media (excluding films). It is aimed particularly at curriculum-oriented collections. The same author's *Selecting Instructional Media: A Guide to Audiovisual and Other Instructional Media Lists* (3rd ed., Libraries Unlimited, 1983) includes lists of audiovisual materials, as well as free materials, government documents, etc. *Audio Video Market Place* (annual, Bowker) can be used to identify producers and distributors of audiovisual materials, as well as equipment dealers, laboratories, and other service companies. *Children's Media Marketplace* (3rd ed., Neal-Schuman, 1988) performs a similar function for children's materials.

Two major libraries in the United States maintain and publish records of audiovisual materials. Since 1953, the Library of Congress has been providing some bibliographic control of motion pictures, filmstrips, sound recordings, etc., through various parts of its catalog series. These catalogs have varied in coverage, and even in title. The *National Union Catalog, Audiovisual Materials* (NUC.AV) now includes new LC MARC records for most video formats. Since January 1983, the NUC.AV has appeared as a register with full bibliographic information and name, title, subject, and series indexes. It is issued quarterly on microfiche with cumulative indexes. The National Library of Medicine has developed a computerized database, available as AVLINE, for locating audiovisual materials in the health sciences. *NLM Audiovisuals Catalog* is the print version of AVLINE.

Two series of indexes to audiovisual materials—one emphasizing free and inexpensive materials—have been produced for educators. The national Information Center for Educational Media (NICEM) has, since 1964, published indexes based on its computerized database, which includes most types of audiovisual materials. There are separate NICEM indexes to 16mm educational films and videotapes (annual); 35mm educational filmstrips (8th ed., 1985); educational overhead transparencies (6th ed., 1980); educational audiocassettes (annual); educational slides (4th ed., 1980); and producers and distributors (6th ed., 1985). There are also several multimedia catalogs, focused on particular curriculum areas. The NICEM database is now available online and on CD-ROM. The Educators Progress Service of Randolph, Wisconsin, publishes the *Educator's Guide Series*, which includes lists of free audio and video materials, free films, and free filmstrips.

Many of the current reviewing sources that feature reviews of audiovisual materials are limited to one or two formats, but four of the most popular general sources for book reviews—*Booklist, Choice, Library Journal*, and *School Library Journal*—also include reviews of selected 16mm films, videocassettes, filmstrips, sound recordings, slides, multimedia kits, and (in the case of *Choice*) computer software. *Media Review Digest* (Pierian Pr.) has, in the years it has been published, indexed reviews from a variety of journals featuring audiovisual materials.

Films, Filmstrips, Slides

Films were among the first audiovisual materials to be incorporated into library collections, and, in spite of the rising popularity of video recordings that offer the same or similar content, films continue to be collected by libraries. The 16mm film was the first motion picture format to become popular for educational purposes, and many large library systems gathered extensive collections of 16mm films. Later, when the 8mm film and the super-8mm appeared, material in these formats was also added by some libraries. The film loop, which requires no threading, rewinding, or unnecessary handling, has been especially popular in schools.

Motion pictures in the 16mm film format are popular for large group viewing because of their sharp image and good sound. This format also has an advantage over certain others in equipment compatibility. Most

16mm films may be shown using any 16mm projector. The projectors for 8mm and super-8mm film are more portable and less expensive than those for 16mm film, but have less compatibility. These formats, as well as the film loop, are more often used for short presentations. Selection of films is governed by the general criteria for evaluating any library material: suitability of content to the intended audience, possible uses, physical features, comparative merits, and cost. With this format, however, more emphasis may be placed on evaluation of technical aspects, such as the quality of photography, sound, lighting, editing, narration, etc. A major consideration will be whether film is actually the most effective medium for presentation of the particular content.

A major problem with acquiring films is the high cost. In fact, the cost of 16mm films has forced most libraries into systems of cooperative ownership or rental. Although large libraries and library systems purchase films, most small and medium-sized libraries depend upon centralized collections of 16mm films, such as those at state library agencies, state universities, or cooperative film circuits. Sometimes a library uses a combination of these sources. When an individual library *does* purchase films, its staff has ordinarily previewed each item, before making a final decision to purchase. Fortunately, most films are available on a preview basis.

The sources of information about films, their producers, distributors, and printed evaluations do not present as neat a pattern as the sources about books and their publishers. Files of producers' catalogs are important in the acquisition of films. *Audio Video Market Place* (Bowker) lists producers of these and gives addresses and information about their products. Catalogs of film loan and rental collections may be useful in identifying films; and excellent film catalogs are available from the audiovisual centers of many large universities. An important listing of new films, which might be appropriate for library collections, is the *National Union Catalog Audiovisual Materials* (mentioned in a previous section). It lists motion pictures, filmstrips, and videotapes of educational value, as well as some theatrical films, released in the United States or Canada and added to the collections of the Library of Congress. The National Library of Medicine's *Audiovisuals Catalog* also includes film formats.

Another extensive listing of educational films is the *Educational Film/ Video Locator* of the Consortium of University Film Centers (3rd ed., Bowker, 1986). It annotates approximately 48,000 film and video titles available for sale or rental from the members of the Consortium. The NICEM indexes (mentioned earlier) include lists of 16mm educational films, 35mm filmstrips, 8mm motion cartridges, educational slides, and educational overhead transparencies. *A Directory of Feature Films on*

16mm and Videotape Available for Rental, Sale, and Lease, compiled and edited by James L. Limbacher (8th ed., Bowker, 1985), lists and indexes over 22,000 titles. The *American Film Institute Catalog of Motion Pictures Produced in the United States*, when finished, will provide a decade-by-decade listing of feature films, short films, newsreels, etc. *The Motion Picture Guide* (distributed by Bowker) is a 12-volume set, containing basic details on most American films released in the United States from 1910 through 1984. More than 45,000 sound and silent films are listed and indexed. *The Motion Picture Guide Annual* provides annual updating for the basic set.

The publications that provide reviews of film formats may also be useful acquisition tools. *Media & Methods, Sightlines, Film Video News, Sight and Sound, Film Quarterly, Booklist, Choice, Library Journal, School Library Journal*, and *Science Books & Films* regularly include reviews of films and, in many cases, of filmstrips, videotapes, and slide sets. Oryx Press has published a two-volume *Film Review Index*, containing citations to reviews in popular and trade journals of more than 7,000 motion pictures, from 1882 through 1985.

Filmstrips—another film format, consisting of lengths of 35mm film containing a series of still pictures—are popular in some libraries. While they do not provide the motion which makes 16mm and 8mm films so attractive, filmstrips may be designed to suggest motion and may be accompanied by sound. Relatively low cost and ease of viewing are among the factors that have made filmstrips particularly popular in school library media centers and children's collections of public libraries. One children's specialist has pointed out the value of filmstrips in helping children learn how to look at an illustration, by focusing on specific features and their relationships.[5] She has also suggested that the lack of true motion in a filmstrip makes viewing it an experience closer to the actual reading of a book or hearing a story.

In general, selection criteria for filmstrips are similar to those for other library materials, but, as with other audiovisual formats, technical quality—particularly visual images and sound (where included)—should be high. Since filmstrips, like films, are restricted to a predetermined sequencing, the organization of material presented in the filmstrip is very important. The educational objectives to be met by the filmstrip should be clearly evident to the one who selects it and effectively presented to the viewer.

Many of the current reviewing sources and other sources that list films also include filmstrips. In addition, the Educators Progress Service series and the NICEM database both include information on educational filmstrips.

Slides (single frames of 35mm film secured in a 2"×2", 2 1/4"×2 1/4", or 3 1/4"× 4" mounting) share some of the advantages of filmstrips. They are relatively inexpensive and their projection equipment is easy to operate. In addition, they offer flexibility of sequence and pacing. Multi-screen presentations, with sound and specially treated slides, can hold an audience's attention as well as a fast-paced motion picture. For educational purposes, color, resolution, and focus of the visual image on the slide are important selection considerations.

Slides are included in some of the acquisition and selection sources mentioned previously—*Audio Video Market Place, Booklist, Choice, Library Journal, School Library Journal*, the Educators Progress Service series, and the NICEM database. *Slide Buyers' Guide: An International Directory of Slide Sources for Art and Architecture* (Libraries Unlimited, 1985) lists, describes, and indexes by subject, sources in the United States, Canada, and selected foreign countries which rent, sell, or exchange slides.

Video Recordings

Video recordings include videotapes, videocassettes, and videodiscs—any form in which visual images have been recorded magnetically or by laser and can be viewed through a television set. The videodisc is a 12-inch platter, silver in appearance and without visible grooves. It may contain digital, motion, audio, or still images, and is read by a laser. Videotapes, most often distributed in cassette form, are strips of polyester with magnetic signals. Videocassettes have been produced and sold to the public in 3/4-inch U-matic, 1/2-inch Beta, 1/2-inch VHS, and 8mm formats. Each requires different playback equipment. The videodisc, which requires still another type of player, is superior to videotape in picture and sound quality, in durability, and in access to specific parts of the recorded content. It can also store a greater range of signals (digital, motion, still, etc.). At the present time, however, the variety of content available on videocassettes is much greater than that available on videodiscs.

Library collections of video recordings may contain locally recorded events and productions, as well as those produced commercially. Videotapes, particularly the locally produced variety, have been common in academic libraries for some time; but now that videocassettes are widely available for the home market, many public libraries collect and lend these cassettes as they do the more traditional formats. The collection development policy for video recordings should specify—in addition to goals of the collection and general selection criteria—which types of materials (feature, nontheatrical, children's) the library will collect and how these will be judged.

The purchase of video formats presents complications not common in the acquisition of other special materials. The technology of video recording is developing rapidly which makes selection of particular formats and related equipment unusually difficult. Initial high cost and possible obsolescence are two of the problems the librarian faces. The ease with which video recordings can be copied raises a host of legal questions, and also means that free preview of video recordings is far more limited than for films. In spite of the collection development difficulties, video recordings are replacing films in some libraries.

Acquiring video recordings involves a number of problems, not the least of which is identifying what is available. It may be necessary to approach feature, nontheatrical, and children's materials differently. Feature videos—full-length dramatizations—are now widely available to libraries and individuals. Many of the sources that help librarians identify films also cover videos. It is relatively easy to find out about the content of feature videos, but harder to learn about technical qualities of a particular release. Nontheatrical videos—general interest nonfiction or fiction works with an educational focus—present a greater challenge to the librarian. Both content and technical quality are hard to determine, and educational videos generally cost more than those aimed at the home market. Some producers of nontheatrical videos also charge higher prices to libraries than to individuals.

Sometimes it will be necessary to purchase a video directly from the producer or distributor (and sometimes the discount will be better), but book wholesalers are now making videocassettes available. In general, feature videos are more easily purchased through wholesalers. Nontheatrical videos *can* be purchased that way, but costs may be higher than through direct purchase. The timing of purchases of nontheatrical videos can mean a big difference in cost to the library, because those that are eventually released to the consumer market will go down significantly in price. Legal off-air taping is another way to build the video collection. The Public Broadcasting System, for example, offers an off-satellite taping license for many of its productions at a cost lower than that of purchasing the videocassettes. Librarians have also found it economical to band together in consortia for the purpose of obtaining large group discounts on educational videos.

The number of guides to video recordings is increasing. General guides already discussed, such as *Audio Video Market Place* and most of those listing films, are useful for video selection. The *NICEM Index to Educational Videotapes* provides useful coverage for education-oriented video recordings, as does the *Educators Guide to Free Videotapes*, on a more limited basis. The *Video Source Book* (9th ed., National Video Clearinghouse, 1988) lists more than 50,000 prerecorded video programs, available from more than 1,000 sources. For entertainment-oriented materials, such as feature films, sports specials, cartoons, travelogs, concerts, plays, etc., the catalogs of individual producers and distributors are a good source of information. *Variety's Complete Home Video Directory* (distributed by Bowker) carried annotated entries and the ordering information for more than 25,000 video titles in its 1988 edition. Review coverage of new video recordings is improving, although it covers only a small portion of the releases. *Booklist, Choice, Library Journal,* and *School Library Journal* are examples of the journals that provide a limited number of reviews.

Sound Recordings

Sound recordings include the familiar phonodisk or phonograph record, the newer compact audio disk, and magnetic tape in all its various packages. Tapes may be 1- or 2-track monaural, 4-track stereo, or 8-track stereo, stored on open reels or in cartridges or cassettes. The materials available on sound recordings cover a broad range. Music predominates, but plays, poetry, and foreign-language instruction are frequently presented through this medium.

Since the same content may be available in several forms, selection of sound recordings first means deciding whether to purchase a phonograph record, a compact disk, or an audiotape. Phonograph records are usually less expensive than compact disks or high-quality tapes, but they are easily scratched and less portable than tapes. Furthermore, the quality of their sound tends to deteriorate with use. On the other hand, the sound quality of phonograph records is likely to be better than that of lower-priced tapes. Compact disks are reputed to have the best quality of sound, but they are still expensive and playback equipment is not as widely owned as that for other types of sound recordings. Although it is more difficult to locate specific parts of recorded material on a tape than on a disk, cassettes and cartridges are convenient to play and are not particularly easy to damage. Audiotapes often provide the sound for filmstrips or slide presentations, because they can be programmed to operate the projectors for those media.

The variety of audiotape formats presents another group of selection concerns. The length and thickness of the tape, as well as its speed, construction, and packaging all affect quality of sound and durability. Long-playing cassettes have thin tape, which can more easily be caught in the mechanism of the recorder and ruined. Thin tape is also likely to stretch and transfer signals from one layer to another; both conditions distort sound. Fast tape speeds (7 1/2 ips and 3 3/4 ips) provide higher sound fidelity, but 1 7/8 ips is the normal speed for prerecorded cassettes. The material composition of audiotapes also varies, and less expensive prerecorded tapes are not very durable. Of course, the options for packaging—open reel, cassette, cartridge—and the number of tracks that may be recorded provide producers with a variety of possible combinations, each of which requires its own special playback equipment.

Information on audiotapes may be found in several sources. The Educators Progress Service provides information on audio materials in its annual guide series to free materials. The previously mentioned NICEM database also includes educational audiotapes. The National Center for Audio Tapes in Boulder, Colorado, publishes a triennial catalog. National Public Radio regularly publishes a catalog of cassettes available from its programs. *On Cassette* (annual, Bowker) is an important source of information for spoken-word audiocassettes, listing in the 1988–89 edition more than 33,000 tapes with annotations.

Some of the bibliographic sources for sound recordings are limited to music, but others include any type of sound recording. For example, *American Record Guide*, *High Fidelity*, *Stereo Review*, and the *Notes* of the Music Library Association provide evaluations of musical recordings; *Booklist*, *Choice*, *Library Journal*, and *School Library Journal* review nonmusical recordings. The most comprehensive bibliography of sound recordings is the Schwann catalog. The *Schwann Compact Disc Catalog* is published monthly and carries new listings of electronic music, classical collections, musicals, movies, current popular, jazz, etc. There is also a quarterly Schwann publication that claims to be "a complete guide to all available CDs, LPs, and cassettes" and an artist issue. Schwann serves as a records-in-print list, but it does not include educational materials, recordings sold directly by the artist, or those sold only on a subscription basis. The Library of Congress' *Music, Books on Music, and Sound Recordings*, issued semiannually and cumulated annually, describes sound recordings of all kinds that have been cataloged by the Library of Congress or one of several outstanding North American music libraries.

Some librarians purchase phonograph records and audiotapes through one of the nationally known jobbers, seeking the optimum combination of discount and service; but others prefer to order directly from producers or distributors. A local dealer probably will be unable to offer as much discount as a jobber, but, as with book purchases at local bookstores, librarians may find other advantages in doing at least some of their purchasing locally. A friendly relationship may be valuable when a recording is needed quickly or when it is important to listen to a recording before purchase. Some manufacturers have standing order plans that offer libraries substantial discounts. It is necessary to write them directly for information or watch for their advertisements.

Purchase orders for sound recordings should include the manufacturer's number and the price, as well as the name of the author, composer or performer, and/or title. The possibility of error through choosing the wrong entry appears to be minimized by using the label-number as the sequencing device.

MAPS

Libraries of all types need reference materials that visually present the features of the earth and other celestial bodies. These materials include sheet maps and atlases; globes; aeronautical, navigational, and celestial charts; aerial, satellite, and space photographs; etc. Because it is possible to illustrate the geographic position of so many different things (or combination of things), the number of map types is almost limitless. In recent years, satellite photography and other large-scale, high-speed remote-sensing techniques have greatly expanded the number and types of maps available. Maps may be physical, emphasizing natural features of the land; political, showing boundaries of governmental units; or special topic, showing such information as historical events, manufacturing, crop production, weather patterns, or religious movements. Cadastral maps identify land areas for purposes of recording ownership and establishing tax rolls. Meteorological maps show the relationship between the atmosphere and weather conditions. Topographic series or sets—that is, groups of sheets on which contiguous areas are mapped on the same scale and which show physical and cultural features—make up a large portion of most map collections. Most countries produce at least one topographic map series. Not all libraries will need to collect all types of maps; in fact, small libraries are likely to limit their acquisitions to carefully selected examples.

The media on which the content of maps is stored also offer variety. Maps have traditionally been distributed on paper, with more modern maps often being produced on plastic impregnated paper, which provides tear resistance and ease of handling. Microphotography is also being used to preserve the content of maps; it is especially popular for aerial photographs and satellite remote sensing images. Some mapping projects have experimented with optical and digital technologies.

The scale of a map is an important consideration in selection. Scale may be expressed as a ratio (for example, 1:25,000, meaning that one unit on the map equals 25,000 units in nature); verbally, using words to express the relationship; or with a bar scale, using marked intervals to indicate relationships. Generally, maps are considered small if the scale is 1:250,000 or smaller; intermediate, if 1:250,000 to 1:50,000; and large, if 1:50,000 or larger. Small-scale maps cover more area, but provide less detail.

The amount of cartographic material now available may help explain the concern in the literature about the need for establishing priorities and preparing collection development policies for the map collection. Policies typically identify the users who will be served by the map collection, the types of maps a library will collect, the geographic areas to be covered, and the formats (sheet, bound, microform, etc.) in which the maps will be acquired. Public libraries may serve such user groups as business persons, travellers, and genealogists. Academic and special libraries may focus on the needs or interests of faculty members and graduate students in particular departments. Anticipating how maps will be used by a particular clientele helps in narrowing the range of maps that should be acquired. Policies may also specify acquisition procedures for maps in sets or series; some libraries buy only complete sets.

Because of the special acquisitions, storage, and reference requirements associated with individual sheet maps, large research libraries tend to house them in special map collections. While order preparations, bookkeeping, and ultimate approval of payments rest with the acquisitions unit in most libraries, selection, verification, and upon-receipt identification should be done by a person knowledgeable about maps. This may be a bibliographer in the acquisitions unit, but it will more likely be a member of the staff of the map collection.

Identifying and acquiring maps can be a challenge, requiring persistence and creativity on the part of the map librarian. The bibliographic sources are not well organized or widely known among librarians who do not specialize in maps, and the library without such specialists cannot rely on approval plans to provide automatic delivery. Delay in identification of desired maps may produce a collection with major gaps, because maps are often printed in limited quantities and go out of print quickly.

Published information about maps and atlases can be found in geographical journals, which regularly carry lists of new maps and atlases and some reviews. Examples of new publication lists may be found in the *Bulletin* of the Special Libraries Associations' Geography and Map Division; *Base Line*, the newsletter of the American Library Association's Map and Geography Roundtable; and the Western Association of Map Libraries' *Information Bulletin*. National bibliographies that contain entries for maps are also useful. The *National Union Catalog. Cartographic Materials*, started by the Library of Congress in 1983, includes citations to all of LC's single- and multisheet thematic map sets, atlases, and maps treated as serials, as well as contributions from other libraries. NUC.CM is issued quarterly on microfiche, in the form of a register, accompanied by five indexes: name, title, subject, series, and geographic classification code.

Most of the maps published in the United States come from federal, state, and local agencies. In fact, the U.S. government is probably the largest map publisher in the world. At the federal level, the *Monthly Catalog of United States Government Publications* may be useful for identifying the map catalogs of the agencies that issue them. The U.S. Geological Survey is the most active mapping agency of the federal government. It produces topographic maps in a variety of scales, as well as geologic, hydrologic, and mineralogic maps. Other federal agencies of interest to map collectors are the Defense Mapping Agency (aeronautical and nautical charts and topographic maps); the Central Intelligence Agency (various political maps and city plans); the National Ocean Survey (nautical charts); the Bureau of Land Management; and the U.S. Forest Service.

State governments also produce maps, including mineralogic and geologic charts, as well as highway maps. Public libraries buying maps for prospective travellers may find the state travel bureaus to be valuable supplies. Other important sources of map information are the current acquisitions lists of major map libraries and the catalogs of publishers and dealers. The *Bibliographic Guide to Maps and Atlases* (G. K. Hall) lists materials cataloged during the previous year by the New York Public Library Map Division and the Geography and Map Division of the Library of Congress. This guide serves as a supplement to the *Dictionary Catalog of the Map Division* of the Research Libraries of the New York Public Library (G. K. Hall, 1971).

The most important publisher of topographic sets in the United States is the U.S. Geological Survey, which also maintains a depository system for American libraries that agree to store and make the maps available for public use. *Guide to Obtaining USGS Information* (U.S. Geological Survey Circular 900; revised 1986) explains how to obtain USGS products. *New Publications of the U.S. Geological Survey*, a monthly publication, and its annual version, *Publications of the Geological Survey*, are essential sources for those libraries that acquire maps extensively.

The National Cartographic Information Center (NCIC) was started in 1974 to be a central source for information about the availability of maps, charts, aerial photographs, satellite imagery, digital mapping data, and other kinds of cartographic products. This unit is a part of the National Mapping Division of the U.S. Geological Survey. It also has a network of affiliated offices in most states, to which it provides reference materials and training in exchange for information about cartographic data available in the state. The information held by NCIC can be accessed by calling the headquarters in Reston, Virginia, or one of the state network offices.

Although maps can sometimes be ordered from the same dealers who handle books, maps are usually ordered directly from their publishers, who ordinarily have larger stocks and can provide quicker service. There are map publishers and dealers that provide international coverage, as well as others that concentrate on the national, state or provincial, county, or city level. Most countries have at least one national mapping agency and many of them publish map catalogs.

The acquisition of foreign maps from certain countries presents special problems. In addition to the usual complications of currency exchange and foreign correspondence is the issue of national defense. There has always been a tendency for countries to restrict the mapping of certain sensitive areas, but in recent years more governments have had reason to refuse to distribute detailed maps of their countries. Topographic sets produced by national surveys in other countries may not be available to American libraries, even when the sets are listed in catalogs.

MICROFORMS

Microforms come in three basic formats—microfilm, microfiche, and microopaque—each of which has several variations. Microfilm is usually produced from high-contrast photographic film, 16mm or 35mm, usually in black and white, although some materials are available in color. Microfiche resembles microfilm in that it contains a series of micro-images on film, but instead of the images that appear in a row on a roll of film, they are arranged in a grid pattern on a sheet of film. The standard size for microfiche is approximately 4 by 6 inches (105mm × 148mm), but other sizes are sometimes available. Library materials are also produced on two kinds of microopaques, each of which uses a different process for transferring the images to opaque card stock.

Reduction ratios for microforms usually run from 1:12 to 1:20, but may be as high as 1:150. Microfiche tends to have higher reduction ratios than microfilm. Most microfilm is available on open reels, but some publishers offer microfilm in cartridges or cassettes. All these variations—microfiche, microfilm on open reels and in cartridges or cassettes, and both types of microopaques—require different types of reading equipment and copiers.

Microforms have been hailed as the most cost-effective solutions to conserving shelf space and reducing binding costs in libraries. Many periodical titles, as well as monographic sets, are available for purchase. Microforms also serve a preservation function; rare and out-of-print materials can be more widely available. The great drawback to making microform purchases a major part of collection development is user resistance. Microforms must be viewed in the library, on the proper machine, and in appropriate lighting conditions. Users' objections can, however, often be overcome with careful planning. Harrington identifies the following factors as contributing to successful use of microforms in a university library: establishment of a centralized microform collection, development of guidelines for acquisition and handling of microforms, provision of a comfortable and pleasant study environment, well-maintained readers and reader-printers, adequate bibliographic control, and enthusiastic, well-trained staff.[6]

Micropublishing, or the production of microforms, is often an on-demand publishing process; that is, duplicate microfiches or rolls of microfilm are produced from the master microform when there is a specific request. It is therefore a particularly appropriate form of publication for materials with limited demand, and there are three major types: (1) reprinting or preservation of works that were originally published in a paper format, (2) publication of original works, such as dissertations or research reports, and (3) simultaneous publication of certain works in both paper format and microform. Out-of-print monographs, current serial subscriptions, backfiles of journals, working copies of rare books and manuscripts, and government or international agency documents are examples of the type of materials most often acquired in microfilm. The U.S. Government Printing Office is beginning to issue more and more documents on microfiche only.

There have been a number of microform projects in which difficult-to-obtain materials (often out-of-print monographs or reports) are gathered by period or subject and offered for sale as a block, sometimes being issued over a number of years. These large sets or long series present special collection development considerations: whether the coverage of one set overlaps that of a similar set offered by another publisher; whether the manufacturer will guarantee the physical quality of the set; and whether users can gain easy access to individual items in the set. Sometimes it is useful to consider the sponsoring institution that may have put the set together and its apparent reason for doing so. The qualifications of the editor of the set and the kinds of guides that have been produced to accompany it (or the indexes that already exist for that block of material) are also important factors in making a selection decision. Production standards that ought to be considered include type of film used, focus and legibility of film images, and capability of making good copies on standard reader-printers.

Some micropublishers also issue hardcover books as enlargement from their stores of microforms. These publications may be called reprints, and some of the micropublishers are reprint publishers. Most, however, do on-demand publishing; that is, they enlarge one copy of a book when a purchaser orders it. The economics are not the same as for regular reprint publishing, but this makes no difference to libraries. If a book is cheaper as a demand reprint than as a regular reprint or an out-of-print copy and the quality of the copy is at least as good, a library should buy the demand publication.

Microforms are usually ordered directly from their publishers. The number of commercial houses is relatively small; their chief customers are libraries; and much of their contact with their customers is through direct mail. A useful source of information about microform acquisitions is *Guidelines for Handling Library Orders for Microforms* (American Library Assn., 1977), prepared by the Bookdealer-Library Relations Committee of the ALA/RTSD Resources Section. Microform orders cover both subscriptions to periodicals in microform and subscriptions to the large projects issued over periods of years. It is sometimes necessary to have a current subscription to a periodical in its original format before a microform subscription will be honored; but some journals are issued in both forms, and subscriptions will be accepted for either or both.

Apart from commercial publishers, libraries are the main sources of microforms. They are not usually purveyors of micropublications, but holders of negative films that another library may want copied—or, more often, holders of original materials that a purchaser wants copied. If the owning library has a copying laboratory, the purchaser may prefer to have the materials copied there. Also, the owning library may require that the materials be copied on its premises. The *Directory of Library Reprographic Services* (6th ed., Microform Review, 1976) may be used to discover the copying services available in major libraries.

If a library borrows material to be copied, it may have the work done in its own laboratory or have it sent to a commercial firm. The different sources will have different prices, and these should be taken into consideration. Permission to copy must be obtained from the lending library and sometimes from the copyright holder, and it should be understood that in some instances a library that owns a desired book will not permit it to be copied, because copying would damage the book or because the library wishes to preserve the unique character of its holdings. Buying microforms from other libraries is so often an aspect of interlibrary lending that the forms in common use, the Interlibrary Loan Request Form and the Library Photoduplication Order Form, may become purchase orders, rather than conventional acquisitions forms.

A method of acquisition of microforms that is sometimes proposed to libraries is the exchange of backfiles of serial sets for microform copies.

These offers come from commercial firms that may expect to use the backfiles to make the microform, as well as sell the backfiles to purchasers who prefer them to microforms. Such exchanges may be legitimate, but a history of malpractice in this business should constitute a warning to librarians to examine the offers thoroughly. In particular, they should be sure that value to be received is equal to or greater than value of the material to be released; that the firm is able to perform as promised; that the procedures for exchange are consistent with good business practices for the library; and that there is no secrecy about the transaction. The Bookdealer-Library Relations Committee, a part of the Resources Section of ALA's Resources and Technical Services Division, stands ready to give librarians assistance in evaluating offers to exchange full-size originals for microform copies.

In the past, librarians often have had trouble discovering what exists in various microformats and locating evaluations of these materials. That situation has been improving somewhat. The most comprehensive bibliographic tool is *Guide to Microforms in Print* (annual, Meckler), a cumulative listing of books, journals, newspapers, government publications, archival materials, and collections and other projects which are currently available in microform from organizations throughout the world. Theses and dissertations are excluded (see *Dissertation Abstracts International* for these), but other titles are included when they are "offered for sale on a regular or current basis." *Subject Guide to Microforms in Print* (annual, Meckler) lists the same titles under appropriate subject headings.

The Library of Congress publishes two useful sources of information on microforms. *National Register of Microform Masters* is an annual listing of materials which have been microfilmed and for which master negatives exist. It includes foreign and U.S. monographs, pamphlets, serials, and foreign dissertations; it excludes technical reports, typescript translations, foreign or U.S. archival manuscript collections, U.S. doctoral dissertations, and master's theses. Another annual publication from the Library of Congress, *Newspapers in Microform*, covers American and foreign newspapers that have been reduced to microform and are held by libraries in the United States, Canada, and other countries, and by domestic and foreign commercial producers.

The catalogs of publishers of microforms are also useful to the acquisitions librarian. Such publishers are listed in *Microform Market Place*, an international, biennial directory published by Meckler. Reviews of large microform sets and other information on developments in the field can be obtained from *Microform Review*, a bimonthly journal, and now from *Choice*.

MUSIC

A distinction must be made between the printed version of a musical work (music score) and works about music. The acquisitions of books and journals about music is no different from the acquisition of other books and journals, although bibliographic listings may cite both types of material, and dealers who specialize in music scores also usually specialize in books about music. The material that requires particular acquisitions knowledge and handling are the scores. Scores designed for performance may come as close scores, conductor's scores, condensed scores, organ-vocal scores, piano scores, piano-vocal scores, short scores, or vocal scores. Scores may also be reduced in size and called miniature scores, pocket scores, or study scores.

The amount and type of printed music or scores collected varies widely from one type of library to another. For example, small to medium-sized general libraries may acquire study scores, but usually do not stock orchestral and choral scores or parts for performance; these are more likely to be collected by libraries of music attached to choirs, orchestras, or other performing groups. Large libraries and special music libraries often have the collected sets of composers' works, while small libraries may have no music beyond folk and children's song books, and perhaps miniature or pocket scores. Lein suggests that, in their collection development policies for music scores, librarians must specify the extent to which they will collect or reject the following materials: solo or chamber music for specific instruments; band music; orchestral music; vocal music (solo, parts, choral); stage works (for example, operas, ballets, etc.); popular music; folk music; music of specific formal or generic types (for example, sonatas, fugues, etc.); music of specific styles or schools of composition; arrangements and transcriptions; and different editions of a work.[7]

Preorder searching for music and music recordings requires an expertise that is best supplied by (or developed in) a person who knows both music and languages. Titles of works are often translated from one language to another; parts of large works may have separate titles; works sometimes have more than one title; and a popular title may be recorded in place of an opus number. A well-built catalog to a music collection should lead the searcher to the correct entry, but few catalogs can provide for all possibilities. Searchers should know when to be suspicious of the information associated with an order that is being searched. As with other special materials, an acquisitions department in a large library may have a music specialist, but more frequently the specialist is in the reference department or in the music or fine arts unit.

There are three principal sources for the purchase of music: the publisher, the local music dealers, and general dealers or jobbers who specialize in music. The advertising section of the Music Library Association's *Notes* has names, addresses, and offerings of many dealers. Most music that is published outside the United States is imported and is quickly and conveniently available from domestic dealers, but libraries with large-volume purchases may work directly with European dealers and publishers. Discounts to libraries for in-print music are customary. For out-of-print music, there is a large trade with specialist dealers in the United States and abroad, most of whom publish catalogs. Many of these dealers also handle books about music.

There is no reference work of books in print for music; the library's collection of publishers' and dealers' catalogs must serve as the in-print listing for most music. Having the library placed on mailing lists for catalogs that list in- and out-of-print music may be done by writing to advertisers in MLA *Notes* and in the standard music journals. All music published in the United States and in foreign countries that is deposited for copyright is listed in the U.S. Copyright Office's *Catalog of Copyright Entries: Music*. The Library of Congress' *Music, Books on Music, and Sound Recordings* contains descriptions of music, musical and nonmusical sound recordings, librettos, and books about music and musicians. It covers materials received by the Library of Congress and by other American libraries that participate in its cooperative cataloging program.

PAMPHLETS

Pamphlets can provide up-to-date material to supplement other library holdings and furnish a variety of viewpoints on controversial issues. Most pamphlets are added to the vertical files in public service units and do not receive full cataloging. While cataloging costs can be bypassed in this way, acquisitions costs, unfortunately, cannot. In some cases, free or inexpensive pamphlets cost more to obtain than expensive sets of books, either because they are difficult to identify or because their publishers or vendors are hard to locate.

Many pamphlets, even though their life spans are short, are as valuable to library users as important and expensive reference books, and these pamphlets deserve as much acquisition time and expense as are necessary to obtain them. However, librarians should guard against spending *more* time on acquisition of a pamphlet than it is worth. Preorder searching to avoid duplicating a one dollar pamphlet may be better left undone, as the cost of a duplicate is less than that of the time spent searching.

The sources for pamphlet selection are almost endless, and there are many guides to them, including library periodicals and indexes, *Library Journal, Wilson Library Bulletin, Booklist, Public Affairs Information Service Bulletin*, and the *Vertical File Index* (monthly, Wilson). Associations, corporations, and various government agencies publish pamphlets with current, concise information. The publications of the Educators Progress Service and other guides to free and inexpensive materials, many of them devoted to special subjects, are useful identification tools for many libraries.

Orders for pamphlets and requests for free materials are usually made directly to the publisher or distributor. Although some pamphlets cost as much as books, most are inexpensive or free. Many can be obtained by sending a form letter or form postcard. For priced pamphlets, payment should, when possible, accompany the library's order because the process of invoicing will cost several times the price of the pamphlet. A personal letter, not a form, may be desirable in making a special request or writing to an agency that does little distribution by mail. Having the library placed on the mailing list for publications may require a personal letter signed by a library officer.

Form letters and postcards, in addition to requesting specific publications, may ask the publisher to place the library on the mailing list for future publications as they are issued. When it is uncertain whether there is a charge for a publication, the letter or card may ask that the library be notified, before the publication is sent, about any charge; or if the library has enough fiscal freedom, the librarian may ask the publisher to ship the item and send an invoice, or otherwise notify the library of the cost of the pamphlet. Return mailing labels may be enclosed with letters requesting free pamphlets, to assist the sender and expedite the shipment, and the labels can be coded to note the location of an order record.

Purchase records for priced pamphlets are maintained in the same way as other order records, but there is some question about maintaining order records for free materials. If requests for free items are centralized in a medium-sized or large library, but more than one vertical file is maintained (business and economics, travel, etc.), it will be necessary for the acquisitions department to have a record that will permit the forwarding of pamphlets to the proper unit. Sometimes it is also desirable to avoid duplicate requests to a particular publisher. When it is necessary to keep a file of free pamphlets that are on order, the best plan is probably to arrange the file by source—that is, the place from which shipment is to be received—and then by title. Many pamphlets do not have personal authors, and establishing their corporate authors before receipt is difficult, if not impossible.

PICTURES

Pictures (including art prints and art reproductions) present visual information—as do films, slides, microforms, etc.—but they require no projectors, reading devices, or other equipment for viewing. Pictures may be
used by anyone—scholars, technicians, children, or the average adult who
just enjoys looking at them. The subject matter in pictures is practically
limitless: places, people, customs, buildings, machinery, equipment,
events, etc. Pictures can be original works of art or reproductions of works
of art. Ordinarily, an engraving, etching, lithograph, or woodcut (printed
from a plate prepared by the artist) is called an art print, and any mechanically reproduced copy of it, or of any other work of art (painting, sculpture,
etc.) is called an art reproduction.

Picture collections are typically built for archival purposes (preservation of the image is the primary objective); commercial purposes (images
to be used for sale or business purposes); or educational purposes (images
to be used for instruction or personal study). The type of library and the
special needs of its clientele will determine the most useful sources for
acquiring appropriate pictures. If the library supports specialized research, more detailed and higher-quality pictures will be needed, such as
original photographs or photographic prints obtained from other special
collections. Picture collections for a general audience can be built from
plates in discarded books, clippings from periodicals, dust jackets, posters, and all sorts of advertising material. Free pictures can often be
obtained from travel agencies, airlines, tourist bureaus, public relations
offices of corporations, and various kinds of local, national, and international agencies. Museums and art galleries can usually supply reasonably
priced museum catalogs, exhibition catalogs, sales catalogs, and individual prints.

In general, printed pictures are less expensive than photographs.
Since many pictures are available free, ordering routines for them are
similar to those for other solicited gift materials. Purchased pictures will
ordinarily be obtained directly from the publisher. When the publisher is
a museum, learned society, or government agency, payment may be
required with the order.

Librarians who search for art reproductions or art prints will find
several helpful guides to the various museums, art galleries, and private
collections that make reproductions from their collections available. In
1950, UNESCO sponsored *The International Directory of Photographic
Archives of Works of Art* (London, Crosby Lockwood), which was supplemented in 1954. UNESCO has also published two catalogs of painting
reproductions, with illustrations: *Catalogue of Colour Reproductions of
Paintings Prior to 1869* (10th ed., UNESCO, 1977) and *Catalogue of*

Reproductions of Paintings 1860–1973 (UNESCO, 1974). Two national listings, *Directory of British Photographic Collections* (Heinemann for Royal Photographic Society, 1978) and *Picture Sources 4. Collections of Prints and Photographs in the U.S. and Canada* (Special Libraries Assn., 1983), provide information on the contents of public collections.

World Museum Publications (Bowker, 1982) has a section that lists thousands of prints and audiovisual items available from museums around the world, together with descriptions and ordering information. *Art Museums of the World* (Greenwood, 1987) gives information about the availability of slides and photographs in its entries on individual museums. *Museums of the World* (3rd ed., K. G. Saur, 1982) provides a subject approach to 17,500 museums in 150 countries. Other directories of possible use in identifying sources for art reproductions are *International Directory of Arts* (Berlin: Deutsche Zentraldruckerei), *American Art Directory* (52nd ed., Bowker, 1988), and the *Fine Arts Market Place* (3rd ed., Bowker, 1977). *Audiovisual Market Place* (annual, Bowker) lists commercial producers who supply study prints. The *Picture Researcher's Handbook: An International Guide to Picture Sources and How to Use Them* (3rd ed., Van Nostrand Reinhold, 1986) is one of the more extensive guides to commercial and other picture sources.

BIBLIOGRAPHY

Audiovisual Materials

American Library Association. Audio-Visual Committee. *Guidelines for Audiovisual Materials and Services for Large Public Libraries.* Chicago: American Library Assn., 1975. 35p.

Bratton, Barry, Mark Albanese, C. Michael Brooks, Gloria J. Holland, James Jackson, and Connie Kohla. "Selection and Acquisition of Audiovisual Materials by Health Professionals." *Bulletin of the Medical Library Association*, 75(October 1987):355-361.

Cabeceiras, James. *The Multimedia Library: Materials Selection and Use.* 2d ed. New York: Academic, 1982. 290p.

Caldiero, Wendy A. "The Selection and Use of Children's Audiovisual Materials in Public Libraries." *Catholic Library World*, 57(March/ April 1986):212-215.

Irvine, Betty Jo. *Slide Libraries: A Guide for Academic Institutions, Museums, and Special Collections.* 2d ed. Littleton, Colo.: Libraries Unlimited, 1979. 321p.

Lewis, Shirley. "Nonprint Materials in the Small Library." *Library Resources & Technical Services*, 29(April/June 1985):145-150.

Nonbook Media: Collection Management and User Services. Edited by John W. Ellison and Patricia Ann Coty. Chicago: American Library Assn., 1987. 388p.

Rehrauer, George. *Film User's Handbook: A Basic Manual for Managing Film Library Services.* New York: Bowker, 1975. 301p.

Serebrin, Ray. "Video in Public Libraries: A Guide for the Perplexed." *Library Journal*, 113(May 15, 1987):29-33.

Stevenson, Gordon. "Sound Recordings." *In Advances in Librarianship*, vol. 5, pp. 279-320. Edited by Melvin J. Voigt. New York: Academic, 1975.

Whichard, Mitchell. "Collection Development and Nonprint Materials in Academic Libraries." *Library Trends*, 34(Summer 1985):37-54.

Electronic Delivery of Information

Association of Research Libraries. Office of Management Studies. System and Procedures Exchange Center. *Microcomputer Software Policies in ARL Libraries.* Washington, D.C.: Association of Research Libraries, 1986. 114p. (SPEC Kit No. 123)

Boss, Richard W., and Susan B. Harrison. "Optical Media for Libraries." *Library Technology Reports*, 23(November/December 1987):783-896.

"Data Libraries for the Social Sciences." Issue editor, Kathleen M. Heim. *Library Trends*, 30(Winter 1982):321-509.

Dudley, Claire C. "Microcomputer Software Collection Development." *Choice*, 23(January 1986):704-706.

Galloway, Margaret E., Kenneth Lavender, George Mitchell, and William Floyd. "The Expanding Universe of Special Formats." *College & Research Library News*, 47(November 1986):650-654.

Gatten, Jeffrey, Judy Ohles, Mary Gaylord, and Harvey Soule. "Purchasing CD-ROM Products: Considerations for a New Technology." *Library Acquisitions: Practice and Theory*, 11(1987):273-281.

Heim, Kathleen M. "Social Scientific Information Needs for Numeric Data: The Evolution of the International Data Archive Infrastructure." *Collection Management,* 9(Spring 1987):1-53.

Holmstrom, Larry W. "Electronic and Media Delivery of Information: Matching New Techniques to Products and Markets." *Reference Services Review*, 16(1988):7-19.

Jones, Ray, and Colleen Seale. "Expanding Networks: Reference Services for MRDF." *Reference Services Review*, 16(1988):7–12.

Lowe, John B. "Gambling on CD-ROM." *Library Journal*, 113(July 1988):37-39.

Management of Microcomputer Software Collections. Edited by Sheila S. Intner and Jane A. Hannigan. Phoenix, Ariz.: Oryx Pr., 1988. 192p.

"Numeric Databases." Issue editors, Charles R. Claydon and Dagobert Soergel. *Drexel Library Quarterly*, 18(Summer/Fall 1982):1-219.

"Perspectives on CD-ROM for Information Storage and Retrieval." Issue editor: Lois F. Lunin. *Journal of the American Society for Information Science*, 39(January 1988):30-66.

Stewart, Linda. "Picking CD-ROMs for Public Use." *American Libraries*, 18(October 1987):738-740.

Strauss, Diane. "A Checklist of Issues to Be Considered Regarding the Addition of Microcomputer Data Disks to Academic Libraries." *Information Technology and Libraries*, 5(June 1986):129-132.

Maps

Allison, Brent. "Map Acquisitions: The Major Sources." *Wilson Library Bulletin*, 60(October 1985):21-24.

Cruse, Larry. "Cartography's Photographic Revolution: Microcartography." *Wilson Library Bulletin*, 60(October 1985):17-20.

Farrell, Barbara, and A. Desbarates. *Guide for a Small Map Collection*. 2nd ed. Ottawa: Assn. of Canadian Map Libraries, 1984. 101p.

Ives, Peter B. "State Atlases by State Agencies: An Historical Survey." *Government Publications Review*, 15(March/April 1988):113-136.

Larsgaard, Mary. *Map Librarianship: An Introduction*. 2d ed. Littleton, Colo.: Libraries Unlimited, 1986. 382p.

"Map Librarianship and Map Collection." Issue editor, Mary L. Larsgaard. *Library Trends*, 29(Winter 1981):371-562.

Noga, Michael M., and Charlotte R. M. Derksen. "Map Collection Development, Processing and Public Services in an Academic Earth Sciences Library: Stanford University." *Science & Technology Libraries*, 5(Spring 1985):1-12.

Stevens, Alan R. "The National Cartographic Information Center: An Information Resource on Mapping Products for the Nation." *Science & Technology Libraries*, 5(Spring 1985):25-38.

Microforms

American Library Association. Bookdealer-Library Relations Committee. *Guidelines for Handling Library Orders for Microforms*. Chicago: American Library Assn., 1977. 14p.

Folcarelli, Ralph J., Arthur C. Tannenbaum, and Ralph C. Ferragamo. *The Microform Connection*. New York: Bowker, 1982. 210p.

"Guidelines for the Handling of Microforms in the Yale University Library." *Microform Review*, 9(Winter 1980):11-20; 9(Spring 1980): 72-85.

Harrington, Sue Anne. "The Development and Management of a University Microforms Collection." *Collection Management*, 9(Winter 1987): 43-59.

Microforms in Libraries: A Manual for Evaluation and Management. Edited by Francis Spreitzer. Chicago: American Library Assn., 1985. 63p.

Patterson, Elizabeth. "Microforms for College Libraries: A Core List of Resources." *Choice*, 26(September 1988):58-70.

Saffady, William. *Micrographics.* 2d ed. Littleton, Colo.: Libraries Unlimited, 1985. 254p.

Unsworth, Michael E. "Evaluating Primary Sources on Microform." *Microform Review*, 17(May 1988):76-79.

Music

Bradley, Carol J. *Reader in Music Librarianship.* Washington, D.C.: Microcard Editions Books, 1973. 340p.

Brown, Peter Bennett. *Ordering and Claiming Music Materials: Tips from a Dealer.* Beverly Hills, Calif.: Theodore Front Musical Literature, 1981. 21p.

"Collecting Popular Music." Issue editor, Tim LaBorie. *Drexel Library Quarterly*, 19(Winter 1983):1-164.

Krummel, Donald W. "Observations on Library Acquisitions of Music." *Music Library Association Notes*, 23(September 1966):5-16.

Thorin, Suzanne E., and Carole Franklin Vidali. *The Acquisition and Cataloging of Music and Sound Recordings: A Glossary.* New York: Music Library Assn., 1984.

Pamphlets

Miller, Shirley. *The Vertical File and Its Satellites: A Handbook of Acquisitions, Processing, and Organization.* 2d ed. Littleton, Colo.: Libraries Unlimited, 1979. 271p.

Spencer, Michael D. "Pamphlet Collection Development." *Bookmark*, 41(Winter 1983):91-98.

Thomas, Joy. "Rejuvenating the Pamphlet File in an Academic Library." *Library Journal*, 110(October 5, 1985):43-45.

Pictures

Coulson, Anthony J. "Picture Libraries: A Survey of the Present Situation and a Look into the Future." *Art Libraries Journal*, 13(1988):9-12.

Houghton, Beth. "Acquisition of Exhibition Catalogues." *Art Libraries Journal*, 9(Autumn/Winter 1984):67-78.

Quigley, Suzanne. "Beyond Art and Architecture: Broadening the Visual Resources Collection to Serve the Entire College." *Art Libraries Journal*, 13(1988):13-16.

"Sources of Art Prints for Children's Collections." *Top of the News*, 37 (Winter 1981):198-201.

TEN

Acquisition of Serials

DEFINITION OF A SERIAL

ONE OF THE BASIC PROBLEMS associated with acquiring and handling serials effectively is defining exactly what is included in the term "serial." Although the library profession has put forward a generally accepted definition, the term may be interpreted slightly differently in various types of libraries, resulting in a need to identify the local definition before trying to understand the acquisitions procedure in a particular setting.

In 1978, British, Canadian, and American librarians agreed upon the definition of a serial as:

> A publication in any medium issued in successive parts bearing numeric or chronological designations and intended to be continued indefinitely. Serials include periodicals; newspapers; annuals (reports, yearbooks, etc.); the journals, memoirs, proceedings, transactions, etc., of societies; and numbered monographic series.[1]

The definition further refers to the term "series" as:

> A group of separate items related to one another by the fact that each item bears, in addition to its own title proper, a collective title applying to the group as a whole. The individual items may or may not be numbered.[2]

Analysis of these definitions reveals that the only significant factors in recognizing a serial are the presence of a collective title, the fact that it is issued in successive parts with or without specific numbers, and the intention of the person or group that issues the publication that it be continued indefinitely.

The indefinite continuation of a serial is very likely the most important characteristic from the standpoint of the acquisitions unit in a library.

While other publications may be ordered once and their receipt, processing, and payment completed, in most instances within a year, serials continue arriving, and their records must be almost perpetually maintained. To be sure, serials do die—sometimes to be resurrected subsequently—and others are born, but these events are not under library control. Serials-acquisitions personnel establish order procedures and record keeping techniques with the expectation that serials will continue arriving forever.

Another characteristic of serials not mentioned in the definition is their value for conveying current and vital information to library users. Since many serials, particularly periodicals and newspapers, are issued frequently, it is essential to good library service that they move through the acquisitions and processing routines very quickly. Few delays frustrate the library user more than those that prevent the timely arrival of an important periodical or newspaper issue.

CATEGORIES OF SERIALS

The definition of a serial enumerates several types of serial publications in particular: periodicals, newspapers, annuals, proceedings, and monographic series. Each type has its own characteristics, which sometimes require special consideration.

Periodicals

The most recognizable characteristic of a periodical is its regularity and frequency of issue. Ordinarily, a periodical appears at predictable intervals, more often than once a year. Because of this predictability, periodicals are sometimes treated separately from other serials. Indeed, some libraries accord periodicals a simplified cataloging and merely arrange them on the shelves in alphabetical order by title, while others incorporate them into the regular cataloging and classification system used for both monographs and serials.

In general, periodicals are easy to acquire and record, but their frequency of issue makes it imperative that they be monitored to prevent unnoticed problems from developing; for example, a subscription that suddenly disappears or is interrupted without explanation. Since individual issues of periodicals often go out of print rather quickly, it is important to detect promptly the fact that issues are missing or subscriptions have gone awry.

Newspapers

Although newspapers may be viewed merely as a special category of periodical, their publication frequency usually occasions a different type of handling. In many libraries, particularly small ones, newspaper subscriptions are placed directly with local publishers or dealers, and very little record keeping is done. Outdated issues may simply be discarded. If permanent copies are to be maintained, they are acquired on microform. In the past, it was common to bind newspapers and store them for research use, but many large libraries now routinely discard them in favor of permanent retention on microform. Some subscriptions are arranged to include the microform as well as the paper version right from the start.

Annuals and Proceedings

While some proceedings appear annually and some annuals incorporate the proceedings of meetings or conferences, they are not technically synonymous. The term "annual" implies a regularity of frequency not always observed by proceedings. In many libraries, however, these two serial categories are handled similarly because of their relative infrequency of issuance, compared with periodicals and newspapers.

Another common difference lies in the fact that many annuals and proceedings are issued hardbound rather than in paper binding. Lest the difference be pushed too far, however, it should be noted that a large number of annuals and proceedings come in paperback, particularly those from foreign sources, while some periodicals have been known to appear hardbound.

The difference between a periodical and a serial, specified to include only annuals, proceedings, and perhaps pseudoserial items, discussed herein, may be obscure to the library user. However, acquisitions units quite often use the distinction to separate items that are processed much as monographs are, with full cataloging and classification, from those that are given less detailed cataloging and arranged alphabetically rather than by classification symbol.

Monograph Series

Perhaps the most difficult type of serial for a nonlibrarian to visualize is the paradoxical monograph series. Such publications cause problems for the acquisitions staff because they participate in two worlds: the world of monographs, since each item can be fully identified for retrieval by its author and title, and the world of serials, since each item also carries the collective title of a publication meant to continue indefinitely. If the series specified by a collective title is numbered, the item can be equally well identified by serial name and number as by its author and title. This dual means of retrieval causes the library to record each issue of a numbered monograph series in two ways if it is to be fully accessible; that is, both as a monograph and as a series.

Unnumbered monograph series may also need this dual identification. However, in such cases, knowledge of the series name is not enough to retrieve the item without some clue to its author, title, or particular subject matter as well. For this reason, libraries sometimes ignore the series relationship of monographic items in unnumbered series or record the series connection only for internal record keeping and payment purposes. In addition, some numbered monograph series, in which the numbering is assigned by the publisher merely as a means of inventory control, are given minimal identification by series for record keeping purposes only.

Pseudoserials

Any publication that appears in separate parts or editions, under a consistent title, and continues for more than one or two years is likely to be handled as if it were a serial, even though it does not fully match the technical definition. These often are referred to as pseudoserials.

A number of publications display some of the characteristics of serials, but fail to have all of them. For example, a publisher may decide to issue a dictionary or encyclopedia in parts over a period of several years. But publication of the parts, while having a collective title and appearing in parts, is not meant to continue indefinitely; the title is expected to be completed at some time in the future. Such publications are sometimes called continuations while they are being issued and sets when they are complete. Some libraries, for reasons primarily of convenience in receiving and keeping records on such materials, handle these continuations as if they were serials rather than monographic sets.

Other publications, such as successive editions of reference works, behave very much like serials, even though, technically, they are not issued in parts; the content of each new edition is not unique. Examples of such materials are directories, cumulative bibliographies, biographical lists of the "who's who" type, and handbooks for special disciplines. Again, because these publications continue over a long period of time, it is often more convenient for libraries to treat them as if they were serials rather than separate editions.

ROLE OF SERIALS IN THE LIBRARY'S COLLECTION

Various estimates have been made concerning the number of serials and monograph series published. At one time, the Library of Congress indicated that between 70 and 80 percent of the materials it cataloged had a series relationship. Series are viewed as highly important resources for current information, and in certain disciplines such as the physical and life sciences, medicine, and engineering, for example, they are much more vital to research than are book materials.

Without question, one of the knottiest problems in many large research libraries is the distribution of limited acquisitions money between monographs and serials. In allocating the acquisitions budget, the percentage to be expended on serials takes on special importance because the purchase of a serial subscription commits the library to a long-term acquisition process, involving repeated payments over the years the serial is available. While subscriptions can be canceled, there is a tendency to renew them routinely unless the price of the serial rises dramatically or someone raises a question about its value under current collection-development policy.

Serials are somewhat costly in terms of their handling and permanent storage. For each subscription, particularly to periodicals, the library commits staff time to receiving and checking in each issue, preparing claims for missing issues, recording lost issues, collecting issues for binding, maintaining binding records, reporting holdings to union lists, and generally dealing with the myriad small problems associated with keeping the issues coming, and making necessary payments not only for the serial but for such associated items as title pages and indexes, supplements, and special issues.

Many serials are high-cost items. Some are even priced higher for libraries than for individual subscribers, since libraries make a serial available to many readers and often provide facilities for users to make photocopies of its articles.

In view of the cost and processing time associated with serial publications, most libraries have in recent years tended to formalize their procedures for selecting and canceling serials. Evidence of such formalization can be found in comprehensive statements of serials collection-development policy, committees charged with reviewing requests for all new serial subscriptions, and empirical studies of how various groups such as high school students, college undergraduates, engineers, and political scientists, for example, actually use serial publications.

A number of libraries have adopted procedures to discourage casual initiation of new serial subscriptions. In some settings in which budgets have become particularly tight, a new serial subscription cannot be entered unless one of equal cost is discontinued. Furthermore, in libraries that divide their budgets according to subject fields, the commitment to purchase a serial may permanently reduce future allocations for the purchase of monographs.

Core lists of journals basic to a discipline, considered essential for a particular group of library users, are often compiled to assist in selection and cancellation decisions. Various techniques have been used to develop these lists, but all are aimed at determining journal worth, which, presumably, will be highly correlated with future use. Core lists have been developed by using one or more of several criteria such as volume of past use of individual journal titles, subjective ratings of experts, frequency of citation of a journal in other journals in its field, rapidity with which articles in a journal are cited in other journals, frequency of publication, number of pages or articles published in a year, number of places a journal is indexed or abstracted, and subscription cost. Rather than adopt published core lists of journals, some libraries develop their own, taking into account local use patterns and judgment of local experts, as well as the number of volumes of the journal owned by the library, and the availability of each journal in other libraries nearby.

A typical cost/benefit procedure for developing a core list of journals was developed by Kraft and others as part of a research project for the National Library of Medicine. Using this procedure, the first step in developing the list for a particular library is to identify those journals that should be considered for possible selection and acquisition. Each selected title is then evaluated by comparing its total cost, expressed in dollars, to its total benefits, also expressed in quantitative terms:

> The total annual cost to the library to own a given title for a year = acquisition and processing costs + (the storage and maintenance cost, including binding and replacement of missing items + the cost per use of the item × the annual usage of the item) + the subscription cost for a year.[3]

While cost estimates may be difficult to obtain in some libraries, the most important element in the journal selection model, also difficult to calculate, is the estimate of benefits to be derived from an individual journal.

Three primary factors are usually weighed when determining journal worth: usage, relevance, and availability elsewhere. Usage may be estimated by gathering statistics on circulation outside the library, use in the library, photocopying, interlibrary loan requests from the library's clientele, and interlibrary loan requests from other libraries.

Relevance, the second major factor contributing to a journal's overall worth, is typically measured more subjectively. Sometimes an estimate of relevance is based simply on the professional judgment of a librarian or a library user. Relevance may also be determined by citation analysis. The number of times a journal title is retrieved in online bibliographic database searches and the number of times articles within a journal are cited by authors of other articles are useful indicators of possible relevance. Since frequency of citation of a journal may be related to the number of articles the journal contains, which may itself be related to the size or frequency of publication of a journal, raw citation statistics can be misleading.

Subramanyam describes two ways of gaining more pertinent information from citation statistics: calculating an "impact factor" and an "immediacy index."[4] An impact factor is a measure of the average number of times articles in a journal were cited during a specified period of time. The immediacy index attempts to measure how rapidly the articles in a journal are cited, determined by dividing the total citations to articles published in a journal in a particular year by the total number of articles published in that journal during the same year. Availability elsewhere, the third factor in the journal decision model, is a subjective estimate of the ease, expense, and delay of getting articles in that journal from another source.

The final estimate of a journal's potential benefit or total worth is a weighted sum of the three factors previously discussed: usage, relevance, and availability elsewhere. Each factor may be assigned a weight that represents its significance to the collection development plans of the library developing the core list. For each journal on the original list of potential selections, the estimate of cost, explained previously, is divided by its benefit or worth figure to provide a cost/benefit ratio or a measure of the cost per unit of worth to the library. All journals can then be ranked on the basis of these cost/benefit ratios, and those journals with the best ratios form the core of the list.

Depending on the goals of a library and the type of use its serials collection receives, decisions must be made whether to bind each serial subscription, leave some titles unbound, discard older issues after a specified time, or maintain backfiles of journals in microform. In some cases, a decision may be made to bypass paper editions completely and to purchase certain serials in microform only.

The online serials database, a fairly recent phenomenon, adds to the expense of the collection but is almost indispensable for research libraries. Some of the databases represent computerized versions of printed abstracting and indexing services issued serially, while others incorporate information that is periodically augmented or updated by computer. Examples of the latter include general news, stock market quotations, and summaries and census reports. Although some of the cost of these databases may be recovered through user fees, the library usually bears a percentage of the charge for having the service and for maintaining the equipment needed to access the information and print the results of a search.

In most instances, user fees are assessed on the basis of the connect time to a database; that is, the actual amount of time required for the host computer to complete the search as requested. Added to this may be the cost of printing and mailing abstracts or texts of any documents retrieved by the search if such services are provided by the database vendor and desired by the user.

One factor influencing the cost to libraries of using a database is the coupling of access to the computer-based system to the additional purchase of a printed or hardcopy version of the index or bibliography. Clearly when such commitments involve several hundred or several thousand dollars annually, they cannot be made lightly.

SOURCES OF SERIAL PUBLICATIONS

The complexity of keeping up with a variety of serial subscriptions, even in small libraries that purchase no more than twenty or thirty titles, is often surprising to nonlibrarians. If each serial is ordered directly from its publisher, it is likely that the subscription expiration dates will be scattered over the year. The acquisitions staff must be especially careful not to let a renewal time slip by unnoticed, since it may be even harder to replace missed issues than to devise a system to anticipate renewals.

When libraries begin to acquire serials by the thousands, as many research institutions do, the problem of making sure that each is properly renewed and correct payment submitted can be solved only by employing numerous competent staff members or by shifting the responsibility for placing, renewing, and paying subscriptions to some organization outside the library. The subscription agent, much like the jobber, acts to mediate between the library and the publisher in acquiring publications speedily and consolidating payment procedures. While the jobber tends to specialize in supplying monographs, the subscription agent's attention is devoted to obtaining serials on the library's behalf.

For various reasons, some serial publishers will not or cannot make their titles available through a subscription agent. The online databases also tend to be acquired differently, usually through some sort of broker, although the broker's services in many ways parallel the activities of an agent. As a result of this diversity of supply, libraries that buy more than a small group of commercially published periodicals will probably be involved in direct purchase of some serials, as well as, perhaps, buying the majority through a subscription agent.

It should also be noted that many monograph series can be acquired item by item as well as by subscription. Titles that are popular may be available as monographs through a jobber and, at the same time, obtainable on subscription from an agent.

Publishers

Most publishers accept subscription orders for their serials, although a few make their publications available only through agents or exclusively through a general purchase arrangement such as a standing order or a membership in the publisher's parent organization. Occasionally, a subscription, particularly for a serial issued by an educational institution or a learned society, may be obtained solely as a gift or exchange. In a few other cases, a serial such as a monograph series must be requested issue by issue, as no subscription is possible.

SUBSCRIPTIONS. Depending on the publisher and the subscription terms, a library ordering a serial directly from the publisher may obtain a reduced price, compared with the rate offered an individual. Sometimes the rate is available only for multiple-year subscriptions. However, libraries that are supported by public funds may be prohibited by law or regulation from ordering for more than one year at a time.

While discounts might be achieved by ordering a subscription direct from its publisher, it is often the case that in-house costs of handling renewals and payments in effect raise the price of the serial. Many publishers, moreover, assess a library rate on their serials that far exceeds the purchase price for individual subscribers. In such instances, it may be to the library's advantage to work through an agent, since the agent is more likely to obtain a discount rate than is the library.

Some serial publications are not marketed through an agent and must be ordered directly from the publisher. Typically, the serials issued by educational institutions and organizations and by scholarly societies that maintain a nonprofit status have to be obtained by subscription from their publishers. Even then, exceptions exist. A few serials from nonprofit groups are available exclusively through agents, while others can be obtained only as a gift, on exchange, or through membership in the group. It is thus imperative that the serials-acquisitions staff be aware of these variations and be prepared to accommodate whatever procedure is required by a publisher.

STANDING ORDERS. The difference between a subscription and a standing order may appear slight, and in some cases placing a standing order for a monograph series means exactly the same thing as placing a subscription for a periodical; it is merely a matter of the publisher's terminology. In other instances, however, a standing order implies that the library wants all publications from a particular source, including monographs *and* serials. As in the case of subscriptions, certain publishers refuse to sell their output except through a standing order placed by the library directly with the issuing body.

The library may obtain a significant price discount by instituting a standing order with a publisher for its serials. If the total output of the publisher is of interest, such an arrangement may have distinct advantages.

MEMBERSHIPS. In many ways, obtaining publications by taking out membership in the body that issues a serial or group of serials is similar to placing a standing order. Some groups will not sell their serials except to members, while others give discounts or provide their publications as part of the membership perquisites, so that the cost of a membership is clearly less than purchasing desired publications separately. Some subscription agents will undertake to handle standing orders and memberships for participating libraries, but the library will very likely encounter organizations that will not allow an agent to be involved in the transaction.

GIFTS, EXCHANGES, DEPOSITS. Exchange or gift arrangements may be more effective than direct purchase or the efforts of a subscription agent to locate items, particularly in the acquisition of serials published in other countries under the auspices of academic institutions or scholarly groups. Such arrangements must be monitored carefully to ensure that an exchange is operating as initially established or that the gift subscription is arriving regularly and on time. Because of the special care required to keep the arrangements working properly, these subscriptions are not free; in fact, they may be more costly than if they were purchased.

In a number of cases, however, purchase is not an option, since, for various reasons, the titles may be available only through an exchange arrangement or by gift. In these instances, the acquisitions staff should be certain that the value of the materials outweighs the time required to negotiate and maintain the arrangement.

Deposits are much like gifts and exchanges, except that they may not be officially the property of the receiving library. It is important to know in detail the terms of a depository agreement before accepting it, especially for serial publications. Libraries have upon occasion lost an extremely valuable periodical run because the organization that made the deposit decided to reclaim the material.

Another factor to consider in accepting a depository arrangement for serials—indeed, any gift or exchange—is whether the library would be willing to pay for a subscription if the agreement were suddenly terminated. It is generally unwise to spend staff time on items that are of marginal importance to the collection, since it is probable that the entire serial file will eventually be discarded if the gift, exchange, or depository arrangement disappears.

The future status of a subscription is relatively unimportant if it is for a current-issues-only title. Some serials have value for the topical and timely information that each issue presents, but need not be retained. These are ideal materials to acquire by gift or exchange, since they do not have to be monitored to any great extent. It is unlikely that the library would want to accept such items on deposit, however, since without their clear ownership, the library would be unable to dispose of outdated issues with impunity.

Subscription Agents

Many libraries find that their serials are more effectively and reliably purchased through a subscription agent than directly from the publisher. Although these agents formerly offered, in addition to the clerical services performed in placing and renewing subscriptions, the lure of sizable discounts, many have not only eliminated the discounts but instituted service charges. Among the reasons advanced for the change in pricing is the general disappearance of discounts by publishers to agents.

Although the library staff might be tempted to reinstitute direct purchase of serials when agents' fees rise, a careful analysis of the in-house costs to place, renew, and pay for subscriptions may demonstrate that the agents' fees are a bargain compared with what would be required for the library to perform these services for itself. If, however, a subscription agent is ineffective, a fee increase may cause the library to reconsider direct purchase, especially if the staff already handles a number of direct orders for serials.

GENERAL PURCHASE AGREEMENTS. Large libraries with a variety of serial purchasing needs often contract with several subscription agents who specialize in different fields. In particular, some agents are more adept than others at acquiring serials published in other countries or written in unusual foreign languages. In negotiating a contract with an agent, the library should specify its requirements as precisely as possible and indicate what kinds of reporting and billing procedures are expected. Agents who primarily handle foreign serials, however, are not always able to place subscriptions as quickly as those who tap the domestic market, and contractual adjustments may be incorporated to allow for an agent's special problems.

Many agents are interested in limiting their services to the placement, renewal, and payment of subscriptions and prefer not to try to solve problems relating to missing issues or other subscription irregularities. Agents that do undertake to transmit claims for missing issues are often those that have computer-based record keeping systems. In order for these claims to be processed, the library will have to notify the agent promptly of the failure of an issue to arrive. Libraries must, therefore, keep accurate records of the arrival of serials and forward notices either to the agent or to the publisher, as appropriate, concerning the need for replacement issues. Even using the services of an excellent subscription agent does not relieve the library of the responsibility for keeping its own serials records in an accurate and up-to-date manner.

The particular specifications drawn up by a library for its subscription agent will, of necessity, reflect the needs of that library and the expectations of its users. As Harry Kuntz phrased it in his article on the selection and evaluation of serials agents, "The rapid placement of orders, speedy handling of claims, and prompt attention to renewals are basic to any serials operation, large or small."[5] In *The Serials Librarian: Acquisition Case Book*, a checklist of services is provided to help in the selection of an agent.[6] This list also offers a starting point for developing performance specifications for the agent. For example, agreement must be reached on the amount of lead time required by the agent for processing an order for a new subscription; once this is done, the library can expect either that issues of the new serial will begin arriving within a specified time period after the order is placed, or that the agent will explain any delay.

If the subscription agent undertakes to process claims for missing issues, the library may wish to stipulate that the agent supply preprinted claim forms, acknowledge the receipt of each claim request, adhere to an agreed maximum length of time for transmitting a claim to the publisher, and submit claims reports at specified intervals. If the library uses computerized record keeping, it may wish to locate a subscription agent that accepts orders and claims requests in machine-readable form.

In order to speed communication, a library may decide to deal only with agents that provide a toll-free telephone number and agree to supply written acknowledgment of inquiries transmitted by telephone. The library may also stipulate the frequency and format of the billings received.

BID CONTRACTS. Depending on the library's relationship to its parent body, giving a contract to a subscription agent may require a bidding procedure. While such procedures are more likely to be mandated in institutions supported by public funds, they exist in private organizations as well. The purpose of bidding is to obtain for the library the best service at the least cost, although it is sometimes difficult to maximize both aspects. Since, at present, a library is not likely to save money on the subscription price by working through an agent, it becomes imperative that the quality of the agent's service be high. Unfortunately, it is easier to measure discounts than good service; and the bidding process, if it results merely in award of a contract to the lowest bidder, can cause more problems for the library than it solves. The library staff must thus become sophisticated in writing performance specifications and in monitoring that performance to identify ineffective subscription agencies to which contracts should not be awarded in the future.

Most librarians dislike the use of a bidding process to secure a subscription agent. As Andrew Osborn has noted, negotiating bids is both time consuming and generally financially unrewarding for the library and the agent.[7] Daniel Melcher, long associated with the publishing industry and even more adamant in his objections to the bidding process, has referred to it as a fallacy.[8] Some of the difficulties associated with the process are illustrated in detail by the case studies in *Purchasing Library Materials in Public and School Libraries*, by Evelyn Hensel and Peter D. Veillette.[9]

In general, bid specifications for a serials agent should include a description of the types of serials to be acquired, such as whether they are all domestic publications of the periodical type; the length of time given the agent to place the subscription or report on its status; frequency and form of billing; and discount and fee structure. Failure to live up to the terms of the contract should result in penalties, also specified at the outset.

Libraries ought to recognize, however, that even though penalties may be successfully invoked, the library's serials acquisitions program will always be weakened by contractual interruption. Agents with poor performance histories should be avoided whenever possible, since it may cost the library a considerable amount of money to straighten out its subscriptions once they are confused by an ineffective agent.

While it is always disruptive to change a library's dealer or jobber, it is especially difficult to change a major serials agent. For this reason, many librarians have worked to exempt serials, if not all library materials, from the bidding process. Where such an exemption cannot be negotiated, the staff has a particular obligation to ensure that the agent lives up to expectations and to maintain a history of dealings with agents so that the lowest bid will not necessarily result in awarding the contract to a company with a poor performance record.

SERIALS RECORD KEEPING PROCEDURES

The records kept for serials are quite similar to those maintained for monographs and include copies of purchase orders, encumbrance records of general budget and special funds, and accounts of receipts, billings, and payments. The records differ primarily in longevity, because record keeping for a serial continues indefinitely, just as publication of the title is expected to do.

Record of the Subscription

The initial subscription to a new serial, or one new to the library, may be handled in much the same way as a purchase order for a monograph. Bibliographic information about the serial, such as its title, issuing body, publisher, etc., must be located, along with such an identifying symbol as the ISSN. Because purchase of a serial represents a long-term budgetary commitment, the bibliographic information, including subscription price, may be reviewed by a library committee prior to authorization of a purchase order. At that time, the committee or a library selection officer may consult with other libraries in the area to determine which of them has placed or intends to place a subscription to the item, especially if its cost is substantial.

Once purchase is authorized, the library acquisitions unit, or the special serials acquisition unit if there is one, will prepare an order, whose form may vary according to whether the subscription is to be placed directly with the publisher or sent to an agent. In either case, the library will retain a copy of the purchase record and will encumber the appropriate amount against the serials budget and against any special funds that will be used to pay for the item.

Although acquisition of a serial through an exchange or gift arrangement does not require a purchase order, a record of the agreement is usually created so that the title is not duplicated by purchase. Once the initial issue of a serial is received, however, a current check-in record is ordinarily developed for the title, no matter how it was obtained.

Record of Receipt

Since serials are expected to continue indefinitely, they differ from monographs in that a record of receipt of individual issues must be created and maintained indefinitely. As noted earlier, some items that do not technically fit the definition of a serial are treated as if they were, for convenience in handling.

CHECK-IN SYSTEMS. Once a serial is ordered and begins to arrive, a record of continuing receipt must be established. This checking record, or check-in record as it is often known, documents the arrival of each serial issue and provides directions concerning its handling; for example, whether an issue goes to a branch library, where it is to be shelved, and how long it is to be retained. Because serials appear at different intervals ranging from once a day to only once every two years or even less often, the format of the checking record must be capable of accommodating almost any frequency imaginable. In addition, some libraries find it useful to attach to the checking record information about such matters as subscription status, decisions about binding, availability of cumulative title pages and indexes, price, fund to which the serial is charged, and source of receipt.

The checking record may be kept in a number of different formats. Libraries that record the receipt of their serials manually usually log them in on cards filed alphabetically in some type of storage unit. These files may be housed in regular catalog drawers, in flat trays, or in rotating drums or wheels. The use of cards hinged into flat trays has, however, been perhaps the most common manual system in use since the end of World War II.

The proliferation of serial publications after 1945 occasioned the search for new methods to keep track of them, especially systems that would avoid the creation of multiple files for routines such as checking issues into the library, claiming missing issues, developing binding records, and making subscription payments. While centralized serial control helped to reduce the proliferation of separate records, the use of the computer as a tool to maintain a single, complete file on each serial was viewed as the ideal, particularly if the computerized record could be made accessible to staff and users at remote stations. For a more complete description of serial record keeping, reference should be made to Andrew Osborn's *Serial Publications*.

The transfer of serial records to the computer has clearly improved and simplified many library record keeping processes and made the preparation of claims notices and payments routine rather than tedious and time consuming.

Most of the automated systems anticipate the arrival of the next issue through the creation in advance of a machine-readable record that is utilized during check-in. The system prompts the staff with the volume and number of the next issue expected to be received. All the staff has to do is to acknowledge to the system that, indeed, the expected issue has been received. Other systems simply enable the staff to key the volume and number information for an issue which is received. Still other systems enable staff to manually change a holdings statement to reflect the new issues received; for example, the staff would change the holdings statement, "vol.1, no.1–vol.12, no.11" to "vol.1, no.1–vol.12, no.12" when the next issue is received.

Detecting missing issues, either manually or by computer, is predicated upon one of two events: a new issue arrives before its predecessor has come, thereby triggering a claim for the earlier one; or each issue arrives on a predictable schedule, but the latest issue failed to come when predicted, again triggering a claim. It is common in an automated system that, if an issue is not received when expected, or if a previous issue is missing when an issue is checked in, the system will include the missing issue on an exception report to be evaluated by staff to determine whether or not a claims notice should be sent. Knowing *when* to claim an issue of an irregularly published serial is a problem not easily solved by either manual or automated techniques.

Unfortunately, the advent of automated serials-control systems has not eliminated the possibility of human error. While each approach can speed the check-in process, neither assures that the person who matches the serial with the computerized record will not mistake it for another or fail to note that it is not the issue that was expected.

PROBLEM MATERIALS. While check-in records suffice to document the receipt of most serials, they often have to be supplemental to reveal unique or unusual aspects of particular titles. For example, some publishers issue separate title pages and indexes for their serials, while others include them as part of the basic subscription price and provide them automatically. Other titles either occasionally or regularly include a special issue or a membership directory as part of the subscription, but some of these items have to be purchased separately. The check-in record commonly shows these patterns or special situations and is used as a basis for claiming items that are part of the subscription price.

Other problems associated with the receipt of serials include a change of title of a subscription, causing it not to be recognized for check-in; division of a serial into parts, requiring adjustment of the subscription to include the new titles; merger of titles to form a new publication; combined issues and issues released as part of more than one serial; and titles that are suspended or cease publication. In addition, some serials, especially those in foreign languages that use non-Roman scripts, are so difficult to read that inexperienced staff may be unable to locate the check-in record or, more seriously, may check issues in on the wrong record.

If the library uses one or more subscription agents in obtaining its serials, the checking staff must be clear about which problems are to be negotiated with the agent and which with the publisher. For this reason, the terms of the contract with the agent become especially important, for the library cannot afford to lose serial issues because the staff does not know to which organization to address questions about a subscription's status.

Payment Records

Key to maintaining a successful serials acquisitions program is development of a reliable system for estimating and recording payments. In some large libraries, the serials expenditures may account for well over half the materials budget. If payments are not made promptly and accurately, the whole budget can be in jeopardy.

DIRECT PAYMENTS. If a library purchases any of its serials directly from the publisher, then the staff will have to recognize the obligation to renew these subscriptions, sometimes at odd intervals. To minimize the possibility of allowing a subscription to lapse because of inattention or poor budget allocation procedures, the library must keep careful records of its subscription expiration dates and the cost of each title. If subscription-price increases are announced, these must be factored into the budget. For this reason, some libraries try to arrange their purchases of new serials to coincide with the beginning of a budget year, although this can prove to be awkward if the serial begins its volume in January and the fiscal year starts in July. At minimum, if the library has any direct purchases, the staff should establish a record keeping system that will predict the expiration dates of these serials and occasion their renewal in an orderly fashion.

PAYMENTS TO A SUBSCRIPTION AGENT. The problems associated with renewing a wide variety of serials during different times of the year often constitute one of the major factors that prompt transfer of the process to a subscription agent. The agent's staff, knowing that these problems must be routinely handled, will of necessity establish a workable system to deal with them. So long as the agent performs effectively, the library can benefit significantly by releasing staff to other, more user-oriented services.

Failure of an agent to handle placement of new subscriptions, renewals, and payments satisfactorily can have a devastating effect on the library. For this reason, the library must have from the agent a workable list of all subscriptions placed or renewed and their cost submitted at regular intervals, no less frequently than once a year. The list should be in a sequence either alphabetically by title or by some characteristic such as ISSN that can be easily recognized by the library staff and related to its manual or automated checking system. When the agent's invoice arrives, the staff must examine the list for accuracy and certify that the total is correct. Between invoices, the agent may be required to submit supplementary reports showing the placement of new subscriptions, cancellations, and changes in subscription status or price. The library, in turn, must notify the agent of intent to place new subscriptions or to cancel subscriptions in effect.

Most libraries that use a subscription agent will probably place their orders on a "till forbid" basis; that is, they expect the agent to continue renewing the subscription until the library specifies cancellation. In such cases, it is very important for the library to receive notification of any changes in subscription prices so that its budget may reflect the alteration. Other libraries, because of regulations relating to expenditures or the necessity of participating in a bidding procedure, may in effect have to resubscribe to their serials each year. If the subscription agent is not changed, this procedure is relatively routine; however, transferring to a new agent generally entails a transition period of several months and puts a special burden on the library's acquisitions staff.

To anticipate the level of payment required of the library to maintain its serials subscriptions, the budgeting staff will undoubtedly make advance estimates based on the general rate of inflation as applied to the current budget. Since serial prices may be linked to inflation rates all over the world, if the acquisitions program is extensive, the use of price indexes for serials may prove to be more accurate than employing the national inflation rate. Unfortunately, serial prices have tended to increase faster than general cost-of-living rises. A good automated serials control system should assist the library in estimating its subscription renewal costs by providing reports projecting the subscription budget required, given a specific inflation factor.

Special consideration must be given, as well, to serials that are enhanced or replaced by computer-based services. The cost of these services and of the equipment needed to use them may dramatically change the serials acquisitions cost total.

Other Records

Depending on the size of the library and the complexity of its serials subscription list, the staff may maintain a variety of additional records to assist in receiving, processing, and distributing serial materials.

FUND RECORDS. If the library apportions its serials budget among various departments or divisions, the staff may need to establish a record of the titles purchased for each unit. In recent years, some libraries have allocated a total amount to each unit, leaving the unit free to specify what percentage of the budget will go toward serials subscriptions and what percentage toward monographs. As annual budget decisions are made, the list of serials charged to each fund becomes an important tool in determining how much money will be left to acquire monographs after the serials are purchased.

BINDING AND REPLACEMENT RECORDS. Serials gathered for binding, those replaced by a publisher-supplied bound copy or microform version, and those for which missing issues or replacement microform copies have been ordered are generally recorded either through the checking record or by means of separate files. One of the benefits of an integrated serials record maintained by computer is that all such transactions can be attached to a basic record for the subscription and, if the system is online, viewed when needed.

RECORDS FOR UNION LISTS AND COOPERATIVE PLANS. Libraries that participate in cooperative relationships often supply records of newly acquired serials, discards, and lists of volumes or issues obtained to complete gaps in a serial run to a local, regional, or national union list. Through such lists, cooperating libraries are able to determine which member holds a title and, in many cases, what volumes of the title are held. Commonly, these lists are kept on computer. Participating libraries may consult the list in some instances by an online connection to the database or through a microform produced from the computerized information.

A further means of cooperation is advanced listing of serials being considered for purchase, so that libraries in the same area will be able to avoid costly duplication of titles that will receive little use within any one institution. Although publishers sometimes object to this kind of arrangement as interfering with the sales of certain serials, there is reason to believe that, under severe budget constraints, none of the libraries would be able to buy expensive, little-used titles unless a cooperative agreement were negotiated.

While continued participation in union listings and cooperative purchasing negotiations may be something of a burden to the staff, particularly in small libraries, it is expected that the costs of participation will be recouped through the library's use of interlibrary loan and purchase of photocopies, rather than placing a subscription to a title expected to be used infrequently. For this reason, the library staff should report accurately and regularly to those cooperative structures and establish internal record keeping devices to assure that this is accomplished.

SERIALS STANDARDS

Several important serials standards are now being utilized by libraries.

The Serials Industry Systems Advisory Committee (SISAC) of the Book Industry Study Group (BISG) has been the primary promulgator of the standards.

The International Standard Serial Number (ISSN), like the International Standard Book Number (ISBN) for monographs, uniquely identifies each serial publication. There is a special MARC format for serials. Other standards provide for recording and display of serials holdings at the summary level for union lists; for recording and displaying all levels of serials holdings for serial check-in, circulation, interlibrary loan, and union list systems; for describing holdings and location data for specific serial titles in a communications format suitable for electronic data transfer; for creating a unique serial issue identifier and a unique serial article identifier suitable for electronic data transfer and encoded symbology; and for describing serials for automated ordering and claiming of serials at the title and issue level, in a communications format suitable for electronic data transfer.[10]

BIBLIOGRAPHY

Brown, Clara D., and Lynn S. Smith. *Serials: Past, Present, and Future.* 2nd rev. ed. Birmingham, Ala: EBSCO Industries, 1980.

Clapper, Mary Ellen. "Standards for Serials." *Serials Review*, 12 (Summer and Fall 1986): 119-131.

Coplen, Ron. "Subscription Agents: To Use or Not to Use." *Special Libraries*, 70 (December 1979): 519-526.

Collver, Mitsuko. "Organization of Serials Work for Manual and Automated Systems." *Library Resources and Technical Services*, 24 (Fall 1980): 307-316.

DeGennaro, Richard. "Wanted: A Minicomputer Serials Control System." *Library Journal*, 102 (April 15, 1977): 878-879.

Farrington, Jean Walter. "Automated Serials Control: Preparation and Planning." *Drexel Library Quarterly*, 21 (Winter 1985): 77-86.

Fowler, Jane E. "Managing Periodicals by Committee." *Journal of Academic Librarianship*, 2 (November 1976): 230-234.

Gleaves, Edwin S., and Robert T. Carterette. "Microform Serials Acquisition: A Suggested Planning Model." *Journal of Academic Librarianship*, 8 (November 1982): 292-295.

Green, Paul Robert. "The Performance of Subscription Agents: A Preliminary Survey." *Serials Librarian*, 5 (Summer 1981): 19-24.

Hanson, Jo Ann. "Trends in Serials Management." *Serials Librarian*, 8 (Summer 1984): 7-12.

Kuntz, Harry. "Serials Agents: Selection and Evaluation." *Serials Librarian*, 2 (Winter 1977): 139-150.

Leatherbury, Maurice C. "Serials Control Systems on Microcomputers." *Drexel Library Quarterly*, 20 (Fall 1984): 4-24.

Lomker, Linda. "Serials Acquisitions and Control." *Serials Review*, 11 (Summer 1985): 67-70.

Lupone, George. "The Effect of Local Serials Systems on Subscription Agents: Back to the Basics." *Serials Review*, 13 (Fall 1987): 69-71.

The Management of Serials Automation: Current Technology & Strategies for Future Planning. "A Monographic Supplement to *The Serials Librarian* (Volume 6, 1981/82)." Edited with an Introduction by Peter Gellatly. New York: Haworth Press, 1982.

McQueen, Judy, and Richard W. Boss. "Serials Control in Libraries: An Update of Automated Options." *Library Technology Reports*, 21 (May/June 1985): 231-343.

_____, and Richard W. Boss. "Serials Control in Libraries: Automated Options." *Library Technology Reports*, 20(March/April 1984): 89-282.

Milkovic, Milan. "Continuations: Some Fundamental Acquisition Concepts and Procedures." *Serials Librarian*, 5 (Spring 1981): 35-43.

Osborn, Andrew D. *Serial Publications: Their Place and Treatment in Libraries.* 3rd ed. Chicago: American Library Assn., 1980.

Paul, Huibert. "Are Subscription Agents Worth Their Keep?" *Serials Librarian*, 7 (Fall 1982): 31-41.

Sabosik, Patricia. "SISAC: Standardized Formats for Serials." *Information Technology and Libraries*, 5 (June 1986): 149-154.

Tuttle, Marcia. *Introduction to Serials Management.* Greenwich, Conn.: JAI Press, 1983.

White, Herbert S. "Factors in the Decision by Individuals and Libraries to Place or Cancel Subscriptions to Scholarly and Research Journals." *Library Quarterly*, 50 (July 1980): 287-309.

ELEVEN

Gifts and Exchanges

METHODS OF ACQUISITIONS discussed in previous chapters generally require direct payment by the library for materials received. This chapter will concentrate on the two most common ways of acquiring library materials without direct purchase: by gift and by exchange. Gift and exchange operations are often integrated because neither involves direct financial payment, neither is responsible for a large percentage of most libraries' new acquisitions, and unneeded gifts often provide material to pass on to exchange partners. Another advantage of integrating gifts and exchanges is that staff members in this area tend to work with the same kinds of materials, and assigning both functions to the same staff allows them to develop expertise in handling such materials.

Gift and exchange activities may be (1) centralized into a single unit, usually operating as a part of the acquisitions department; (2) organized as two separate units, one for gifts and one for exchanges; or (3) absorbed into various other departments, such as serials, government documents, or reference. The size of the library and the volume of gift and exchange receipts appear to be the main determinants of the location of these functions in the organizational structure of a library. Only a few large libraries can support separate departments for gifts and for exchanges. Most large, research-oriented libraries have one centralized gift and exchange department, while medium-sized and small libraries assign gift and exchange responsibilities to a variety of units and individual staff members.

Regardless of how the handling of gifts and exchanges is organized, many departments within the library will have some connection with this activity. Reference, other public service departments, and all staff involved directly in collection development may advise on the likely usefulness of proposed gift and exchange materials. Technical service

216

units, particularly the cataloging department, must be consulted about the way in which gifts and materials received through the exchange program will fit into the cataloging and processing routines. The director and other high-level staff members are likely to be involved in soliciting and receiving particularly important gifts. Although even the centralized gift and exchange units in a large library may have a small staff (typically no more than one professional and two or three paraprofessionals or clerks), the actual involvement of a library staff in gift and exchange activities may be extensive.

Even though few professional librarians have full-time assignments in gifts and exchanges, those who do have full-time assignments have enough special problems—separate from, or in addition to, ordinary problems of collection development and acquisitions—that they have their own group organized within the American Library Association's Resources and Technical Services Division. The Gifts and Exchanges Discussion Group meets regularly at ALA Conferences to consider the latest legal developments regarding gifts and to share information on administrative procedures for handling gifts and exchanges.

GIFTS

For many libraries, gift materials and funds have been very important in building their collections. The library collection may be enhanced by solicited and unsolicited gifts, and by gifts of money. Solicited gifts range from free vertical file material (routinely requested by clerks in various public or technical service departments) to the rare books, manuscripts, and other important collections that come to a library only after sustained and tactful solicitation by high-level staff members. Since a decision was presumably made about the appropriateness of such a gift before it was requested, solicited gifts do not present the same kinds of problems that unsolicited (and sometimes unwelcome) gifts often do. Gifts of money, to be used for the purchase of library materials, are usually welcome— unless the donor attaches undesirable qualifications to the way in which the money is to be used.

The Tax Reform Act of 1984, which became effective on January 1, 1985, has been viewed with apprehension by many librarians involved in gift and exchange work. Because the U.S. Internal Revenue Service has established stricter guidelines for reporting by donors, there has been fear that gifts may decrease. Library record keeping responsibility has also been increased. The new legislation requires libraries to account for any significant gifts that are not kept for more than two years. "If property is sold, exchanged, or otherwise disposed of by the receiving institution within two years after its receipt, the institution must make a statement for the IRS and the original donor giving: a) the name, address, and TIN of the donor; b) a description of the property; c) the date of the contribution; d) the amount received on the disposition; e) the date of such disposition."[1]

A clearly written and widely understood policy on the solicitation and acceptance of gifts for the library collection is essential in even the smallest library. Certainly, the larger the volume of gifts and the wider the staff participation in all activities relating to gifts, the more important the written policy becomes. The gift policy should be consistent with general collection development policy, and is often included within that policy statement. Because of the many difficulties that can develop with unsolicited (and sometimes even solicited) gifts, it is not unusual for libraries without a full collection development policy to have at least a detailed, written policy on gifts.

Gift policies are ordinarily based on the premise that materials acquired as gifts should meet the same standards as materials that are purchased; therefore, gifts deserve, and should receive, the same care and processing as other materials. Most policies make clear the conditions under which a library will accept gifts—typically, that gifts become the property of the library and that the library administration reserves the right to determine the final use and disposition of all gift items. Other topics often covered in policy statements are criteria to be considered when solicited and unsolicited gifts are evaluated; identification of staff members with the authority to accept various types of gifts; the library's position in regard to legal title, appraisals, and other matters with tax implications; acceptable and unacceptable restrictions on gifts (in regard to processing, housing, access, etc.); and the final disposition of unwanted materials.

Some policy statements are developed for internal use by the library staff; others are produced in a form that can be given to prospective donors. In many cases, the general statement of library policy concerning gifts is supplemented by a procedures manual, detailing the step-by-step operations to be used in soliciting, accepting, recording, processing, and disposing of gifts.

Solicitation and Selection of Gifts

Gifts can provide valuable additions to the collection of any library, if proper care is taken in their solicitation and selection. Historically, academic and other research-oriented libraries have benefited most from large gift collections of valuable materials and endowments established from monetary gifts; but any size or type of library may receive important small gift collections and single-item donations. These materials or funds may come from people in the community or those associated with an educational institution as teachers, alumni, or trustees, as well as from research and educational institutions, and various organizations.

The collection development implications of donations of special collections to public libraries was studied by Little and Saulmon, who suggested that it is possible "to tie the issues of gifts, donations, collection development, long-range planning, and limited materials budget into a cohesive plan."[2] If donations of money or materials for special collections can meet identified, sustained community needs that are not being met elsewhere in the community, then acceptance of the special collection may be justified. There are other conditions relating to library control, open access, and long-term commitment on the part of the donor that may also need to be met. Sometimes community organizations with specific, narrow interests will be interested in supporting a special collection at the public library.

In many libraries, many of the gifts are not useful because of their physical condition, their inconsistency with the library's collection development plan, or their duplication of items already owned by the library. A survey conducted in 1976 of 51 members of the Association of Research Libraries indicated that 33 percent of the libraries processed 25 percent or less of the gifts they received; only 7 percent of the libraries processed as much as 75 percent of their receipts.[3] Lane, in his manual of procedures for gifts and exchanges, suggests that a library should probably not accept a gift collection "when almost certainly 90 percent of the material would duplicate library holdings"—although he notes that there may occasionally be good reason to ignore this rule of thumb.[4]

Some of the considerations that affect evaluation of a prospective gift include whether the offered material matches the needs of the collection and whether the library should assume responsibility for processing and housing this material—or can gain access to other copies of the material through resource-sharing arrangements. The library must have enough staff to catalog and process the gift, as well as sufficient space to store it while it is awaiting processing, and an acceptable place to house it after processing is finished. Other points to be considered are whether the library can afford to maintain the collection and keep it up to date. Some gifts require special handling, beyond the library's ordinary routines, and their acceptance may therefore be impractical. As each gift offered to the library presents a different set of potential problems, each gift should be considered individually.

Solicitation of gifts may occur at several levels. Taking advantage of free materials from corporations, associations, institutions, etc., requires continual review of publication lists and other sources that describe materials available on request. In libraries in which there is an effort to obtain gifts of money, individual items, or entire collections, knowledgeable staff members develop regular patterns for identifying and maintaining contact with prospective donors. In some libraries, a Friends of the Library organization is used effectively. If gifts are a significant source of acquisitions for a library, staff members must be continually aware of what is or may be available, and try to nurture collectors' interest in the library.

One public librarian (in a community of approximately 26,000 population) has reported on a successful project to increase magazine subscriptions through gifts. Citizens of the community were asked to "adopt" a magazine by donating money to the library to cover its subscription costs. After four years of the adoption program, eleven organizations and 22 individuals were contributing enough to support 35 subscriptions, supplying about 15 percent of the amount spent on periodicals.[5] Some of the participants—particularly the organizations— supported magazines costing more than $100 a year, and most of those participating renewed their support each year.

An important feature of a successful donor relations program is to keep donors informed of how their gifts will be handled. A library should accept gifts with the understanding that they will be used to the best advantage of the library, with the library exchanging, selling, or discarding unwanted materials. All donors should be informed of this so that there will be no misunderstandings. It is good practice to supply prospective donors with a printed statement that tactfully describes the conditions of gift acceptance.

Gifts should always be acknowledged. A form letter or postcard is sufficient in most instances, especially in responding to publishers of material offered for free distribution. Gifts of special value, including most donations from individuals, should be acknowledged with a personal letter, often signed by the library director, curator, university president, etc. Most librarians, if they work with gifts, are aware that a small and possibly unimportant gift may mark the beginning of a relationship beneficial to the library collection and, at the same time, aid the donor in finding a suitable repository for a prized collection.

Sometimes it will be necessary to reject a gift—a difficult task that must be handled tactfully. Probably the best way to deal with the situation is to suggest an alternative to the prospective donor. For example, another library or institution that needs such material or a local charity that sponsors book drives might welcome such a gift. It is desirable never to offend a person who wants to make a donation to the library. Even though the first gift offered may be unacceptable, the next could be highly valuable.

Appraisals

Those who donate materials to libraries often want to claim their gifts as tax deductions. For that reason, the library should provide donors with a written statement which describes the contributed property and states the date of its receipt. In general, the library should not make appraisals, because it is an interested party in the transaction and because it may not have the staff expertise to carry out an evaluation. Some libraries have policy statements that forbid staff members to evaluate gifts to their own institution—although they are allowed to suggest the names of professional appraisers or to help donors find sales and auction records in order to make their own evaluations. Under the Tax Reform Act of 1984, appraisals for gifts over $5,000 are mandatory. The Internal Revenue Service tends to give less weight to opinions of appraisers who are associated with either the donor or the receiving organization, and appraisers whose work has been considered unacceptable in the past are not allowed to submit subsequent appraisals. The Rare Books and Manuscripts Section of the Association of College and Research Libraries has prepared a statement of recommended library policy regarding appraisals that points out the advantages of hiring an independent appraiser. The appraisal of a gift is the responsibility of the donor, and is ordinarily paid for by the donor. It is also the responsibility of the donor (and the donor's appraiser) to present evidence supporting the fair market value reported.

Gifts of small monetary value may not require professional appraisal. For a standard collection of books that is unexceptional in monetary value but important to a library, the cost of the appraisal may be greater than the donor or the library can afford, and in some cases may be greater than the value of the books. When the value of a gift is nominal, the library staff may assist the donor in finding prices for materials by using the standard bibliographies and dealers' catalogs. Donors may be referred to sources of prices, such as *American Book-Prices Current* (Columbia University Press) and *Bookman's Price Index* (Gale Research). Evaluation of many collections of materials that are not unusual can be assisted by reference to the original list price, using the *Cumulative Book Index*, *Books in Print*, and the other standard bibliographies that contain price information. Librarians have sometimes found it useful to prepare and print a statement drawing attention to some of the facts of book values. For example, a book is not always valuable just because it is old; condition, binding, edition, illustrations, and other details must be taken into consideration. Such a statement can be offered to prospective donors, as well as to people who ask for assistance in evaluating their own books.

Records and Procedures

Procedures for handling gift receipts may vary, depending on whether the gift is solicited or unsolicited and whether it is an individual item or a collection. When specific titles are solicited, the procedure is similar to that for any individual order. Searching is done to prevent unwanted duplication, to gather enough information to send out a request, and to establish basic cataloging information. When a request is sent, a record is added to the library's order file to avoid later duplication and to assist in forwarding items to their proper destination upon arrival.

Gift collections and unsolicited items are usually screened to remove materials in poor condition or obviously inappropriate for the library's collection. In some libraries, faculty members or others involved in collection development can review gifts and offer suggestions about their disposition. Anything selected for addition to the collection is then entered into the regular processing routine, although the processing priority assigned to gifts may be low in relation to purchased materials. Some gifts may go unprocessed for years.

All gifts, as they are received, are recorded and acknowledged. As noted earlier, acknowledgment may range from signed postcards for minor gifts to personal letters from the library director for major gifts. Identification of the source of an item is important. Procedures for this vary from one library to another, but many libraries use a special bookplate to identify gift materials. Some libraries maintain a file in which each item received as a gift is recorded and its disposal (i.e., whether it is added to the library, or exchanged, or sold, or discarded) is indicated.

Donor files are a typical part of record keeping on gifts. A card or sheet is made for each donor, and each gift by that person is recorded, indicating the type of gift and the date received. Some libraries also provide each donor with a copy of this record. In large libraries, other files may be established to keep records of donors by subject field and by geographical location. Computer control of donor records facilitates this.

Serials that come to the library as solicited gifts should join purchased items in the serial check-in files and be handled in the same manner as other titles, except that they may require different procedures for claiming missing issues. The claim form may be worded differently, and the library unit in charge of gifts may wish to have claims routed through its hands, or may establish special conditions for claiming some gifts where a routine claim might be inappropriate.

Unsolicited serial publications present more processing problems, because it is not easy to determine if the issues received are one-time samples, ongoing gifts, new publications coming with existing subscriptions or memberships, or just mistakes by the publisher or dealer. Kovacic suggests that the three primary factors affecting how these materials will be handled are the source of the material, the reason for its receipt, and the possible pattern of receipt.[6] For example, unsolicited serials from a commercial publisher may be sample issues, a new part of an existing subscription, or a gift subscription placed without knowledge of the library staff. Holding these issues (perhaps for a year) will establish the pattern of receipt and help to identify the possible reason for receipt. Those publications received from associations, societies, institutes, etc., may appear as part of the benefits of a membership, as an exchange item, or for any of the other reasons cited above. It is often useful to keep all unsolicited serials together in a holding area until pattern of receipt can be established. This process usually involves setting up a simple control file, either on cards or using a microcomputer database or file management package.

Disposition of Unwanted Material

Well-meaning donors who do not understand a collection's needs often give the library a large amount of unwanted materials. To these materials can be added items weeded from the library's collection, accidental duplicate purchases that cannot be returned, etc. The volume of these materials awaiting disposition in some libraries (especially those with limited storage space) can present serious problems.

Unwanted material can be thrown or given away, exchanged, or sold. In the 1976 survey of 51 members of the Association of Research Libraries, 88 percent offered some of their unaccepted gifts to other libraries, 51 percent sent some of them to Universal Serials and Book Exchange, Inc., and 41 percent sold some of them.[7] Choice of method sometimes depends on the legal restrictions of a state or municipality that specify what can be done with the property of tax-supported institutions.

A portion of the library's policy statement on gifts may indicate the options available for disposing of unwanted material, and may also rank these options—presumably in a way that brings most benefit to the library. Exchange or sale of unwanted materials will probably bring the most return for effort, if those options are legally available and if the materials in question appeal to prospective buyers or exchange partners. In other cases, destroying the materials or donating them to other libraries or organizations may be the least expensive way of handling unwanted material.

DEPOSITS

Although a deposit may be handled in much the same way as a gift, it is usually considered to be a temporary donation to the library, rather than a permanent one. Some individuals and organizations wish (for various reasons) to retain title to a collection, but would like to have the materials available for use and prefer to place them in the care of an experienced library staff. The library that is offered a deposit may accept it—and the cost of housing the collection and making it available—because it contains materials that will enhance the library's collection and perhaps attract the attention of other donors.

There are risks attached to accepting a deposit. If the library has no legal title to the collection, the owner can remove it almost at will, although the conditions stipulated by the library in accepting the deposit may preclude its being removed without prior notification. Loss of a deposit cannot only create a gap in the library's holdings but also discourages other donations—in addition to producing undesirable publicity for the library and the institution to which it is related. Further, the cost of removing all records of a depository collection and preparing it for shipment is high. The library must therefore be certain, before accepting a deposit, that it will be extremely valuable to its users and is not likely to be withdrawn in the foreseeable future.

So far as the library's acquisition unit is concerned, a depository collection is processed in the same way that any gift collection is handled. An in-process record will, in many cases, be prepared for each item to prevent its being duplicated unnecessarily while it is being cataloged. In other cases, the collection may be processed as a whole, bypassing the acquisitions unit entirely, or it may be handled somewhat differently than a purchased item or gift material. Some deposits, for example, receive a special type of cataloging or classification, especially if they have integrity as a collection and the library staff wishes to minimize the cost of withdrawing the materials, should they be recalled by the depositor.

For all intents and purposes, many deposits are gifts to the library. In such instances, it is desirable for the library to enter into legal agreements with depositors concerning disposition of the material upon their deaths. While a depositor may not be eager to reclaim the collection, the donor's heirs sometimes view the situation differently, seeing the materials as a valuable part of their estate.

Probably one of the best-known types of deposits is governmental. Federal, state, county, and municipal bodies often find it to their advantage to make sure that their documents are available in libraries that service their constituents. Certain religious groups and social organizations frequently deposit their archives (often including valuable manuscripts) in an appropriate library, primarily to obtain its organizational and preservational services.

Clearly, deposits can be a valid way to develop a library's collection quickly and offer users access to unique materials. However, they should probably be accepted only with a clear understanding, on the part of both donor and library staff, that they will eventually belong to the library and will not be withdrawn without negotiation that would allow the library to purchase the material (if it wishes to do so).

EXCHANGES

The exchange of materials between and among libraries has a long history and, in some libraries, has contributed significantly to the development of valuable collections. Exchange agreements are often established for materials published outside the United States, some of which may not be available in any other way. These materials often fail to appear in regular book trade channels, or are produced in countries for which there is no book trade usable by American libraries. Sometimes frustrations encountered while trying to purchase foreign materials have led librarians to value the exchange procedure. In the 1976 survey of 51 members of the Association of Research Libraries, 52 percent of the libraries using international exchanges reported that 75 percent or more of their exchange agreements were with foreign organizations.[8]

Exchanges with some countries, particularly in Eastern and Central Europe, are based on political and economic considerations. Librarians in those countries cannot export dollars to buy the American publications they want, but they can provide publications from their own institutions through exchange programs. In cases where publications from the United States ordinarily cost more per item than their domestic publications, foreign institutions also find it advantageous to institute an exchange arrangement.

Some advocates of exchange as a method of acquisition stress the possible financial savings. Materials sent out on exchange may have originally been gifts, or have been purchased at a special discount, but in return they bring library items of greater value. Exchanges are a useful way to dispose of duplicates, discards, or other items of potential use that are not appropriate for the library's collection. In fact, as Lavigne noted in 1983, when fewer university publications become available to the library to use for exchange, and when those that are available become increasingly expensive to the library, "the economics of duplicate lists begin to look more attractive."[9]

Exchanges are usually arranged directly between institutions, but international exchange may be conducted indirectly through national exchange centers. Libraries may also exchange material through cooperative programs, either regional or national ones (often sponsored by library associations). Direct exchanges offer speed; indirect arrangements offer economy in negotiation, and sometimes in transportation. Large libraries are more likely to conduct exchanges—even international ones—directly.

Exchanges can be based on (1) the trade of one piece of material (perhaps a monograph) for a similar piece; (2) title for title (often the basis of serial exchanges); (3) value for value (which involves keeping records on list prices and foreign exchange rates); (4) page for page (which sometimes ensures closer equivalency than the piece-for-piece or title-for-title methods); and, occasionally, (5) one library's trading everything it has available for everything another library is offering at that time. In general, piece-for-piece or title-for-title exchanges are more common, because they are easier and less time consuming. Some foreign libraries, however, prefer the value-for-value or page-for-page method.

Even the smallest libraries may exchange materials, but most activity takes place in university and special libraries, large public libraries, and scholarly societies. Since many materials received through exchange are foreign publications, nontrade publications, research reports, etc., they are primarily of interest to research collections. When users of small or nonresearch libraries need this type of material, they ordinarily rely on interlibrary loan. Small libraries that do participate typically belong to cooperative exchange programs and tend to be the recipients of duplicates from large libraries.

Among research libraries, serials are the type of publication most often exchanged, but some valuable additions to the monograph collection may also be acquired from time to time. The needs of foreign exchange partners are likely to differ from those of U.S. libraries. Lavigne reported on a study of what Stanford University's exchange partners requested from its duplicate lists over a six-month period. He found that Eastern European exchange partners favored science books. Eighty-five percent asked for science books from the exchange list, compared to 65 percent making requests for books in the humanities and 48 percent in the social sciences. Sixty-nine percent of the Latin American exchange partners requested books in the humanities; 42 percent made requests for social science books, and 39 percent for science books. Fewer of the Western European libraries requested books. From that area, 44 percent favored the humanities; 39 percent, the social sciences; and 29 percent made requests in the sciences.[10] Reference books in all subjects were popular.

The organization of exchange operations in a library ought to be consistent with its overall collection development policy and goals. This point is worth emphasizing because with exchanges, as with gifts, there is a tendency to let selection decisions be swayed by availability and cost considerations. The purpose of establishing exchange agreements is to acquire material that cannot be obtained any other way, or for which exchange is a more economical method of acquisition than direct purchase. This is probably why research libraries with large serial holdings and a strong international orientation are most likely to be heavily involved in exchange programs.

Written policy statements on exchange activities, which are not as widespread as policies on gifts, tend to cover such points as types of publications (monographs, serials, documents, etc.) to be covered by exchange agreements; the institutions (sometimes identified only by geographic areas) that will be considered as possible exchange partners; and from what source the library will obtain the materials it offers to exchange partners (some university libraries restrict this to publications of their own institution). Ideally, the written exchange policy will be incorporated into the total collection development policy of the library. Barker reports that this approach was taken at the University of California, Berkeley. The policy there "explicitly states that all materials received on exchange must be reviewed and accepted by the selector for the collection where the materials are to be shelved."[11] There is also a provision that exchange receipts are to be judged by the same criteria as purchases and gifts.

Sources of Exchange Material

The effectiveness of an exchange program will probably depend on the kind of publications a library has available to use for exchange purposes. In theory, any type of library material could be exchanged. In practice, however, American libraries are likely to have three types of materials to offer for exchange: (1) their own publications and publications of the institutions of which they are a part, (2) surplus duplicates, and (3) materials specially purchased to send to the exchange partner (sometimes referred to as "bartered exchanges").

The library may have a great variety of its own and institutional publications to use for exchange: from the library's bulletin, through university press publications, agricultural experiment stations bulletins, and the reports of institutes and other units. Some of these publications are free, and others must be purchased. Since most university presses are now required to operate at a profit, or at least without subsidization, libraries usually buy press publications when they are used for exchanges. Sometimes special discounts or remainder offers are available from university presses.

Libraries may also have to pay for publications from units other than the university press. Surplus duplicates are usually the parts of gift collections that are not added to the library but are appropriate for the holdings of other libraries. Offering them on exchange is one means of disposing of them, with benefit to the libraries involved. Some libraries purchase books at the request of their exchange partners and forward them on exchange. They may do this because they do not have enough or appropriate materials to offer in exchange for needed materials.

Several sources exist to help librarians identify potential exchange partners or specific titles that may be available through exchange. One of the most useful is the *UNESCO Handbook on the International Exchange of Publications*, which contains extensive explanations and discussions of international exchanges. It is supplemented by the *UNESCO Journal of Information Science, Librarianship and Archives Administration* (published four times a year) that contains a section on exchange, listing publications wanted or available for distribution. *The World of Learning* (Europa), *Yearbook of International Organizations* (Union of International Associations), *International Library Directory* (A. P. Wales), *World Guide to Libraries* (Bowker), and other directories are important sources for identifying issuing bodies and their addresses. Faculty members who travel abroad and attend international conferences may also obtain information useful for establishing exchanges.

Procedures and Records

The typical procedure for establishing a direct exchange arrangement begins with the identification of desirable material that is available this way. An exploratory letter is sent, suggesting an exchange, proposing specific titles and terms, and often including sample copies of items offered. Sometimes an exchange may be established through a formal contract, but usually correspondence will be sufficient to set up the agreement.

Exchanges tend to require a great amount of paperwork, particularly to establish them and to acknowledge receipts. In exchange programs based on duplicates, one of the most time-consuming tasks is preparing the lists to be sent to exchange partners. In addition, libraries maintain records to show that the expected material is arriving and that the library is receiving value for effort expended. A library with extensive exchange receipts will probably have a master file (formerly on cards or in loose-leaf notebooks, now more likely to be in machine-readable form) of all exchange agreements, noting complete address of the exchange partner, date and subject of all significant correspondence, and titles, number, and value of materials sent and received. Record systems should be kept as simple as possible but detailed enough for control and evaluation of the exchange program. Claiming exchange materials can be difficult. The usual form letters often do not suffice, but merely confuse foreign recipients.

In some libraries, items received on exchange—particularly if they are serial publications—are integrated into the regular automated processing routines of the library. At one large research library, "materials acquired on exchange blend in with other materials, and any technical difficulties of acquisition, cataloging, or record maintenance are invisible to the public."[12] Another librarian complains that "exchange serials are, in fact, so fully integrated into the files that it is difficult to extract some kinds of information about them that would be useful in our systematic review of exchanges."[13]

Cooperative Exchange Programs

Cooperative programs for the exchange of duplicates have been organized by groups of librarians in special types of libraries—medical, theological, law libraries, etc.—and some operate on a regional basis for other, less specialized libraries. Duplicate exchanges provide an inexpensive way to ensure that material not needed in one library can fill in missing issues or provide out-of-print books for only the cost of shipping (plus costs of preparing and distributing the exchange lists required of members).

The Duplicates Exchange Union (DEU), administered through a committee of the American Library Association's Resources and Technical Services Division, is an example of a national cooperative exchange program with a general membership of several hundred libraries. The DEU has been operating under the same basic procedures since 1944, one of which requires a member library to distribute at least one duplicate exchange list per year to the other members. Small colleges and public libraries in the United States form a majority of the membership, but the number of overseas libraries included on the membership list has been increasing. Periodical issues are the main type of material exchanged, but other items—books, documents, microforms, even audiovisual materials—may be exchanged.

Duplicate exchange programs of this type vary slightly in their operating procedures. Some charge a membership fee while others do not, but most require a participating library to prepare and distribute lists of the materials it is willing to offer to other participants. Sometimes the lists are sent directly from one library to all the others; in other programs the lists are sent to a central office, where they are duplicated and mailed. Libraries that receive these exchange lists check them against their collection needs, select the titles they want, and usually place orders directly with the offering library, reimbursing the sender for the cost of shipping. In some state and regional exchange programs, libraries are not required to prepare and distribute lists. Instead, a central deposit area is established to which members can send appropriate duplicates, and which they can visit to select materials for their collections.

The USBE (now Universal Serials and Book Exchange, Inc., but known as the United States Book Exchange from its establishment in 1948 until 1975) is another type of duplicate exchange. Established as the successor to an agency involved in the worldwide restoration of war-damaged libraries after World War II, USBE describes itself as a clearinghouse of publications from all countries and covering all subject fields. It is a private, nongovernmental, nonprofit membership corporation that accepts, holds, and distributes publications. The stock held by USBE at any one time numbers in the millions, most of which are individual issues of serial publications. Any library or library organization may join USBE by paying the annual membership fee; other costs involve shipping and handling charges for all materials received. Members agree to deposit unwanted materials with USBE and to pay the costs of shipping those materials.

USBE provides, on request, monthly lists of titles in specified categories, and information on holdings is now available to member libraries through online search services. Representatives of member libraries may visit the USBE warehouse (in the Washington, D.C., area) to select materials.

EVALUATION OF GIFT AND EXCHANGE PROGRAMS

There are differences of opinion about the cost effectiveness of various types of gift and exchange programs. Many libraries have given up, or substantially reduced, their exchange programs because analyses of costs indicate that it is sometimes less expensive to buy books and serials than to obtain them on exchange. The costs (in library staff time) of correspondence, record keeping, and special handling may exceed regular acquisitions costs. At one time, libraries, especially those in universities, were able to obtain without charge many of the university press or bureau or institute publications needed for exchanges. Now the trend is to charge the library for these publications, thereby reducing the sources of supply for exchange agreements.

Only a few cost studies on gift and exchange programs have appeared in library literature—perhaps because of the lack of detailed gift and exchange records in some libraries, the time required to do the necessary cost estimates, and the marginal place that gifts and exchanges occupy in the collection development efforts of many libraries. Studies at some libraries, however, have indicated that gift and exchange programs can be cost effective.[14] These studies are usually conducted by determining the total costs of the library's gift and exchange operation—salaries, supplies, postage, value of exchange publications sent, etc.—and comparing that cost with an estimate of the total current retail value of the material added to the collection.

Another approach to evaluating the contribution of a gift or exchange program to the collection development process is to measure the amount of use such items receive after they are added to the collection. Diodato and Diodato chose use as the measure for determining cost-effectiveness of the gift program at one large academic library.[15] Taking into account the dollars needed to acquire and process a nongift book, the dollars needed to acquire and process a gift book, the number of uses per nongift book, and the number of uses per gift book, they produced a formula for determining the point at which the cost/use of a gift book equals or surpasses the cost/ use of a purchased book. These cost/use ratios may vary from one part of the collection to another, as well as from one library to another.

BIBLIOGRAPHY

Association of Research Libraries. Systems & Procedures Exchange Center. *Gifts & Exchange Function in ARL Libraries.* Washington, D.C.: Assn. of Research Libs., 1976. 129p. (SPEC Kit No. 28)

Barker, Joseph W. "A Case for Exchange: The Experience of the University of California, Berkeley." *Serials Review*, 12(Spring 1986):63-73.

"Brief History of USBE." *Library Resources & Technical Services*, 14(Fall 1970):607-609.

Carter, Harriet H. "Setting Up an Exchange Operation in the Small Special Library." *Library Resources & Technical Services*, 22(Fall 1978): 380-385.

Diodato, Louise W., and Virgil P. Diodato. "The Use of Gifts in a Medium Sized Academic Library." *Collection Management*, 5(Spring/Summer 1983):53-69.

Dole, Wanda V. "Gifts and Block Purchases: Are They Profitable?" *Library Acquisitions: Practice & Theory*, 7(1983):247-254.

Falk, Gretchen. "Adopt-a-Magazine." *Library Journal*, 110(June 15, 1985):34.

Galejs, John E. "Economics of Serials Exchanges." *Library Resources & Technical Services*, 16(Fall 1972):511-520.

"Gifts and Donations for the Library." *Unabashed Librarian*, No. 60 (1986):27-29.

Han, Jean C. "The Exchange Program with the People's Republic of China at the East Asiatic Library, University of California at Berkeley." *Library Acquisitions: Practice & Theory*, 11(1987):341-345.

Handbook on the International Exchange of Publications. 4th ed. Edited by Frans Vanwijngaerden. Paris: Unesco, 1978. 165p.

Kovacic, Mark. "Controlling Unsolicited Serial Publications." *Serials Review*, 13(Spring 1987):43-47.

_____. "Gifts and Exchanges in U.S. Academic Libraries." *Library Resources & Technical Services*, 24(Spring 1980):155-163.

Lane, Alfred H. *Gifts and Exchange Manual*. Westport, Conn.: Greenwood, 1980. 121p.

Lanier, Don, and Glenn Anderson. "Gift Books and Appraisals." *College & Research Libraries*, 40(September 1979):440-443.

Lavigne, Jonathan. "Duplicate Exchange Lists: A Study of Costs and Response Patterns."*Library Acquisitions: Practice and Theory*, 7 (1983):195–202.

Leonhardt, Thomas W. "Gift Appraisals: A Practical Approach." *Library Acquisitions: Practice and Theory*, 3(1979):77-79.

Little, Paul L., and Sharon A. Saulmon. "Gifts, Donations, and Special Collections." *Public Libraries*, 26(Spring 1987):8-10.

McKinley, Margaret. "The Exchange Program at UCLA: 1932 through 1986." *Serials Review*, 12(Spring 1986):75-80.

Miller, Edward P. "International Library Exchanges." *Library Acquisitions: Practice and Theory*, 11(1987):85-89.

Moran, Michael. "Foreign Currency Exchange Problems Relating to the Book Trade." *Library Resources & Technical Services*, 17(Summer 1973):299-307.

Nelson, Milo. "Washington Transfer: The Precarious but Enduring Services of the USBE." *Wilson Library Bulletin*, 55(May 1981):672-675.

Payne, John R. "A Closer Eye on Appraisals." *College & Research Libraries News*, 46(February 1985):52-56.

Richards, Daniel T., and Joy K. Moll. "International Exchange of Scientific Literature by U.S. Academic Health Sciences Libraries: A Literature Review and Survey of Current Activities." *Bulletin of the Medical Library Association*, 70(October 1982):369-373.

Schenck, William Z. "Evaluating and Valuing Gift Materials." *Library Acquisitions: Practice & Theory*, 6(1982):33-40.

"Statement on Appraisal of Gifts." *College & Research Libraries News*, 34(March 1973):49.

"Statement on Legal Title."*College & Research Libraries News*, 34 (March 1973):49-50.

Stevens, Jana K., and Jennifer Swenson. "Coordinated System of Processing Gift or Exchange Serials at the University of Utah Library." *Library Acquisitions: Practice & Theory*, 4(1980):157-162.

_____, Jade G. Kelley, and Richard G. Irons. "Cost-Effectiveness of Soviet Serial Exchanges." *Library Resources & Technical Services*, 26(April/June 1982):151-155.

Studies in the International Exchange of Publications. Edited by Peter Genzel. New York: K. G. Saur, 1981. 125p. (IFLA Publication No. 18)

Volkersz, Evert. "Gift Development in Academic Libraries." In *Academic Libraries: Myths and Realities*, pp. 290-292. Edited by Suzanne C. Dodson and Gary L. Menges. Chicago: Assn. of College and Research Libraries, 1984.

Yu, Priscilla C. "Berkeley's Exchange Program: A Case Study." *Journal of Library History*, 17(Summer 1982):241-267.

_____. "Duplicates Exchange Union: An Update." *Serials Review*, 11(Fall 1985):59-64.

_____. "International Gift and Exchange: The Asian Experience." *Journal of Academic Librarianship*, 6(January 1981):333-338.

TWELVE

Evaluation of the Collection

T̲HE PROCESS OF DEVELOPING a library's collection does not end when the chosen materials are received in the library. Collections must be continuously maintained by evaluating what has been obtained, replacing lost or deteriorating materials, duplicating heavily used titles, discarding unneeded items, sending little-used materials to storage, and preserving the valuable items in the collection. Information on the scope, usefulness, accessibility, and quality of a collection must be accumulated systematically if those in charge of the collection are to assure that its development will be consistent with current and anticipated needs.

Collection evaluation is concerned with how good a collection is in terms of the kinds of materials in it and the value of each item in relation to items not in the collection, to the community being served, and to the library's potential users. Collection management goes beyond the relative or absolute value of the collection and looks at how its availability (and eventually its use) may be enhanced through informed decisions about binding, microfilming, duplication, replacement, discarding, storage, security, and preservation.

Various techniques can be used to get some idea of the quality of a library collection, the habits of its users (or nonusers), and the ways in which the effectiveness of the library might be improved. Some techniques involve qualitative judgments: checking standard lists, asking opinions of users, etc.; but others emphasize development and manipulation of quantitative data: holdings in various subject areas, growth rates, circulation statistics, etc. Quantitative measures are easier to apply, on average, than qualitative assessments, and they are generally easier to explain. There are problems, however, with the lack of uniformity in the way such statistics are collected and reported and in the way they are interpreted.

Another way to classify the techniques commonly used in collection evaluation is to determine whether they focus primarily on the collection itself or on the users of the collection. The 1987 draft of the *Guide to the Evaluation of Library Collections* compiled by the Collection Management and Development Committee of ALA's Resources and Technical Services Division defines *collection-centered techniques* as those "employed to determine the size, scope, or depth of a collection or segment thereof, often in comparison with an external standard."[1] Techniques for analyzing the collection include both quantitative —compiling statistics, checking lists, etc.—and qualitative—evaluation by subject experts, etc. *Use-centered techniques*, as defined by the *Guide*, measure "whether and/ or how often a book, periodical, or segment of the collection is used and/ or by whom. Emphasis may be on the use or on the users."[2] Circulation studies, citation studies, and surveys of users are examples of use-centered techniques.

Certain kinds of quantitative data required for collection development and management can be most effectively gathered through automated systems, usually as a byproduct of the automation of another library function. Perhaps it is no accident that interest in compiling information about the composition and use of collections has increased as the application of automation to library processes has spread. Circulation statistics, in particular, offer many quantitative data to be analyzed and manipulated. Questions such as which books circulate and how often, which subjects circulate heavily, what portion of the collection is in circulation at any given time, how many copies of heavily used items are needed to satisfy demand, who are the borrowers and what are their characteristics, and what is the average circulation per user for a specified period can ordinarily be answered by manipulation of circulation records. Acquisitions systems can collect and summarize information on new materials: their distribution by subject, price, publisher, or fund charged. Some systems are capable of sorting new purchases by the bibliographer or other selector originating the request, so that unusual variations in buying patterns may be detected. Online catalogs can be manipulated to provide a detailed profile of the present collection, subdivided in a variety of ways. When a library's total holdings are recorded in machine-readable form, it may also be possible to do comparative studies using other bibliographic databases. With proper planning, automated systems can be designed to produce a wide variety of collection evaluation and management data on a continuous basis as a normal byproduct of regular system operation.

Profiling the Collection and Monitoring Growth

One of the first steps in collection evaluation and management is to understand what is already in the collection and what is currently being added. The absolute size of the collection, the holdings of the library in certain types of materials, the size of the collection in relation to the total number of users or potential users, the money spent on the collection as a whole and by categories, and the growth rate of the collection as a whole and by categories are examples of collection characteristics that may be used for comparison with the performance of the library in previous years or with the holdings of other libraries of a similar size or type. Periodical holdings can be characterized by length of backfiles, completeness of backfiles, and coverage of indexing services. A profile may also be constructed of the new materials acquired over a specified time.

Many automated acquisitions systems have the capability of providing extensive management data and may provide much data for profiling the collection and monitoring growth by summarizing new acquisitions by subject, publisher, fund charged, etc. Tendencies to buy books from certain publishers can be identified. In academic libraries, the buying patterns of departments can be traced.

In educational or research institutions, the collection may be partially profiled by asking faculty members and researchers to describe their courses and research interests in terms of the subject classification scheme used by the library. A summary of the chosen class numbers can then be compared with the library's shelflist to determine how closely present holdings match perceptions of needs. This technique can also provide insight into cross-disciplinary use of materials. Piccinni describes a project at SUNY, New Platz, which used HEGIS codes and the Library of Congress Classification to analyze the relationship between the collection and the academic community.[3] HEGIS, created in 1971, is a classification of academic fields of study. There are 32 major areas of study with enough subdivisions to produce approximately 550 HEGIS codes. When HEGIS codes can be correlated with a standard library classification scheme and combined with machine-readable data on library holdings and university enrollment, it is possible to do extensive analysis by academic program.

In a small library, it may be rather easy to construct a profile based on data for the whole collection. In a large library, however, a sample of the collection may be the only realistic way to estimate such characteristics of the collection as publication dates, country of publication, language, type of publisher (trade, academic, private, etc.), type of format (monograph, serial, government document, etc.). Large libraries have also profiled their collections through shelflist counts, using a fairly detailed breakdown of the classification scheme and measuring the number of shelflist cards for each section of the classification. Such counts provide a quick and easy estimate of the size of the library's holdings in any specified subject area. These estimates of holdings have sometimes been used to compare libraries and to identify particularly strong collections.

Among the disadvantages to the shelflist-count method of profiling a collection is the fact that classification practices vary over time and from one library to another. Not only may different libraries classify the same book differently, but a high percentage of titles in a given subject may not have been classified consistently in the *same* library.

One of the most common techniques for monitoring collection size and growth is the use of formulas for determining collection adequacy. An example is the Clapp-Jordan Formula, published in 1965 at a time when standards for college libraries did not give enough guidance in estimating the minimum number of volumes that would be acceptable for libraries serving undergraduates.[4] The Clapp-Jordan Formula states the number of volumes required for a basic collection, and specifies the number of additional volumes needed for each faculty member, student, and academic program.

Others have worked with variables similar to those used by Clapp and Jordan—size and research activity of the faculty, curriculum profile of the institution, range and depth of programs, etc.—and have devised formulas for large academic libraries. Some states have developed similar collection-size formulas for use in planning higher education budgets, and the latest revision of the standards for college libraries (1986) includes a formula for estimating the number of volumes to which a library should provide prompt access. The standards for university libraries do not provide a formula but *do* suggest analytical techniques for studying such relationships as library materials expenditures to total library operating expenditures or number of current serials to number of total volumes held. Previous editions of standards for school media centers also include specific recommendations on size of holdings. The latest guidelines for school library media programs (1988) contain summary statistics on collection size drawn from a survey of "high service" programs at each school level.

In addition to size of present holdings, the rate of growth of a library is a useful indicator of the collection's probable ability to satisfy the demands upon it. In 1975, Voigt suggested a model for determining the minimum annual acquisitions rate for a university library supporting extensive doctoral programs.[5] Concerned only with current imprints, the model started from a basic acquisition rate of 40,000 volumes and adjusted that figure on the basis of such factors as number and type of advanced graduate students, dollar value of sponsored research contracts or grants, and travel time required to reach other research libraries. Others have experimented with similar groups of variables to gain insight into the meaning of different growth rates and acquisition rates for library effectiveness.

The point of all this manipulation of statistical data is to gather information on whether or not the collection is actually growing in a way that is consistent with long-range collection development goals. Loertscher has proposed an evaluation technique for school library media centers, called collection mapping, that goes directly to the question of how well the collection matches instructional needs. He begins with the assumption that a collection ought to be tailored specifically to the school it serves. The total collection owned can then be counted and profiled from three points of view: as a basic collection serving a wide variety of interests (representing breadth of collecting); as a group of general emphasis collections (supporting broad areas of the curriculum and representing intermediate depth in a collection); and as a group of specific emphasis collections (supporting individual units of instruction and representing greater collection depth). "The mechanism by which a collection is divided into the three main collection segments, evaluated, and then managed has been titled collection mapping."[6]

Part of the collection mapping process involves constructing a graphic representation of general emphasis and specific emphasis areas. These emphases can easily be compared with courses and units of instruction taught in the school, weak areas noted, and collecting efforts redirected if necessary. While the initial procedures of collection mapping are quantitative—based on comparing items/student ratios—there is a qualitative aspect to the procedure. School library media specialists are encouraged to evaluate each general or specific emphasis area at the time it is used during the academic year. For example, teachers and students may be asked to rate the materials used for a unit on such points as diversity of formats available, currency and relevance of the information provided, adequacy of duplicate copies, and appropriateness of reading/viewing/listening levels.[7]

Checking Lists, Bibliographies, Reviews

Perhaps the most widely used technique for evaluating a collection is comparing a library's holdings with one or more lists of selected titles. Such standard lists as the *Elementary School Library Collection*, the *Public Library Catalog*, or *Books for College Libraries*, comprehensive subject bibliographies, literature reviews, and selected lists of best books have been used as guides to check the effectiveness of a library's collection development efforts. Evaluation by standard lists is based on the assumption that such lists, which represent the composite judgment of many specialists, include the most important titles in a given subject field. Checking the library's holdings against the standard list produces a figure that represents the percentage of the titles on that list which the library holds. This figure, of course, does not indicate what percentage of the titles *ought* to be on the shelves, and can be seriously misleading if the library has been using that particular standard list as a buying guide.

A variation of checking a library's holdings against a published subject bibliography or standard list is to construct such a checklist from citations (footnotes, references, etc.) which appear in significant works in the field or fields of a library's interest. Significant works might include whatever is meaningful to the library in question, for example, theses and state-of-the-art publications for a large university library or textbooks and most-used journals for a high school or undergraduate collection. In the case of citations in theses, research reports, or literature reviews, the implied question is whether a scholar could have written that work in the library being surveyed. For the high school library or undergraduate collection, the assumption is made that a student should be able to locate the materials cited in the books and journals used for class reading.

Critics of the checklist method of evaluation point out that any bibliography represents an arbitrary selection of sources. The titles on the list will not be of equal value, and some titles may have been omitted that are better than the titles on the list. The smaller the list, the more arbitrary the selection is likely to be. The materials that a library has, but are not on the checklist, may be just as useful as those on the list. One way to approach this problem is to take a sample of the library's holdings and search for reviews of those specific titles. While the titles on a standard list may be authoritative, if the list does not bear a close relationship to the community served by a given library, checking it will probably be useless.

Comparing a library's holdings against a list is costly and time consuming. It is probably more practical to survey only part of the library collection, with the checking limited to subject areas suspected of being weak.

Collection Overlap Studies

Collection overlap studies—that is, studies of the extent to which libraries' duplicate each other's holdings and acquisitions—have become more common in recent years, although, as Potter pointed out in a review of these studies, objectives and methodologies are not consistent from one study to another, making comparison and generalization difficult.[8] The pressures to plan for resource sharing seem to have encouraged the design of overlap studies, and automated systems have made them much easier to conduct. OCLC archival tapes, for example, have been used to determine overlap of current acquisitions among libraries within state systems. In 1985, the Committee on Institutional Cooperation (CIC), whose membership includes the Big Ten universities plus the University of Chicago, initiated a project using the OCLC and RLG databases to identify relative strengths of the member libraries collections in botany and mathematical analysis. Pointing out one of the weaknesses of automated collection overlap studies, the directors of this project concluded that "earlier suspicions that holdings indicated by the bibliographic networks may not accurately reflect a library's collection" were confirmed.[9]

Most reports of overlap research give the findings of a specific study with some discussion of implications, but limited explanation of techniques. Those who want more explanation of how to conduct an overlap study may find useful Howard White's paper on applications of the Statistical Package for the Social Sciences (SPSS).[10] Detailed explanations of how to create and interpret holdings profiles for coverage, overlap, and gaps are illustrated with sample SPSS commands and tables.

Circulation Studies

As sophisticated automated circulation systems have become more common, librarians have begun to take advantage of those systems' capabilities to collect detailed, long-term data on materials borrowed from libraries. Circulation statistics may be analyzed for selected classes of users, subject categories, or formats. Groups of materials purchased within a certain period or circulated at a particular time of year may be studied separately. Circulation patterns of particular groups of users, such as researchers working on the same project or students taking the same courses, may provide additional data on how widely or narrowly focused are the apparent library needs of these groups, how appropriately distributed are the physical locations of the materials, and how adequate are staffing, service hours, and other policies.

Even very simple circulation data, gathered through a manual system, can provide information on how well a collection development program is operating. Just knowing the way in which circulation is distributed among the various subjects in the collection and whether it has been rising or declining can improve collection planning. However, automated systems make possible the collection of circulation data on individual items, so that the librarian may have access to information of great potential in making intelligent duplication and discarding decisions.

The pros and cons of circulation studies have been sharply debated. Public librarians have been particularly receptive to the use of circulation data as an important element in planning. As one public library director noted, "I believe in output measurement and I believe that actual book circulation is the most appropriate measure of public library effectiveness."[11] But circulation statistics must be viewed with caution, as the same director warned: "But circulation statistics are of no use unless they are analyzed according to the social purpose of the agency. Enormous circulation in pursuit of no social purpose at all is misuse of public taxes."[12] Proponents argue that the use of any item in the library collection is the most valid measure of that item's worth to the library. Recorded circulation has the advantage of showing actual use patterns. The data are collected in the normal course of library operations, and are usually easy to manipulate and analyze. At the same time, such data are severely limited in what they show: the successful matching of expressed needs of active users with materials available on the shelves. Circulation data alone provide no information on the needs of those who choose not to come to the library or of those who come but cannot find what they want.

Axford predicted in 1980 that "there is every reason to believe that the long-term collection use study will become widespread and that it will result in fundamental changes in the way library collections are managed in the decade ahead."[13] Critics of library use studies based solely on circulation data generally agree that circulation studies have some value for collection management, but contend that too much confidence has been placed in this technique. Dudley points out that academic librarians have at least two complementary responsibilities: "one to the student and casual reader and one to the scholar, today's and tomorrow's."[14]

Circulation statistics can provide feedback to selectors who need to know the likelihood that their selections will be used. If an automated circulation system can identify the fund from which an item was purchased or if selectors can be clearly identified with specific subjects, then all persons who choose materials for the library collection can see how frequently their selections are used. Selectors can compare their choices in one subject with those in other subjects as to rate of circulation, and can also compare the circulation of recent acquisitions with that of all the library's holdings in particular subject fields.

Figures on use of materials, obtained from circulation data, are often of most interest when they are compared with certain other internal statistics, such as unfilled requests or interlibrary loan requests. Ratios of circulation to inventory—a way of comparing any subject area's percentage of the library's total circulation with its percentage of total library holdings—are particularly helpful for certain types of libraries. For example, a public library might discover that 20 percent of its collection is classified in the 900s, but only 10 percent of current circulation is accounted for by materials in the 900s—a circulation to inventory ratio of 1:2. The ratio of sports books circulated to sports books held in a school library media center might be 5:1, meaning that sports books account for five times as much of the total circulation as they do of the library's total holdings. These ratios can be obtained for broad or narrow subject classes and for selected periods of time. Subjects for which circulation seems unusually high or low, in comparison to the library's holdings in those subjects, may be targeted for more careful consideration. A subject that accounts for a much lower portion of circulation than its portion of the total collection may need weeding and strengthening, or it may simply be a subject which has declined in interest. A subject that accounts for more than its expected share of circulation probably needs to be strengthened with new titles and, perhaps, titles known to be in great demand need to be duplicated.

If the public library is viewed as a kind of cooperative agency to reduce the cost to taxpayers of obtaining materials they want to use, then much emphasis will probably be placed on circulation studies. Many public libraries give great weight to anticipated user demand when setting collection development priorities, and lean heavily on circulation/inventory ratios as a way of evaluating performance. The starting point is an assumption that the items presently in a collection represent the library staff's best judgment as to the importance of each subject to the library's community. Library users, it is assumed, will communicate their approval or disapproval of the various parts of the collection by their decisions to borrow, or ignore, what the library owns. If the staff's estimate of interests is correct, the circulation in each subject area should be roughly proportionate to the library's holdings in the area. This is sometimes referred to as achieving "supply-demand equality."

Even though circulation studies may provide valuable data for making decisions about the collection, library materials can be used without ever being officially circulated outside the building. Limitations of circulation studies can be partly overcome by studies of in-library use. In-library use, ordinarily determined by counting materials removed from the shelves, left on tables, etc., is harder to measure than use of materials taken outside the library. Such techniques as asking people to leave used volumes on designated tables or shelves, attaching dots to the spines of books found out of place, or stamping the date on an item each time it is used have been tried with varying degrees of success. In general, studies of in-library use have shown that the ratio of in-library use to outside circulation probably differs from one library to another and from one subject area to another, but is relatively stable over time in a given library. This means that one thorough study of in-library use in a given setting may be sufficient to establish ratios of in-library use to outside circulation for various parts of the collection; and these, combined with the circulation data regularly collected, may provide a reasonably complete picture of the use of that library's holdings.

Citation Analysis

When circulation statistics are not available, some librarians turn to citation analysis studies for information on the way in which the library's collections are likely to be used. Citation analysis, in its simplest form, consists of counting the number of times an item is mentioned in the footnotes or bibliographies of published sources such as journal articles, books, reviews, or abstracting and indexing services. Some librarians prefer to use only studies of citations to materials clearly used in the preparation of a paper, article, book, etc., avoiding studies based on counts of citations in separate bibliographies, literature reviews, or abstracting and indexing services. The use of citation analysis studies in collection planning is based on the assumption that citation patterns reflect use patterns and that frequently cited items are likely to be more valuable to a library collection than those that have rarely, if ever, been cited.

One of the most common applications of citation analysis has been to identify core collections of materials for particular types of users. Lists of journals, ranked by the frequency of their citation in the literature of a particular field, provide one way of identifying the most significant or core journals for scholars in that subject field. Citation analysis of carefully selected source items may also be used to identify often cited, presumably basic or classic, books needed by students. Citations in local faculty publications, doctoral dissertations, and other research have been analyzed by some librarians to gain insight into the literature use patterns of their academic communities.

Citation analyses have the advantage of utilizing data that are easily categorized and that do not change while being observed. In general, citation studies are simple to do, once appropriate source items have been selected for the type of user and the subject field to be investigated. The most obvious limitations of this kind of research are that citation analysis is based not on observed behavior, but on assumptions about what bibliographic references really mean to the authors who use them, and that citations often reflect the materials most readily available to those authors, not necessarily those that would have produced the best information.

Document Delivery and Availability Studies

One of the recent trends in collection evaluation is to try to assess a library's capability of providing users the items they need when they need them. This may take the form of studying what is available on the library's shelves at a given time or evaluating total resource adequacy—the holdings of the collection surveyed plus external resources also available to users of that library. One of the early examples of a document delivery test is the Capability Index, developed by Orr and his associates, which emphasizes the speed with which the library can supply items.[15] The test begins with a list of items that a library might be expected to supply to its users, and an effort is then made to secure each item as quickly as possible, either from the test library or a cooperating library. The library's ability to satisfy requests for a list of specific items is then expressed in quantitative terms as its Capability Index.

If the list of items chosen for such a test is appropriate for the situation, the test should simulate a typical user's experiences. The resulting Capability Index should then give an indication of the library's capacity to respond to users' requests, not only through its own collection but also by effective use of cooperative arrangements and interlibrary loans. This method of collection evaluation emphasizes the interdependence of libraries, the importance of which has been recognized in several recent statements of library standards (see Resource Sharing section in chapter one).

Availability studies differ from document delivery tests in that they usually focus on the circulating collection of a specific library and on the probability that certain items can be found readily available on its shelves. In 1986, Mansbridge reviewed more than 40 of these studies, two of them conducted in the 1930s but most dating from the 1970s and 1980s. After comparing these studies, he observed that most studies were based on author or title searches and suggested that there is a need for availability studies based on subject searches, particularly with the increased availability of online catalogs.[16]

One approach to studying availability involves drawing a sample of items published within a specified number of years (perhaps using *American Book Publishing Record* or another national or trade bibliography as the source of titles from which to draw the sample) and checking to see whether the library owns each title and whether the item is actually on the shelf. If a library owns only a small percentage of the items checked, the conclusion may be that either the budget or the current collection development methodology is inadequate. If, on the other hand, the library owns a large percentage of the titles checked, but few of them are available on the shelf at the time of the test, the conclusion might be that more duplication of titles is needed. Similar tests may be devised to evaluate the library's collections of periodicals or nonprint materials.

Another type of availability study starts from specific user requests and attempts to determine how often the library is at fault when a user cannot find an item and how often the user's error causes failure in locating the item. All users, or a sample of them, may be studied for a specified period of time. Those who come to the library to obtain known items are asked to provide, through short questionnaires or interviews, information about their success or failure in locating those items. Searches that end in failure are analyzed to determine the causes, which typically fall in these categories: title not owned by the library; title owned but currently in circulation; title missing or misshelved or otherwise unavailable, due to library error; or title missed in the search because of user's error in copying a call number or failing to locate the item on the shelf. Results of such a test have implications for several types of library policies and procedures, not merely collection development.

Availability analysis has become of special interest to public librarians. *Output Measures for Public Libraries* suggests three ways of looking at availability: title fill rate, subject and author fill rate, and browsers' fill rate. There is, however, some debate on what these fill rates really mean for assessing library effectiveness. D'Elia reported that in one of his surveys of a large public library system "none of the patron search success rates and none of the fill rates were related to the resources available to the patrons within the libraries."[17] He questions "the promulgation of standards, or recommended levels, of performance for libraries based on the fill rates."[18] Van House defends the use of availability analysis in public libraries on the ground that "fill rates are not perfect, but they provide managers with information previously unavailable, another perspective on the library's operations to be added into the information that managers have traditionally used."[19]

Surveying Users and Nonusers

In a comprehensive survey of collection evaluation techniques, Bonn observed: "Of all the ways in which to evaluate a library's collection, finding out what its users think of it comes closest to an evaluation in terms of the library's objectives or missions."[20] Surveying users, rather than collecting circulation statistics, means focusing on people—asking them whether, how much, in what way, or why they use the library, rather than starting with a group of library materials and trying to reconstruct user behavior by determining which items are used and how much. Those who are part of the library's service community but do not choose to use the library may also be surveyed for their opinions about how and why the library's collection and services are not meeting their needs.

Both user and nonuser surveys ordinarily involve gathering responses to specific questions through formal questionnaires or interviews. This can be far more difficult than many librarians realize. Constructing clear and meaningful questions, identifying the users or nonusers to be studied, gaining their cooperation and recording their responses to all questions, and summarizing and interpreting the answers require skill, time, and patience. When a survey is done properly, it may be quite expensive.

Even when the technical problems of the survey can be solved, certain limitations, related to respondents, may remain. For example, many library users have vague and misinformed ideas of what they should expect from their library and therefore have difficulty in judging its adequacy. Some people, to be cooperative, give only the answers they think librarians want. In an article on the uses and misuses of library user surveys, Herb White warns, "there is no library so rotten that many users won't think it is just fine."[21] "If the librarian has been trying to make the point that service is inadequate and even deteriorating, that argument is not likely to be supported by user surveys."[22] He does point out, however, that users are more likely to criticize the collection and hours of service than the services offered by the library. Of course, studies that focus only on people who come into the library, or are otherwise easily available to the surveyors, have obvious limitations on the value of their findings.

Conspectus Approach to Collection Evaluation

The building of collections on a cooperative basis requires collection evaluation based on standard methods for identifying strengths and weaknesses. The 1987 draft of *Guide to the Evaluation of Library Collections* states: "Librarians should standardize techniques of measurement when possible so that the results of evaluation of different collections may be compared."[23] The same guide recommends the conspectus approach and defines it this way: "A conspectus describes collections in a uniform overview or summary format."[24] This approach to collection evaluation and development was discussed in the chapter on collection development policies (chapter two), because the conspectus provides a popular format for recording collection development policy. A conspectus is arranged by the divisions of a standard library classification scheme; codes indicate the strength and special features of various parts of the collection. The assignment of those collecting-level codes requires collection evaluation, using a variety of techniques and, in many cases, taking a regional or national perspective.

Ascertaining the most valid and reliable techniques for determining collecting levels has been one of the difficulties of the conspectus approach. All of the collection evaluation techniques discussed previously may be used, but each has weaknesses, particularly when used in a situation where standardization and comparability are important. In the Research Libraries Group, where the conspectus was first introduced, verification studies have been conducted to try to find objective and quantitative ways to support the assigned codes. These efforts continue. Sanders and others, in a study involving a group of eleven university libraries noted, "the concept of analyzing library collections by comparing their current acquisition patterns to the pool of available monographs was found to be a viable approach to collection evaluation."[25]

Duplication

Among the primary objectives of a collection management program is that of increasing the availability of heavily used materials. Moreover, there is a growing tendency to see duplication as one of the significant factors in determining availability of materials to users. Public librarians are usually concerned with providing sufficient copies of bestsellers, and librarians in educational institutions worry about how many copies to buy of materials that are specifically recommended to students by instructors. Since duplication decisions are ordinarily based on the expected level of demand for particular items, circulation data can be analyzed to look at demand in terms of the number of borrowers who use an item, the number of days an item is off the shelf (and therefore unavailable) in a given period, or the number of requests to reserve an item. Of course, the length of the loan period also affects availability.

In some libraries, the initial reaction to increased demand may be to shorten the loan period; but if demand continues to increase, duplication usually becomes necessary. Since demand, loan period, and duplication all affect availability, loan policy and duplication policy should be planned in coordination. It has been suggested that those in charge of planning these policies might choose one level of demand as a signal to reduce the loan period for one or more items, and another, presumably higher level of demand as an indication of the need to acquire extra copies. Warwick's behavioral model is an example of the attempts that have been made, using economic models, to predict more precisely when to invest in duplicate copies. His research attempted to model demand for reserve books in an academic library (1) by determining the probabilities that students will buy a recommended book, attempt to borrow it from the library, place a reserve on it if it is not immediately available, or return later to try to borrow it, and (2) by categorizing recommended texts by time span of relevance.[26] With the appropriate probabilities determined for a particular library, the librarian would be able to make some differentiation among the titles that may be candidates for duplication.

Inventorying the Collection

An important part of monitoring the collection is keeping track of what is missing and what should be replaced. Replacement decisions may be based on reports of requested items not located and on visual inspection of materials that have been returned and are awaiting reshelving, but the most systematic way to handle replacement is by inventorying the collection. Inventorying the collection is an annual activity in many school and public libraries, but it presents great difficulties in large research libraries.

Where the entire collection cannot receive attention on a regular basis, techniques have been devised to identify areas of the collection most likely to need a complete inventory. A sample of the collection can be surveyed to establish which subjects are sustaining the greatest losses; in other cases, circulation data, pinpointing heavily used areas of the collection, may provide inventory priorities.

The installation of automated circulation or cataloging systems has made complete collection inventory necessary in many libraries. For example, some automated circulation systems require a bar code on each book. When bar codes, prepared from the shelflist, are matched with volumes in the collection, missing items can be easily identified. Even academic libraries with large collections have been forced into an inventory procedure because of automation. Once all items in a collection have received electronically readable bar codes, regular inventories may become possible because of the ease with which individual items may be checked against library holdings using a light wand.

Discarding and Storage

Discarding (often called "weeding") is removal of an item from the library's active collection. Reasons for discarding generally fall under the broad headings of saving money or improving service. More effective use of the library's resources (shelving space, staff required to maintain shelving, etc.) represents one justification for weeding. Little-used materials can be sent to a less expensive building for storage, or can be put into compact storage in a less accessible area of the main library building. This should alleviate space problems and make servicing of the active collection easier. When weeding is justified on the grounds that service to users will be improved, the rationale is that borrowers can more easily find up-to-date and attractive materials, and the general appearance of the library will be improved.

Three groups of criteria are ordinarily used in making weeding decisions: usage, value or quality, and physical condition. Library materials may be weeded because their content is dated or no longer of interest, their use is declining or has ceased altogether, or they have been damaged beyond repair.

The way in which a weeding program is planned and conducted depends on the library in question—on the characteristics of its users, its objectives, its physical facilities staff, and the age and type of collection it holds. Any cooperative agreements in which the library participates probably will affect discarding policies. Ideally, a library will have as comprehensive a plan for weeding the collection as for selecting new materials, and both aspects of collection development and management will be coordinated. Any comprehensive policy for collection development will probably include a section on discarding.

Discarding should be a continuing concern in most libraries, and there are many arrangements which could accomplish this end. In some libraries, a particular time of year is designated for considering a particular part of the collection. The staff responsible for that part of the collection inspects materials for titles which have outlived their usefulness. In other libraries, inventory time is used to identify titles for consideration for discard. An example of the latter approach is the CREW (Continuous Review, Evaluation, and Weeding) manual, aimed at small and medium-sized libraries. The CREW manual makes specific recommendations on establishing guidelines for weeding each part of the collection according to the Dewey Decimal Classification into which it falls, building weeding into the year's work calendar, and combining inventory review with careful consideration of each item in the collection for discarding, binding, mending, or replacement.[27]

In large libraries, such as university research collections, discarding programs have not been popular. The size of a research collection often makes it impractical to consider individual items for discarding and storage; consequently, much effort has been spent on trying to devise decision rules for groups of materials.

Among predictors of future use that have been tested in research libraries are the language in which the material was published, the amount of time that has elapsed since it was published, the number of times it has circulated since the library acquired it, and the amount of time it spends on the shelf between uses. No single criterion has been successful in predicting use for all kinds of materials and all subjects, but many librarians favor some kind of measure of past use as the best way to predict future use for monographs, and favor date of publication as an easy and effective way to select periodicals for storage. However, these simple rules must be used with caution. After applying a Markov model (which "takes into account sudden changes in a book's fortune") to the circulation of social science and literature books in a public library, Kohut warns, "It is clear that the social science and the literature books, to the extent that they show patterns at all, show different ones. Perhaps one of them is predictable, the other not."[28] The basic problem is to predict the point at which the cost in shelf space, staff time, and user frustration of putting into and retrieving from storage a group of titles will fall below the cost of leaving them in the active collection.

Once little-used materials have been identified and withdrawn from the active collection, decisions must be made about their disposition. In libraries with research objectives, many of these materials may be sent to remote storage areas. Some librarians put such materials into compact shelving in the main library buildings; others send them to be stored in facilities separate from the library buildings used regularly by the public. The kinds of storage used will probably depend on the funds the library has to invest in storage facilities, the probable costs of moving materials back and forth, the difficulty of changing library records to show location of materials, and estimates of how much users will be inconvenienced by the remoteness of the materials.

In addition to storage that is planned by an individual library or library system, there is the possibility of joining other libraries in cooperative storage arrangements. In this case, the costs of maintaining the storage area may be shared, while little-used materials in each library are available to users of any of the participants. Cooperative storage is often an integral part of resource-sharing projects. Libraries that accept responsibility for collecting heavily in particular subject fields may also agree to store what other cooperating libraries discard on those subjects. Even if storage is not a formal part of a cooperative plan, any resource-sharing efforts of a library will probably have some effect on its plan for discarding and storage.

EVALUATION OF ACQUISITIONS WORK

For acquisitions work to flow smoothly, it must periodically be evaluated so that any procedures that are not operating properly can be identified and adjusted. Without regular assessment, some procedures may eventually prove to be detriments to the system, perhaps because of mishandling by new staff or seemingly minor changes in the routines used by a vendor. For example, a new employee may be failing to enter a needed element of the order record, which causes trouble when another staff member tries to check the material against the record. Similarly, confusion can emerge because a vendor alters a billing schedule or shifts from a manual to an automated system for invoicing. Even when the current system appears to be functioning effectively, a sudden influx of unexpected material or the extended absence of a key staff member can strain the acquisitions process to the point of breakdown, if no one is monitoring the workflow.

Evaluation should be a recognized part of good management in any type of acquisitions work, no matter how small the staff or how few the materials obtained. This activity, unfortunately, is often given a low priority when the workload in the unit is particularly heavy. In the long run, the cost to the library in loss of confidence in its ability to deliver materials may be much higher than the modest amount required to assure that activities are evaluated regularly and that efforts to correct inadequacies take place.

Goals and Objectives

It is desirable that the goals and objectives of the acquisitions unit be evaluated annually. These goals and objectives should have been established before the beginning of the library's fiscal year or before the beginning of each calendar year. They may be evaluated through the compilation and analysis of statistical reports of activities or through an objective assessment of progress made toward achieving the unit's goals and objectives.

The acquisitions staff should, at minimum, establish goals for the unit that are compatible with those of the library as a whole and with those of any larger organization of which the library is a part. If such goals have never been enunciated, the acquisitions staff may seek to involve staff members from other departments in the development of acceptable goals and in ranking the goals according to their importance. It also is desirable for the acquisitions staff to periodically examine the place of the unit in the library as a whole and to determine whether its activities are furthering the goals of the organization. The acquisitions staff may, for example, place great emphasis on the rapid purchase of current book materials, while giving less emphasis to the purchase of serials. If the library serves a clientele that is currently more interested in the information found in serials than in monographs, the acquisitions priority ought to be revised.

Once the goals are set, specific objectives should be prepared to move the unit toward accomplishing them. Objectives are expected to be achievable within a stated period and to be measurable, and thus are normally phrased rather explicitly in terms of expected performance. Most often, these objectives may be focused on producing output, on improving the quality of output, or on reducing the cost of producing output. The unit that focuses upon rapid delivery of serials, for example, may establish the objectives that a new serial subscription be available in the library, on average, one month after the order request is approved and that this average turnaround time be achieved within two years.

Workflow

Workflow analysis is one tool for determining whether the goals and objectives established for the acquisitions unit are being effectively and efficiently achieved.

Since the acquisitions unit may handle a large quantity of materials and the records for them, one objective of the system might be to minimize the movement of the materials, that is to perform as many operations on them as possible without having to shift them to other locations. A workflow analysis, looking at the movement of items within the acquisitions area, would then become an appropriate tool to achieve such an objective. The purpose of the analysis would be to evaluate whether or not the system is accomplishing its goals. A flow chart can be prepared for an item so that each physical movement through the system, from one work station to the next, is diagrammed. The resulting chart is often very helpful in identifying wasteful movements and streamlining workflow.

Workflow analysis can also lay a base for preparing staff training programs and manuals. The logic achieved in designing an effective system is transferable to teaching the system to new workers. Further, it lays a particularly valuable foundation for the analysis required to change an acquisitions program from manual to machine control.

Caution should be exercised in utilizing workflow analysis in a library for the first time. Unless staff members understand that the technique will be used humanely, that it is not a means of criticizing their performance or replacing them with a machine, they may resist it or participate in the effort with minimal enthusiasm. Staff participation in the design of workflow investigations, in carrying them out, in determining the reliability of the results, and in utilizing the results for workflow redesign is essential if the effort is to be successful. There is no workflow change that cannot be subverted by the staff if that staff is unconvinced of the need for the change and the likelihood of its success.

Another aspect of workflow analysis is anticipation of the effects that changes in acquisitions procedures might have upon other units in the library. In particular, the cataloging function can be severely impeded if the acquisitions staff elects to omit a function that has normally been carried out in that unit. For example, in the interest of achieving greater speed in acquiring new serials, the order staff might decide to reduce the extent of the preorder search that verifies the bibliographic information associated with each item. The time saved, however, could be added when the serials are cataloged, since shortcuts introduced at the order stage can sometimes lengthen the total time the material spends in technical services and thereby subvert the goals of the library as a whole. On the other hand, if the cataloging staff is already double-checking the bibliographic information compiled by the order staff, the acquisitions unit can omit certain verification steps without significantly altering the workflow in cataloging.

Fund Accounting

Another important evaluation is that of the status of the materials budget. Whatever the rigidity or flexibility of budget management under the library's institutional regulations and guidelines, it is likely that the head of the acquisitions unit will be expected to provide understandable and reasonably current status reports of monies budgeted, expended, and encumbered in the various funds utilized by the library, and to do so with no more than perhaps an hour's notice. Depending upon the requirements of the library administration, such figures may have to be gathered and analyzed monthly, weekly, or even, in some instances, on a daily basis. An automated acquisitions system should be able to easily produce such reports. It is therefore necessary to anticipate the need for budget reports and make sure that the system, whether manual or automated, can deliver them when needed.

In some library settings, the acquisitions unit is legally obligated not to overspend the amounts budgeted in the various funds, although it may be possible to shift amounts from one fund to another so long as the total budget is not exceeded. In other settings, overspending may be allowed, even occasionally encouraged, in order to demonstrate the need for an increased level of funding during the following year. More likely, however, is the situation in which an overexpenditure is deducted from the next year's appropriation, thus hampering the balancing of the new budget.

Performance

Another type of evaluation involves the performance of the acquisitions unit, particularly vendor and staff performance.

As in budgetary management, vendor performance is more easily assessed if the acquisitions system is automated. With proper programming, the computer can tally and perform statistical analyses on such quantities as the number of days required by individual vendors to fill orders, the number of cancellations and out-of-stock reports, errors made, average and median prices, discounts given, and the like. Further refinements can create comparative data for vendors who supply specific formats or subject materials. While such figures can be gathered manually, the time and effort required to do so is often prohibitive. For this reason, acquisitions managers are often as much interested in the statistical packages offered by an automated system as in the ability of the system to handle the day-to-day routines of purchasing and budget management.

Figures relating to staff performance are sometimes more difficult to gather, and they are generally more troublesome to interpret. Assessing the work of staff members in quantitative terms, without also reviewing the quality of performance, can lead to a skewed, if not patently unfair, evaluation. Failure to look at any performance statistics, however, can lead to retention of staff members who are not only underproductive but also unhappy in their work. Poor worker attitudes are, unfortunately, contagious and may severely reduce the effectiveness of the entire unit.

BIBLIOGRAPHY

Evaluation of the Collection

Association of Research Libraries. Office of Management Studies. Systems and Procedures Exchange Center. *Collection Description and Assessment in ARL Libraries.* Washington, D.C.: Assn. of Research Libraries, 1982. 117p. (SPEC Kit No. 87)

Bonn, George S. "Evaluation of the Collection." *Library Trends,* 22(January 1974):265-297.

"Collection Evaluation." Issue editors: Elizabeth Futas and Sheila S. Intner. *Library Trends,* 22(Winter 1985):237-436.

Faigel, Martin. "Methods and Issues in Collection Evaluation Today." *Library Acquisitions: Practice and Theory,* 9(1985):21-35.

Grover, Mark L. "Collection Assessment in the 1980s." *Collection Building,* 8(1987):23-26.

Hall, Blaine H. *Collection Assessment Manual for College and University Libraries.* Phoenix, Ariz.: Oryx Pr., 1985. 212p.

Holt, Mae L. "Collection Evaluation: A Managerial Tool." *Collection Management,* 3(Winter 1979):279-284.

Mosher, Paul H. "Quality and Library Collections: New Directions in Research and Practice in Collection Evaluation." In *Advances in Librarianship,* vol. 13, pp. 211-238. Edited by Wesley Simonton. New York: Academic, 1984.

Nisonger, Thomas E. "An Annotated Bibliography of Items Relating to Collection Evaluation in Academic Libraries, 1969-1981." *College & Research Libraries,* 43(July 1982):300-311.

Nutter, Susan K. "Online Systems and the Management of Collections: Use and Implications." In *Advances in Library Automation and Networking,* vol. 1, pp. 125-149. New York: JAI Pr., 1987.

Wiemers, Eugene, Jr., Carol Ann Baldwin, Barbara Kautz, Jean Albrecht, and Linda Haack Lomker. "Collection Evaluation: A Practical Guide to the Literature." *Library Acquisitions: Practice and Theory,* 8(1984): 65-76.

Profiling the Collection and Monitoring Growth

Alt, Martha S., and Richard D. Shiels. "Assessment of Library Materials on the History of Christianity at the Ohio State University: An Update." *Collection Management*, 9(Spring 1987)67-77.

Bolgiano, Christina E., and Mary Kathryn King. "Profiling a Periodicals Collection." *College & Research Libraries*, 39(March 1978):99-104.

Calhoun, John C., and James K. Bracken. "Automated Acquisitions and Collection Development in the Knox College Library." *Information Technology and Libraries*, 1(September 1982):346-356.

Clapp, Verner W., and Robert T. Jordan. "Quantitative Criteria for Adequacy of Academic Library Collections." *College & Research Libraries*, 26(September 1965):371-380.

Ho, May Lein, and David V. Loertscher. "Collection Mapping: The Research." *Drexel Library Quarterly*, 21(Spring 1985):22-39.

Kim, David U. "OCLC-MARC Tapes and Collection Management." *Information Technology and Libraries*, 1(March 1982):22-27.

Loertscher, David V. "Collection Mapping: An Evaluation Strategy for Collection Development." *Drexel Library Quarterly*, 21(Spring 1985):9-21.

McInnis, R. Marvin. "The Formula Approach to Library Size: An Empirical Study of Its Efficiency in Evaluating Research Libraries." *College & Research Libraries*, 33(May 1972):190-198.

Murray, William, Marion Messervey, Barbara Dobbs, and Susan Gough. "Collection Mapping and Collection Development." *Drexel Library Quarterly*, 21(Spring 1985):40-51.

Payson, Evelyn, and Barbara Moore. "Statistical Collection Management Analysis of OCLC-MARC Tape Records." *Information Technology and Libraries*, 4(September 1985):220-232.

Piccinni, James C. "Using the Higher Education General Information System (HEGIS) to Enhance Collection Development Decisions in Academic Libraries." *Collection Management*, 10(1988):15-24.

Saunders, Stewart, et al. "Alternatives to the Shelflist Measure for Determining the Size of a Subject Collection." *Library Research*, 3(Winter 1981):383-391.

Voigt, Melvin J. "Acquisition Rates in University Libraries." *College & Research Libraries*, 36(July 1975):263-271.

Checking Lists, Bibliographies, Reviews

Comer, Cynthia. "List-Checking as a Method for Evaluating Library Collections." *Collection Building*, 3(1981):26-34.

Goldhor, Herbert. "A Report on an Application of the Inductive Method of Evaluation of Public Library Books." *Libri*, 31(August 1981): 121-129.

Lopez, Manuel D. "The Lopez or Citation Technique of In-Depth Collection Evaluation Explicated." *College & Research Libraries*, 44(May 1983):251-255.

Nisonger, Thomas E. "An In-Depth Collection Evaluation at the University of Manitoba Library: A Test of the Lopez Method." *Library Resources & Technical Services*, 24(Fall 1980):329-338.

_____. "A Test of Two Citation Checking Techniques for Evaluating Political Science Collections in University Libraries." *Library Resources & Technical Services*, 27(April/June 1983):163-176.

Porta, Maria A., and F. W. Lancaster. "Evaluation of a Scholarly Collection in a Specific Subject Area by Bibliographic Checking: A Comparison of Sources." *Libri*, 38(June 1988):131-137.

Sandler, Mark. "Quantitative Approaches to Qualitative Collection Assessment." *Collection Building*, 8(4)(1987):12-17.

Collection Overlap Studies

Davis, Charles H., and Debora Shaw. "Collection Overlap as a Function of Library Size: A Comparison of American and Canadian Public Libraries." *Journal of the American Society for Information Science*, 30(January 1979):19-24.

Doll, Carol A. "Overlap Studies of Library Collections in Schools and Public Libraries." *Public Libraries*, 21(Spring 1982):33-34.

Potter, William Gray. "Studies of Collection Overlap: A Literature Review." *Library Research*, 4(Spring 1982):3-21.

White, Howard D. "Computer Techniques for Studying Coverage, Overlaps, and Gaps in Collections." *Journal of Academic Librarianship*, 12(January 1987):365-371.

Circulation Studies

Aguilar, William. "The Application of Relative Use and Interlibrary Demand in Collection Development."*Collection Management*, 8(Spring 1986):14- 34.

Axford, H. William. "Collection Management: A New Dimension." *Journal of Academic Librarianship*, 6(January 1981):324-329.

Broadus, Robert N. "Use Studies of Library Collections." *Library Resources & Technical Services*, 24(Fall 1980):317-324.

Burns, Robert W., Jr. "Library Use as a Performance Measure: Its Background and Rationale." *Journal of Academic Librarianship*, 4(March 1978):4-11.

Dudley, Norman. "A Reaction to Axford's Comments." *Journal of Academic Librarianship*, 6(January 1981):330-332.

Hodowanec, George V. "Literature Obsolescence, Dispersion, and Collection Development." *College & Research Libraries*, 44(November 1983):421- 443.

Konopasek, Katherine, and Nancy Patricia O'Brien. "Undergraduate Periodicals Usage: A Model of Measurement." *Serials Librarian*, 9(Winter 1984):65-74.

McGrath, William E. "Circulation Studies and Collection Development: Problems of Methodology, Theory and Typology for Research." In *Collection Development in Libraries*, pp. 373-403. Edited by Robert D. Stueart and George B. Miller. Greenwich, Conn.: JAI Pr., 1980.

Metz, Paul. *The Landscape of Literatures*. Chicago: American Library Assn., 1983. 143p.

Stiffler, Stuart A. "Core Analysis in Collection Management." *Collection Management*, 5(Fall/Winter 1983):135-149.

Citation Analysis

Broadus, Robert N. "The Applications of Citation Analysis to Library Collection Building." In *Advances in Librarianship*, vol. 7. Edited by Melvin J. Voigt and Michael H. Harris. New York: Academic, 1977. pp. 299-335.

Fitzgibbons, Shirley A. "Citation Analysis in the Social Sciences." In *Collection Development in Libraries*, pp. 291-344. Edited by Robert D. Stueart and George B. Miller. Greenwich, Conn.: JAI Pr., 1980.

Gleason, Maureen L., and James T. Deffenbaugh. "Searching the Scriptures: A Citation Study in the Literature of Biblical Studies: Report and Commentary." *Collection Management*, 6(Fall/Winter 1984):107-117.

Koenig, Michael E. D. "Citation Analysis for the Arts and Humanities as a Collection Management Tool." *Collection Management*, 2(Fall 1978):247-261.

Pierce, Sydney J. "Characteristics of Professional Knowledge Structures: Some Theoretical Implications of Citation Studies." *Library & Information Science Research*, 9(July-September 1987):143-171.

Subramanyam, Kris. "Citation Studies in Science and Technology." In *Collection Development in Libraries*, pp. 345-372. Edited by Robert D. Stueart and George B. Miller. Greenwich, Conn.: JAI Pr., 1980.

Document Delivery and Availability Studies

Altman, Ellen et al. *A Data Gathering and Instructional Manual for Performance Measures in Public Libraries*. Chicago: Celadon Pr., 1976. 171p.

Ciliberti, Anne C., Mary F. Casserly, Judith L. Hegg, and Eugene S. Mitchell. "Material Availability: A Study of Academic Library Performance." *College & Research Libraries*, 48(November 1987): 513-527.

D'Elia, George. "Materials Availability Fill Rates: Additional Data Addressing the Question of the Usefulness of the Measures." *Public Libraries*, 27(Spring 1988):15-23.

De Prospo, Ernest R., et al. *Performance Measures for Public Libraries.* Chicago: American Library Assn., 1973. 71p.

Ferl, T. E., and M. G. Robinson. "Book Availability at the University of California, Santa Cruz." *College & Research Libraries*, 47(September 1986):501-508.

Kantor, Paul B. "Availability Analysis." *Journal of the American Society for Information Science*, 27(September-October 1976):311-319.

_____. *Objective Performance Measures for Academic and Research Libraries.* Washington, D.C.: Assn. of Research Libraries, 1984. 76p.

Mansbridge, John. "Availability Studies in Libraries." *Library & Information Science Research*, 8(October-December 1986):299-314.

Orr, Richard H. et al. "Developments of Methodologic Tools for Planning and Managing Library Services: I-IV." *Bulletin of the Medical Library Association*, 56(July 1968):235-267; 56(October 1968):380-403; 58 (July 1970):350-377.

Radford, N. A. "Failure in the Library—A Case Study." *Library Quarterly*, 53(July 1983):328-339.

Van House, Nancy. "In Defense of Fill Rates." *Public Libraries*, 27 (Spring 1988):25-27.

_____, et al. *Output Measures for Public Libraries: A Manual of Standardized Procedures.* 2d ed. Chicago: American Library Assn., 1987.

Surveying Users and Nonusers

Association of Research Libraries. Office of Management Studies. Systems and Procedures Exchange Center. *User Surveys and Evaluation of Library Services.* Washington, D.C.: Assn. of Research Libs., 1981. 107p. (SPEC Kit No. 71)

Christiansen, Dorothy E., C. Roger Davis, and Jutta Reed-Scott. "Guide to Collection Evaluation through Use and User Studies." *Library Resources & Technical Services*, 27(1983):432-440.

Ford, Geoffrey. "Research in User Behavior in University Libraries." *Journal of Documentation*, 29(March 1973):85-106.

Osburn, Charles B. "Non-Use and Loser Studies in Collection Development." *Collection Management*, 4(Spring/Summer 1982):45-53.

White, Herb. "The Use and Misuse of Library User Studies." *Library Journal*, 110(December 1985):70-71.

Zweizig, Douglas, and Brenda Derwin. "Public Library Use, Users, Uses: Advances in Knowledge of the Characteristics and Needs of the Adult Clientele of American Public Libraries." In *Advances in Librarianship*, vol. 7, pp. 231-255. Edited by Melvin J. Voigt and Michael H. Harris. New York: Academic, 1977.

Conspectus Approach to Collection Evaluation

Farrell, David. "The NCIP Option for Coordinated Collection Management." *Library Resources & Technical Services*, 30(January-March 1986):47-56.

Ferguson, Anthony W., Joan Grant, and Joel S. Rutstein. "The RLG Conspectus: Its Uses and Benefits." *College & Research Libraries*, 49(May 1988):197-206.

Forcier, Peggy. "Building Collections Together: The Pacific Northwest Conspectus." *Library Journal*, 113(April 15, 1988):43-45.

Gwinn, Nancy E., and Paul H. Mosher. "Coordinating Collection Development: The RLG Conspectus." *College & Research Libraries*, 44(March 1984):128-139.

Oberg, Larry R. "Evaluating the Conspectus Approach for Smaller Library Collections."*College & Research Libraries*, 49(May 1988): 187-196.

Reed-Scott, Jutta. *Draft Manual for the National Inventory of Research Collections*. Prelim. ed. Washington, D.C.: Assn. of Research Libraries, 1984.

Sanders, Nancy P., Edward O'Neill, and Stuart L. Weibel. "Automated Collection Analysis Using the OCLC and RLG Databases." *College & Research Libraries*, 49(July 1988):305-314.

Stam, David C. "Collaboration Collection Development: Progress, Problems, and Potential." *IFLA Journal*, 12(1986):9-19.

Duplication

Almony, Robert A. "The Concept of Systematic Duplication: A Survey of the Literature." *Collection Management*, 2(Summer 1978):153-165.

Buckland, Michael K. *Book Availability and the Library User*. New York: Pergamon, 1975. 196p.

Davis, Douglas A. "Maintenance of Circulating Books in an Academic Library." *California Librarian*, 38(April 1977):22-31.

Warwick, J. P. "Duplication of Texts in Academic Libraries: A Behavioural Model for Library Management." *Journal of Librarianship*, 19(January 1987):41-52.

Inventorying the Collection

Cunliffe, Vera. "Inventory of Monographs in a University Library." *Library Resources & Technical Services*, 21(Winter 1977):72-76.

Engeldinger, Eugene A. "Inventorying Academic Library Reference Collections: A Survey of the Field." *Collection Management*, 9(Winter 1987):25-41.

Kohl, David F. "High Efficiency Inventorying through Predictive Data." *Journal of Academic Librarianship*, 8(May 1982):82-84.

Niland, Powell, and William H. Kurth. "Estimating Lost Volumes in a University Library Collection." *College & Research Libraries*, 37 (March 1976):128-136.

Discarding and Storage

Basart, Ann. "Criteria for Weeding Books in a University Music Library." *Music Library Association Notes*, 36(June 1980):819-836.

Douglas, Ian. "Effects of a Relegation Programme on the Borrowing of Books." *Journal of Documentation*, 42(December 1986):252-271.

Fussler, Herman H., and Julian L. Simon. *Patterns in the Use of Books in Large Research Libraries*. Chicago: Univ. of Chicago Pr., 1969. 210p.

Kohut, David R. "A Markov Model Applied to the Circulation of Social Science and Literature Books in a Public Library." *Collection Building*, 7(4)(1986):12-19.

Lancaster, F. W. "Obsolescence, Weeding, and the Utilization of Space." *Wilson Library Bulletin*, 62(May 1988):47-49.

Mosher, Paul H. "Managing Library Collections: The Process of Review and Pruning." In *Collection Development in Libraries*, pp. 159-181. Edited by Robert D. Stueart and George B. Miller. Greenwich, Conn.: JAI Pr., 1980.

Reed, Mary Jane Pobst. "Identification of Storage Candidates among Monographs." *Collection Management*, 3(Summer/Fall 1979):203-214.

Roy, Loriene. "Does Weeding Increase Circulation? A Review of the Related Literature." *Collection Management*, 10(1988):141-156.

Segal, Joseph. *Evaluating and Weeding Collections in Small and Medium-Sized Public Libraries: The CREW Method*. Chicago: American Library Assn., 1980. 25p.

Segal, Judith. "Journal Deselection: A Literature Review and an Application." *Serials Librarian*, 6(Spring 1986):25-42.

Slote, Sidney J. *Weeding Library Collections: II*. 2d rev. ed. Littleton, Colo.: Libraries Unlimited, 1982. 198p.

Verhoeven, Stanley M. "The Expectation of Life Formula Applied to Collection Management." *Collection Management*, 8(Summer 1986):11-29.